A Yiddish Dictionary
in Transliteration

by Harry Coldoff

proclaim

Preface

A Yiddish Dictionary in Transliteration
Transliterated words and phrases in
danger of disappearing from the Yiddish language.

Not for the disciplines of science nor for the technical terminology of sports, but for
the Shtetl folk in our midst who will soon be gone, and for the memorialization of
generations whom we should not forget.

"These are the sufferers:
let not the language of
their ultimate desolation
perish forever"

Harry Coldoff

Dedicated to the memory of
our sister Dorothy
the soul and conscience of
our family

Coldoff, Harry, 1903-1983
  A Yiddish dictionary in transliteration

ISBN 0-919415-03-2

1. English language - Dictionaries - Yiddish.
2. Yiddish language - Dictionaries - English.
3. Yiddish language - Idioms. 4. English language -
Idioms. I. Title.

PJ5117.C64 1988   437'.947   C87-095276-5

Table of Contents

Introduction

Why another Yiddish Dictionary?

Despite the Czernowitz Conference of 1908, despite more than a century of the Yiddish Renascence and the literary tradition of the three classical writers (Mendele, Peretz and Sholem Aleichem) and those who followed, and despite the ever-growing "academization" of Yiddish, one can still occasionally hear from those who should know better "Has it a grammar?", "Has it a dictionary?"

Not that such credentials are required to confirm a language's status and "right to exist". Most modern European vernaculars received recognition without the legitimation of such lexicons. This writer, who makes a hobby of collecting Yiddish dictionaries, has on his shelves some dozen, ranging from Harkavy's efforts in the 1890's to Uriel Weinreich's *opus* and including a curiosity such as a Montreal-published Yiddish-Esperanto dictionary.

At this point only four volumes of *Der groiser verterbukh fun der Yidisher Shprakh* have appeared, completing the letter *alef*. Let us pray that it will be fully completed *bimheyro v'yomeynu*—speedily and in our days! Most of its original editors and editorial advisors are by now *afn oylem ho'emes*. Fortunately a new generation of Yiddish lexicographers has arisen to fulfill their labours though it is fervently to be hoped that it will not take them further decades.

Which brings us to the question at the other end of the spectrum: why another Yiddish dictionary? It might be more helpful if it can be clarified what this dictionary is not. It is not meant to be a work based on historic-linguistic principles, showing the development of the language from its birth in medieval times. It is not intended as an etymological reference, or a thesaurus, or as a guide to grammatical usage. Nor does it dare to compete on the level of scholarship with any other compilation. It has a practical end—to serve the needs and the wants, the interest and the curiosity of those who are familiar with the legacy of Yiddish *ba'al peh* but have not acquired it *bek'sav*; those who have retained something of the oral tradition but have lost the written tradition. To these—and there are more of them than most of us care to admit—as a consequence most Yiddish-English and English-Yiddish dictionaries are literally closed books as they are not familiar with what the late A.A. Coralnick called *di kvadratne oysyes* and those unlettered amongst us should not be cavalierly ignored. Some will tackle the Hebrew *alef-beys* but for most it is too much to expect. Deplore it as we might we have no right to rule this entire element out of our consideration.

It was not my privilege to know the late Harry Coldoff. That he had a deep affection for the Yiddish word, its idiom, its colour and imagery is undeniable—just from a casual look at the present text. From his preface it is clear that it was not meant to be an exhaustive compilation or as an ultimate authority. He was not a scholar of Yiddish or academician or a professional researcher but a private person, a *posheter boser v'dom* who was most anxious to leave something behind that would be a tribute to the *mame-loshn* he loved and at the same time would be a useful compendium to those who had lost the written thread to their cultural heritage. He planned to help them regain and retain this thread and to bring them back to this rich and productive legacy of language, folklore and culture, giving renewed meaning to their enjoyment of life.

Ben Kayfetz

Foreword

The English-Yiddish section of this dictionary will be most useful to English-speaking people who desire to enlarge their knowledge of the Yiddish vocabulary and idiom without the necessity of being able to read the Hebrew characters that are used in most Yiddish-English and English-Yiddish dictionaries. It is to be expected that this section will be most helpful to those seeking the Yiddish equivalents of English words in everyday use. There are therefore more words in this section than in the Yiddish-English section. In many cases, however, it may be advisable to turn to the Yiddish-English section, after finding a word in the first section, to obtain a more elaborate definition and an example of usage.

This dictionary contains only grammatical forms and plurals most commonly used. The infinitive of verbs is not always given if it is not generally employed in conversation. Americanized words which appear regularly in Yiddish-English dictionaries are excluded. *Eleveyter* for "elevator" or *eskeleyter* for "escalator" contribute nothing to the Yiddish language. Highly preferrable as Yiddish forms are *di heybmashin* for "elevator" and *di vikltrep* for "escalator". One can enjoy the sound of words that show imagination in their construction and have not been overworked, such as *di mener-shvakhkeyt* for "impotence".

In separate sections are found interesting Yiddish equivalents of some English words, and a group of Yiddish idioms. All of these idioms are also included alphabetically in the dictionary proper. Included also are sections on trees, vegetables and fruits under the heading "Plant World", and animals, birds and insects under "Animal World". Although the Yiddish language is composed largely of Germanic-origin vocabulary, there is a significant non-Germanic component, mainly Hebraic and Slavic in derivation. The preponderance of Slavic-origin words in these two sections gives rise to thoughts on the life and environment of the East European Jew which I will not pursue and which students of cultural history would be wise to ponder. The social and vital conditions of the people are clearly illustrated in their language. For instance, the words for activity in family life, prayer, and synagogue are understandably from the Hebrew.

Lastly, a couple of pages are devoted to some proper names derived from Yiddish words. It is interesting to speculate on how a family acquired the name *Fingerhut* ("thimble") or *Solway* (from solovey, "nightingale").

I do not presume to offer an exhaustive collection of Yiddish memorabilia or a complete Yiddish-English, English-Yiddish dictionary. Such a work would require probably ten times the space of this book. I am offering rather a modest condensation.

Apart from the lexicon of the most common words with some of their idiomatic usages, this book contains a small collection of some typical Yiddish sayings, expressions and curses (more humourous than venomous), and a few of the many references to G-d and death. I have merely arranged them in alphabetical order.

Many of the sayings I used appeared in Maurice Samuel's delightful book, *In Praise of Yiddish* (New York, 1971). Some of the words are from *Röyte Pomerantsen* (New York, 1947) by Immanuel Olsvanger. The academic compilation by Uriel Weinreich, *Modern English-Yiddish, Yiddish-English Dictionary*, (New York, 1965), has also been consulted.

Larry Goldoff

Notes for the User

Since there are no capitals in Yiddish, I have used none in the transliterated words and, in most cases, none in the English definitions and translations. The exceptions occur in proper names and where there is emphasis to be indicated.

The transliteration generally follows the YIVO system, which is best suited to the average English reader. The letters c, j, q, w, and x are not used. The following table of vowels and consonants should clarify the pronunciation of those letters or combinations where it is not readily apparent.

a as in father	kh as in loch
e as in pet	ay as in eye
i as in pit (in the body of a word)	i as in ee of deer (in articles and pronouns)
ey as in grey	o as in aw of dawn
s as in sit	u as in oo of look
tsh as in ch of chip	g as in get
zh as s in measure	

When s'h appears, this indicates that the "s" and "h" should be pronounced separately.

Note that all vowels are to be pronounced separately, e.g. *toes* as "toe-ess" and *mies* as "me-ess". The accent on syllables varies; where there is some doubt the accent symbol is used.

Written Yiddish generally corresponds to the way it sounds. Exceptions occur when Yiddish words are borrowed from Hebrew. In such cases while the original Hebrew spelling is maintained, the corresponding pronounciation does not resemble the written word, e.g. *kabstn* (pauper) pronounced "kaptsn" (voiced consonant becomes unvoiced) or *bereyshit* (Genesis) is pronounced "bereyshes."

The bracketed initial after a given word indicates—although sometimes only vaguely or indirectly—its derivation. In many cases a word of Hebraic or Slavic origin has a Germanic prefix or suffix. The identification of the different parts' derivation is as follows:

E – English	P – Polish
F – French	R – Russian
G – German	S – Slavic
H – Hebrew	Y – Yiddish
I – Italian	

Where the initials I.O., M.S., or U.W. appear, the works of the authorities Immanuel Olsvanger, Maurice Samuel, or Uriel Weinreich have been followed for the pronunciation, translation or derivation.

Abbreviations

adj - adjective
adv - adverb
coll. - colloquial
E - English
f. - feminine
F - French
G - German
H - Hebrew
hum. - humourous
I - Italian
intr. - intransitive
I.O. - Immanuel Olsvanger
Lat. - Latin
lit. - literally
m. - masculine

M.S. - Maurice Samuel
n - noun
P - Polish
par. - participle
pl. - plural
prep. - preposition
pro. - pronoun
rel. - religious
R - Russian
S - Slavic
sing. - singular
trans. - transitive
U.W. - Uriel Weinreich
v - verb
Y - Yiddish

A prefix or suffix could be Yiddish, Russian or German. *oys* and *op* are Yiddish prefixes. (Pure German is *aus* and *auf*). *ik* and *ak* are Russian suffixes.

Most bracketed words are translations in the vernacular, colloquial or are obsolete.

English-Yiddish Dictionary

A

a, der a; der aleph (H)
abandon, avekvarfn
abandon (v), untervarfn (a child)
able (v), kenen
about (regarding), vegn
about (approximately), an erekh (H),
be'erekh (H), kimat (H), le'erekh (H)
above, oybn
absolutely, durkhoys
absorb, aynzapn
absorbed (mentally), aynzapn zikh,
farklert
absorbent cotton, di vate (R)
abstain, ophaltn zikh fun
abuse (n), der zilzl (H)
academy (Talmudic), di akademye, di
yeshive (H)
accident, di sibe (H), der tsufal, der
umglikfal
accompany, unterfirn
accomplice, der mit'helfer
accomplice in crime, der mitganef
(H)
accomplish, dergreykhn, oysfirn
according to, loyt
accordion, di harmonye (R)
account (n), der khezhbm (H), di
rekhenung
account for (v), opgebn a khezhbm fun
account (on account of), makhmes
(H), tsulib
accounted for, oysgetseylt
accounting (bookkeeping) (n), dos
khezhbm-fireray (H-Y)
accuse, bashuldikn
acknowledge, bashtetikn, moyde zayn
(H-Y), tsugebn
acorn, dos khazernisl (H-Y)
acquaintance, di bakante (f), der
bakanter (m)
acquaintance (knowledge), di
bakantshaft
across, ariber

action, di handlung
actually, leoylem
acumen, dos kharifes (H)
acute, sharf, sickness-akut
Adam (the first man), "der odom
horishen" (H)
add, moysef zayn (H), shteln, tsugebn
addition, der tsugob; (supplement,
enclosure in a mailing) der tsulog
"in addition to", dertsu
admire, bavundern, haltn fun
admission, der arayntret, der tsuloz;
(confession) dos moyde zayn (H-Y)
admit, moyde zayn (H-Y), tsugebn
admit (let in), araynlozn, derlozn
adopt, adoptirn (a child), onnemen
adult (n), der dervaksener, der layt
adversely, lignay (H)
advertise, anonsern, reklamirn
advertisement, der anons, di medoe
(H), di reklame
advice, di eytse (H)
advise, (counsel) eytsn (H), rotn
afar, "From afar"-"fun der vaytn(s)"
affair (business), der eysek (H), dos
gesheft
affairs (communal), di inyonim (H)
affection (brotherly), di libshaft, di
varemkeyt
affliction, di make (H), dos onshikenish
afflictions (list of), di toykhekhe (H)
afraid, dershrokn, moyre hobn (H-Y);
"He is afraid", "di hoyt tsitert oyf im"
after, nokh (also "after all")
after the fact (in retrospect),
bedieved (H)
again, nokh a mol, vayter, vider
against, akegn, antkegn, kegn
age, der elter
agent (commission), der agent
aggravate, farergern, farshverern
agile, flink, rirevdik
agitated (to be a.), oyfrudern, platsn
agnostic, der koyfer-beiker (H)
agonize, oyskrenken
agony, di gsise (H), yesurim (H)

agree, aynshtimen, maskem zayn (H-Y), mushve vern (H-Y)

agreed, maskem; "as agreed upon", "vi der meduber iz" (Y-H)

agreement, der durkhkum, di haskome (H), der tolk (R)

aid, di hilf; (device), der oys'helf

ail, feln, krenken; "What ails you?", "vos felt dir?"

aim (n), der tsil

aim (v), ontsiln, shtrebn

air (n), di luft

air conditioner, der luftkiler

aircraft, dos flivarg

alarm clock, der vekzeyger

alas, a shod

alcoholic drink (liquor, whiskey, not wine), der bronfn, di mashke (H)

alder (tree), di olkhe (R)

alive, baym lebn, bekhayim (H), khay, lebedik

all, ale, alts, gants

allow, bashteyn, derloybn, derlozn, lozn

allusion, der farruf, der remez (H)

Almighty (God), der almekhtiker, der oybershter

almond(s), der mandl(en)

almost, shier (with "nit" or "nisht")

almost, kimat (H), koym

alms, di nedoves, di tsdoke (H)

alone, aleyn

along, leng-oys, paze

alphabet, der aleph-beys (H)

already, shoyn

also, oykh, oykhet

alter, (iber) baytn, genitseven (R)

altered (clothing), genitsevet (R)

although, hagam (H), khotsh (R), khotshbe (R), vi voyl

altogether, besakhakl (H), in eynem, in gantsn, legamre (H)

always, ale mol, shtendik, tomid (H)

am, bin

amazed, fargaft vern, nishtoymem vern (H-Y)

amber, burlantn (R), burshtin

ambush, di ambuskade, der iberfal, der loker

amen, omeyn (H)

amends (to make a.), fargitikn, iberbetn, meytev zayn (H-Y)

ample, genugik

amuse, amuzirn, farvayln

and, un

anecdote, der anekdot

anemic, blutorem

angel, der malekh (H)

angel of death, der malkhamoves (H) (not used literally)

anger, der kaas (H), di rugze

angle, der vinkl

angry, broygez (H)

animal, der bal-khay (H), di khaye (H)

ankle, dos knekhl

anniversary, der yortog, der yoyvl (H), der yubiley (H)

anniversary of death, der yortsayt, (Memorial candles-yortsayt likht)

announce, bakant makhn, ongebn, onzogn

annoy, dergeyn di yorn, duln a kop, "tshepn zikh tsu"

annoyed, derkutshet

annul, anulirn, botl makhn (H-Y), kasirn, opshrayen (revoke)

another, anderer; nokh a

answer (n), der entfer; di tshuve (H)

anteroom, dos firhoyz, der proyzder (H)

anxious (to be a.), naygerik tsu, shtark veln

anxious (adj), bazorgt, umruik

any (not any), keyn; "Any day now", "az nisht haynt, iz morgn"

any (whatever), abi velkher/voser es iz

anybody, ver, ver nor, yeder eyner

anyhow, "say vi say"; "vi es iz"

anything, "abi vos"

anyway, say vi say, yednfals

anywhere, "abi vu"

apart, bazunder

apart from, akhuts (H)

apart (set apart), opgesheyt
(dissociated)
apartment, di dire (H)
apartment (three stories high), der
draygorndik
ape, di malpe
apology, di antshuldikung
apostate, der feltsher, der meshumed
(H) (Jewish), der oykher yisroel (H)
apparel (clothing), di kleydung, dos
onton
apparent, kentik, klor, kloymershtik (H-
Y), niker
apparently, a ponem (H), lekhoyre
(H), mashmoes (H), nibito (R)
appear, vayzn zikh; "to all
appearances", "vi es zet oys"
appearance (facial expression), dos
oyszen, dos ponem (H)
appetite, der apetit
appetizer(s), dos firgerikht(n), dos
forshpayz
applause, di aplodismentn
apple, der epl
apply for, ongebn, onverdn, tsuleygn
tsu
appointee, der memune (H)
approach, dernentern zikh, tsugeyn
approval, di aprobirung, di haskome
(H)
approximately, an erekh (Y-H),
be'erekh (H), le'erekh (H)
apricot, der aprikos (R)
apron, der fartekh
Arab(s), der araber
arc (arch) (n), der boygn
argue, ampern, durkhvertlen zikh,
misvakeyekh zayn (H-Y), zikh taynen
argue it out, oystaynen
argument, der iberred, di tayne
ark (Noah's), di teyve; Holy Ark, der
orn-koydesh (H)
arm (limb), der orem
armchair, der fotel (F), di fotershtul
army, di armey, dos khayil (H)
aromatic (to be) (permeate),
farshmekn

around, arum
arrange, tseleygn, tseshteln
arrange (a feast), oppraven
arrogance, dos gadles (H), di gayve
(H), di khutspe (H)
arrogant man, der bal gayve (H), der
gadlen (H), der khotsef (H)
art, di kunst
article (written), der artikl, der
maymer (H)
artist, der kinstler
as, az, vi; "as is", vi shteyt un geyt; "as
long as", abi, azoy lang vi, kolzman
(H); "as many", azoy fil, vifl
ascent, di aliye (H), der aroyfgang, der
oyfheyb
ash(es), dos ash
ash (tree), der ashboym
ashamed (to be), shemen zikh (H-Y)
ashtray, dos ashtetsl
Asia, di azye
Asia-minor, di kleyn-azye
ask, fregn
ask for, betn, farlangen
asparagus, di sparzhe (R)
aspen (tree), di osine (R), der topol
ass (buttocks), der hintn, der tokhes
(H) (coll.)
ass (donkey), der eyzl
ass (fool), der khamer (H)
assail, bafaln, onfaln oyf
assist, (aroys) helfn
assistant, der asistent, der gehilf
association (group), der farband, di
khevre (H)
astray (go), farblondzhen (Y-R)
at, bay; "at home", bay zikh
atheist, der koyfer-beiker (H)
atonement, dos opkumenish, di tshuve
(H)
atonement (religious ceremony),
kapores (H)
"Attaboy", "a lebn oyf dayn kop", "ot
azoy"
attach, bindn, festikn
attack, bafaln, onfaln
attempt, pruvn

attic, der boydem
attorney, der advokat
attorney (power of), di fulmakht
auction (n), di litsitatsye
audible, herevdik
aunt, di mume
Australia, di oystralye
author, der mekhaber (H), der
  shrayber
authority (expert), der meyvn (H),
  der oytoritet
authority (power), di eybershaft, der
  reshus (H)
authorization (Rabbi's), di smikhe
  (H)
autumn, der harbst, der osyen (R), der
  yeshn (R)
awaken (v), oyfshteyn
away, avek, (not here) nito
awe, der opshay
awkward, kuneleml; (humorous)
  umgelumpert
awkward (to be), hobn leymene hent
ax, di hak

B

babble, balebetshn, plaplen
baby, dos eyfele, dos viklkind
baby carriage, dos gangvegele
back (adj), karik, tsurik
back (anatomy), der rukn; (rear) di
  hintershte zayt
back (backwards), oyf tsurik
back (small of), der krizh (R)
backward, hintershtelik
bad, shlekht
bad (decayed, gone bad, rotten),
  farfoylt, tsefoylt; (tsefoylt also
  decadent)
bait (n), di tsishpayz
bait (v), "tsapn dos blut"
bake, bakn
bald, lise, naket

ball (party), der bal
ball (sphere), di koyl (R); (toy) der
  balem, di pilke
"Baloney!", di bobe mayse, di bovo
  mayse
ban (n), der farver, der kherem (H)
banana, der banan
bandit, der gazlen (H)
bang (n), der trask
bang (v), hakn, klapn, knaln, trasken
bank (edge), der breg
bank (money), di bank
banquet, der banket
baptize, kristikn
barb, di shtekhlke
barber, der sherer
bare, bloyz, hoyl, naket
barefoot, borves
barely, kam, koym
bargain (n), di metsie (H)
bargain (a real b.), "a metsie fun a
  ganef" (a thief's bargain)
bark (tree), di kore
bark (v), biln, havken
barn, der shayer
barrel, di fas, di tun
barrel maker, der bodner
bartender, der barshenker
basement, der keler, der untergorn
basement apartment, di kelershtub
bashful, shemevdik
basin, der bekn, der bit
bask (v), bodn zikh, varemen zikh
basket, der korb, der koshik, der
  koyber, der koysh
bastard, der mamzer (H)
baste (cook) (v), banetsn
baste (sew) (v), strigeven
bat (animal), di fledermoyz
bat (wood), di hilke
batch, dos bintl, dos pekl
bath, di bod, di vane
bath (Jewish ritual), di mikve (H)
bath (take a bath), bodn zikh, "makhn
  a vane"
bath attendant, der beder; (Jewish
  ritual) (female) di tukerin

bathrobe, der bodkhalat
bathroom, der vanetsimer, der
  vashtsimer
bath tub, di vane
battle (n), di shlakht
bazaar, der yarid (H)
be, zayn
beam (light), der shtral
beam (wood), der klots; der shtang
beach, der breg (yam), di plazhe (R)
bead, di krel, di patsherke (R)
beak, der shnobl
bean, dos bebl; (pl.) beblekh, der bob
  (pl. bobes), di fasolye
bear (n), der ber
bear (v), ibertrogn, laydn, oys'haltn
beard (v), di bord
bear out (vocally), unterhaltn
beast, di beheyme (H)
beat (defeat), tseklapn, tseshlogn
beat (hit), shlogn
beat up, tsehargenen (H), tseklapn
beau, der feler; (Yiddish jargon) der
  kavalir
beautiful, sheyn
beautiful (most), shenste
beautiful woman, di krasavitse (R)
beauty, di sheynkeyt
beauty parlor, der sheynkeyt-salon
became, gevorn
because, vayl, vorem, vorn
because of, bizkhus (H), makhmes (H)
become, vern
bed, di bet, di geleger
bed bug, di vants
bedding, dos betgevant; (linen) dos
  batsiekhts
bedroom, der shloftsimer
bedsheet, der laylekh
bedspread, der iberdek, der kape (R)
bee, di bin
beech (tree), der buk (R)
been (has), geven
beet, der burik; (pl.) di burikes (R)
beetle, der khrushtsh (R), der zhuk
beet soup, der borsht (der borshtsh)
  (R)

before, eyder, far
"Before you know it", "eyder vos ven"
beg, betlen, betn
beggar, der betler, der shnorer
begin, onfangen, onheybn
beginning, di haskhole (H), der
  onfang, der onheyb; "in the
  beginning", fun/in onheyb
begrudge, nit farginen, zhaleven
behead, kepn
behind (prep.), hinter, hintn
behind (remain b.), zamen zikh, zayn
  hintershtelik
belated, farshpetikt
belch (n), der grepts
believe, dakhtn zikh, folgn, gloybn,
  shtamen
believer, der gleybiker, der maymen
  (H)
believer (non) (Jewish), der
  apikoyres (H)
bell, der glok
belle, di krasavitse (R), di yefeyfye (H)
bellow (v), ritshn
bellows (n), der blozzak
belly, der boykh
belong, gehern
belongings, dos tsugeher
beloved (adj), balibt, gelibt
beloved (n), di gelibte (f), der gelibter
  (m)
below (adj), untn
below (prep), unter
belt (n), der pasik, der rimen; der gartl
  (Jewish religious)
bench, di bank
bend (v), beygn, onbeygn
benediction, di brokhe (H)
benediction (over bread) (Jewish),
  di hamoytse (H)
bent, ayngeboygn
bequest (n), der izovn (H), der
  opshrayb, di tsavoe (H)
bereaved, farovlt
bereaved person, der ovl (H); (pl.) di
  aveylim
berry, di yagde (R)

beside, bay, lebn
besides, akhuts dem (H-Y)
best man (wedding), der unterfirer
bestow, bagobn mit, bashenken
bet, dos gevet, der vet
bet (v), vetn zikh
betray, masern (H)
betroth (v), farknasn
betrothal, di farknasung, di farlobung
  (obsolete)
betrothal dinner, der knas-mol
better, beser
between, tsvishn
beverage, dos getrank, di mashke (H)
bible (Jewish), der tanakh (H)
bicycle, der bitsikl, der velosiped
bier, di mite (H)
bigot, der fargleybter, der khnyok (R)
bigoted, fanatish, fargloybt
big-shot, "der groyser held", "der
  groyser miyukhes" (H), der hitlmakher (hat maker or brass hat), der
  karpnkop, der knaker
bile, di gal
bin, der zasik
birch tree, di bereze
bird, der feygl, der foygl
bird's-eye-view, der feyglblik
birds of a feather, "fun eyn teyg
  geknotn"
birdies, di eyfelekh
birth, dos geboyrn-(vern), di geburt
birth (give b. to a child), geboyrn,
  geyn tsu kind
birth certificate, di metrike
birthmark, der mutertseykhn
biscuit, der biskvit
bishop, der biskup; (chess), der lafer
bit (small quantity), dos bisl, dos
  brekl, dos shtikl
bitch, di klafte (H)
bitch (dog), di tsoyg
bite (n), bis
bite (v), bisn; "Have a bite to eat",
  "khapn epes"
bitter, biter, galik; "The bitter end",
  "der same sof"

blab, (oys) leymern, piskeven
black, shvarts
blackberry, di ozhene (R)
"Black Hundreds" (Russian
  reactionaries), der shvartsmeyenik
  (G-H-R)
black eye (adj), untergeshlogn
blackbird, der amstl
blackboard, der tovl
blackjack (billy), di nagayke (R)
blackmail (n), der shantazh (R)
blackmail (v), shantazhirn
blacksmith, der kovel (R), der shmid
bladder, der penkher
blade (knife), der kling; "blade of
  grass", dos grezl
blame (n), di shuld
blame (v), hobn tsu . . . far
blank, bloyz, leydik
blanket, der dek, di koldre (R), der
  kotz; "Wet blanket", di bitere tsibele
  (bitter onion), "di zoyere ugerke
  (sour pickle)
blasphemy, der khilel-hashem (H)
blast-off, der aroyfshos
bleach (n), dos bleykhekhts
bleach (v), bleykhn
bleak, trib, vist
blemish, der pgam (H), dos umteyderl
bless, mekhadesh zayn (H)
bless (to say grace), bentshn
blessing (n), di brokhe (H)
blink (eyes) (v), pintlen
blister, der bloter, der pukhir (R)
blizzard, di zaverukhe (P)
blob, der koyk, der shmir
block (v), farshparn, farshteln
blockhead, der khamer (H), der tipesh
  (H)
blood, dos blut
bloodhound, der shpirhunt
bloodshed, di blut-fargisung, di
  shfikhes-domim (H)
bloody (adj), blutik
bloody (v), farblutikn, tseblutikn
bloom (n), der bli, der tsvit
bloom (v), blien

bloomers, maytkes (R)
blossom, dos bliekhts (blossoms), der kveyt
blot (n), der flek, der klek
blotch, der bloter
blotter, der kleker
blouse, di bluzke
blow (wind) (v), blozn
blueberry, di shvartse yagde (Y-R)
blunt (dull), temp
blunt (frank), ofn, sharf
blur (n), der flek, der vish
blurt out, aroysplatsn mit
blush (v), (far)reytlen zikh
board (council), di kolegye
board (food), der pansyon
board (food) (Jewish), di kest
board (wood), di bret
boarder, der kvartirant, der pansyoner
boast (n), der barim, der prol
boast (v), proln
boastful, barimerish, groys'halterish
boat, di lotke (R), dos shifl
bobby pin, di horshpilke
body, der guf (H), der kerper, dos layb
body and soul, "dos layb un lebn"
bodyguard, di laybvakh (soldier); (civilian) der laybvekhter
bog (n), di gruzne (R)
bog down, fargruznet vern
boil (n), dos geshvir
boil (v), kokhn, zidn
bold, bahartst, brav, dreyst, mutik
boldness, di dreystkeyt, der kurazh, der mut
bolt (n), der rigl; (screw) der shroyf
bomb, di bombe
bond (financial) (n), di obligatsye
bond (tie) (n), der bund
bone, der beyn
"More bones than meat", "kay un shpay"
"Make no bones about it", "redn ofene diburim"
book, dos bukh; (pl.) di bikher; der sider (H) (for daily prayers) (Jewish); der seyfer (H) (pl.) sforim (Talmudic)

bookbinder, der aynbinder
bookcase, di bikhershank
book end, der bikher-vinkl
boor, der am-orets (H), der grober yung, der zhlob
boot, der shtivl; (rain, snow) der bot
booze (v), farshikern (Y-H)
bore (n), der nudnik, (colloquial) der nudzh
bore (be a nuisance), nudyen (R)
bore into (drill), (durkh) boyern, (durkh) ekvern
borrow, borgn, layen
bosom, der buzem, der shoys (figuratively)
boss, der balebos (H), der shef
both, beyde
"Both . . . and . . .", "hen . . . hen", "i . . . i", "say . . . say"; "Both you and me", "ikh un dir"
bother, di dayge (H), dos fardreyenish, dos kop-dreyenish
bother (v), shtern, tshepn; "Bothered with", "patshken zikh"; "Don't bother me", "drey mir nit a spodik" (R) (don't turn my fur hat); "Not bothered in the least", "arn vi der farayoriker shney"; "Too much bother", "es loynt nit"; "What bothers you?", "vos art dir?", "vos kotert dikh?"
bottle, di flash, dos fleshl
bottom (adj), untersht
bottom (n), der dek, der dno, der untn
"From the bottom of my heart", "fun tifn hartsn"
bough, di tsvayg
boundary, der grenets, der gvul (H)
bow (bend) (n), der farneyg
bow (violin), der smitshik
bow (weapon), der boygn
bowel movement, der shtulgang
"move one's bowels", hobn dem mogn
bowl (n), di shisl; glass bowl, der klyosh (R)
bowling, di keglyeshpil
bowtie, di mushke (R)

box, der kastn, dos kestl; little box, dos pudele
box (on the cheek), der frask
boy, der/dos yingl; older boy, der bokher (H)
boy (dear little boy), dos zunele
brag, barimen zikh, proln zikh
braggart, der barimer, der flokn-shiser, der knaker
braid (n), der tsop; (pl.) di tsep
braided, geflokhtn
brain, der moyekh (H)
"Brain and brawn", "moyekh (H) un koyekh (H)"
brake, der tormaz (R)
bran, klayen
brandy, der konyak, der shnaps; cherry brandy, der vishnik (R)
brass, dos mesh
brassiere, der stanik
brave, bahartst, brav, mutik
brave man, der khvat (R)
bread, dos broyt; Sabbath bread, di khale; braided white loaf, der koyletsh (R); rye with caraway seeds, der pompernikl
breadbox, di broytnitse
bread crumbs, dos breyzl
break, brekhn; break up, tsebrekhn
breakfast, der frishtik, dos iberbaysn
break out, oysbrekhn
breast, di brust
breastpocket (inside coat pocket), di buzem-keshene
breath (n), der dukh, der hoykh, der otem
breathe, otemen
breathe in-breathe out, oysotemen
breed, hodeven (R) (see Y-E)
breeze, dos vintl
brew (n), dos gebray
brew (v), brayen
bribe (n), der khabar (R), der shoykhed (H)
bribe (v), shtupn, unterkoyfn, untershmirn, untershtupn
brick, der tsigl

bride, di kale (H)
bride and groom's private room, dos yikhed-shtibl (H)
bridegroom, der khosn (H), der man
bride-to-be, di bamante, di basherte
bridge (n), di brik; foot-bridge, di kladke (R) (klatke)
brief (adj), kurts
briefly, bekitser (H)
brilliant (in Talmud), geoynish (H), iluish (H), kharif (H)
brilliant (shiny), blank, glantsik
bring, brengen; bring about, brengen tsu
bring over, ariberbrengen
bring up (children), dertsien, onhodeven, oyfhodeven (R)
broad (adj), breyt
broadminded, breytgaystik, meykldik
broil, brotn
brooch, di brosh
brood (v), dumen
brook, di ritshke (R), dos taykhl
broom, der bezem
broth, der rosl, di yoykh (R)
brothel, dos shandhoyz
brother, der bruder; (pl.) di brider
brother-in-law, der shvoger
brown, broyn
bubble (n), dos blezl
bucket, der emer
bud (n), der buton, der knosp
budge (v), a rir ton
bug (n), der knayper, der zhuk
build, boyen
building (n), der binyen (H), di gebeyde
buffoon, der batkhn (Jewish Ritual) (H), der lets
bulge (n), der poysh (R)
bull, der bik (R), der buhay
bullet, di koyl (R)
bully (n), der britan, der onkhap; "Stand for no bullying", "nit lozn zikh shpayen in der kashe"
bully (v), balebateven, tshepen zikh tsu
bum, der orkheporkhe (H), der shleper

bumblebee, di zhumzhe
bump (blow), der zets
bump (in road), der shtroykhl
bun, di puter bulke; (hair) der grek
bundle (n), dos bintl, dos hayfl, dos
  pekl
bungalow, dos baydl, di (shlof)hayzke
bungle (v), farpartatsheven
burden (n), di last, di mase (H), der ol
  (H), der yokh
"Be a burden", "zitsn oyfn haldz",
  "zitsn oyfn kark"
burdened (with many children),
  metupl (H)
bureau (chest), der kamod (R)
burial, di kvure (H)
burial society, di khevre-kedishe (H)
  (Jewish)
burn (v), brenen
burst (n), der blits, der fleyts, der
  shtrom
burst (v), oyfraysn, platsn
bury, araynleygn, bagrobn, mekaber
  zayn (H)
bush, der kust
business, der eysek (H), dos gesheft,
  der miskher (H)
"Mind your own business", "shtekh
  zikh nit"
businesslike, mayse soykher (H),
  sokhrish (H)
business man, der gesheftsman, der
  soykher (H)
bust (n), der byust
busy, farhavet, farnumen, farshmayet
busybody, der kokhlefl
but, dokh, elo (H), ober
butcher (purveyor), der katsef (H)
butcher shop, di yatke (R)
butter, di puter
butterfly, dos flaterl
buttermilk, di maslinke, di putermilkh,
  di zoyermilkh
buttocks, dos gezes, dos grobe fleysh,
  der hintn, der tokhes
button, dos knepl, der knop
buttonhole, di knepllokh

buy, koyfn
buy up, oyfkoyfn, oyskoyfn
by, fun, lebn

C

cabbage, dos kroyt
cage, di shtayg; "birdcage", dos shtaygl
cake, der kukhn, der lekekh; (soap), dos
  shtikl
calculate, khezhbenen (H)
calculation, der khezhbm (H)
calendar (Jewish dates only), der
  luekh (H)
calendar (non-Jewish), der kalendar
calf (animal), dos kalb
call (n), der ruf; (phone), der klung
call (v), rufn
call (be named), heysn
call girl, dos lebmeydl
call up (telephone), onklingen,
  ontelefonirn
calm, barut, ruik
camel, der keml
camp, der lager
campaign (n), di aktsye, di kampanye
campaign (v), "firn an aktsye",
  kampanyeven
can (v), kenen
"How can this be carried out?", "vi
  kumt di katz ibern vaser?" (how does
  the cat cross the water)
can (charity box), di pushke
can (tin), dos blekhl
cancer, der rak
candle, dos likht
"Synagogue candles", kneytlekh
candy, dos tsukerl, dos zisvarg
"Box of candy", di bombonyerke (R)
candy bar, di shokoladke
candy store, dos zeltserkleytl
cannibal, der mentshn-freser
cannon, der harmat (R)

canopy (wedding), di khupe (H)
(Jewish)
cantaloupe, di dinke (R)
cantor, der khazn (H)
cantor's wife, di khaznte (H)
cap, dos hitl, dos mitsl
cap (skull), di yarmulke (H) (Jewish)
cape (cloak), di pelerine (R)
cape (land), der kap
capital (financial), der kapital
capital city, di ir habiro (H), di
kroynshtot
caraway, der kiml
carbon paper, di kalke
card(s) (playing), di kort(n); "to play
cards", shpiln in kortn
cardboard (n), di tektur
care (n), di dayge (H), di zorg
care (take care), hitn, ophitn
careful, gevornt, opgehit
caress (n), der glet
caress (v), gletn
caretaker (of Synagogue), der shames
(H)
carnation, dos negele
carouse, hulyen (R)
carpenter, der stolyer
carpet (n), der kobrets, der tepekh
carriage, di droshke (R), di karete (R),
der vogn; baby-carriage, dos gangvegele
carrot(s), di mer(n)
carry, trogn
carry away, fartrogn
cart (n), der vogn
"Put the cart before the horse",
"khapn di fish far der netz" (catch the
fish before the net)
cash, dos mezumen (H), mezumonim
(H)
cash (in cash), bimzumen (H)
cask, dos fesl, dos tundl
casket (coffin), dos shketele
Caspar Milquetoast, der/di lemishke
(R)
castrate, mesares zayn (H-Y)
cat, di kats

catarrh, der kater
catch (grab) (n), di khapung (R)
catch (v), khapn (R)
caterpillar, der opfreser, dos shleyerl
cattle, beheymes (H), dos fikh, rinder
cauliflower, dos blumenkroyt, der
kalefyor
cause (n), di sibe (H)
cave (n), di heyl
cedar tree, der tsederboym
ceiling, di stelye, der sufit (P)
celebrate, farbrengen, fayern, oprikhtn,
praven (R)
celebrate the Sabbath, "makhn
shabes" (Y-H)
celebration, di fayerung, di simkhe (H)
celery, di selerye
cellar, der keler
cemetery, der bes-oylem (H) (see
intr.)
century, der yorhundert
certain (to make certain), farzikhern,
hitn
certain (sure), zikher
certainly, avade (H), graylekh
chain, di keyt
chair, dos benkl, di shtul
chalk, di krayd
chandelier, der henglaykhter, der,
kandelaber, di lustre
change (n), der (iber)bayt, di
enderung, di shine (H); (returned
money), der oysgob, der resht; (small
change), dos kleyngelt, dos mints; "for
a change", in a novene (R)
change (v), baytn, endern; (money),
tsebaytn
change clothes, iberton zikh
Channukah, der khanuke (H) (festival
of lights; feast of the Maccabees)
chaos, der khaos, der toyevoye (H)
chapter (of a book), dos kapitl, der
peyrek (H)
character, der kharakter
chariot, di karete (R)
charitable gift (trifling), di nedove
(H)

charity (public), di kitsve (H), di tsdoke (H)
charm, der kheyn (H)
chat (n), der shmues (H)
chat (v), shmuesn (H)
chatter (n), dos geplapl
chatter (v), plaplen
chatterbox, der yabednik (R)
cheap, bezol (H), bilik, volvl
cheat (n), der ramay (H)
cheat (v), bashvindlen, opnarn
checkers (game) (n), di damke; (checkers piece), der tsigl
cheerful, munter, oyfgeleygt
cheese, der kez
cherry, di karsh, der vaynshl
chess, der shokh
chest (anatomy), di brust, der brustkastn
chestnut, di kest
chew (v), kayen
chicken, dos hindl, di hun
chicken coop, der katukh (R)
chicken soup, di gildene yoykh (R)
child, dos kind; (pl.) di kinder
children (little), kinderlekh
chime (n), di gloknshpil
chimney, der koymen
chimneysweep, der koymenkerer
chin, di morde (R)
china, dos portselay
China (country), di khine
Chinese (n), der khinezer, der kitayets (R)
chip (n), dos brekl
chipmunk, der geshtrayfter vevrik
chipper (adj), hoferdik, oyfgeleygt
chips (wood), shpendlekh
chisel (n), der dlot
chit-chat, dos ployderay
choice, di breyre (H), der iberklayb, der oysklayb
choir, der khor
choke (v), dervargn zikh, (der) shtikn
choked, dervorgn
cholera, di kholere
choose, oysklaybn

chop (n), der kotlet (R)
chop (v), hakn
chop-stick, dos es-shtekele
chorus girl, dos blishtshmeydl (R-Y)
Christian (n), der krist
Christmas, der nitl
chubby, poyshik (R)
chump, der frits, der yold
chunk, di payde (R)
chunk (wood), der shayt
church, di kirkh, di tifle (H), di tserkve (R)
chute, der aroploz
cigarette, der papiros (R)
cinder, di holeveshke (R)
cinnamon, der tsimring
circle, der krayz, di rod
circumcise, mal zayn (H-Y), maln (H), yidishn (Jewish)
circumciser, der moyel (H)
circumcision, di mile (act of) (H)
circumcision ceremony, der bris (H) (Jewish)
circumstance(s), der maymed, der umshtand(n); "under no circumstances", "beshum oyfn veyinyen" (H)
circus, der tsirk (R)
citizen, der birger
citron (for Succoth), der esreg (H)
city, di shtot
civil war, di birger-milkhome (Y-H), der briderkrig
claim (n), di khazoke (H), di tayne (H), di tvie (H)
clamour (n), dos gepilder, dos geshrey, der tuml
clan, der klan, der shtam
clap (v), aplodirn, patshn
clarify, klor makhn, oyfklern
clatter (n), dos geklaper, der trask
claw (n), di krel
clay (adj), leymen
clay (n), di leym
clean (adj), reyn
clean (clean up), oyframen
clean (house) (v), ramen

clean (ritually), kosher (H) (Jewish)
cleanliness, di reynkeyt
clean out, oysramen
clear (adj), klor
clearly, bekhush (H), poshet (H)
clerk, der byuralist
clever, geshayt, klug
clever (efficient person), der/di berye (H)
climate, der klimat
climbers (leaves), kleterbleter
clink glasses, tshoken mit
clique, di knufye (H)
clock, der zeyger
clog (v), farleygn, farshtopn
close (v), farmakhn, tsumakhn
closet, der almer, di shafe (R)
cloth, dos gevant, der shtof, dos tsayg
clothes, kleyder, malbushim (H), dos onton
clothes (washed), dos gret, dos vesh
clothesline, der gretshtrik
clothespin, der gretklamer
clothing, di halboshe (H), di kleydung, dos ontuekhts
cloud, der volkn; threatening cloud, di khmare (R)
clove(s), dos negele(kh); garlic, dos tseyndl
club (informal), dos krayzl
club (people), der klub
club (weapon), der flokn
clue (n), der shlisl, der slid; "I don't have a clue", ikh hob nit keyn anung
clump (cluster), dos gezeml
clumsy, kuneleml (col.), umbaholfn, ungelumpert
coach (vehicle), di karete (R)
coachman, der balegole (H)
coal, koyln
"Carry coal to Newcastle", "firn shtroy keyn mitsrayim" (carry straw to Egypt)
coarse (common), grob, prost (R)
coat (as worn by religious Jews), der kaftn, di kapote (R)
coat (paint), der shikht

coat (top), der mantl; jacket, dos rekl
coax, aynredn
cobbler, der shuster
cock-a-doodle-do, kukeriku
cockroach, der tarakan (R)
coconut, der kokosnus
c.o.d., der nokhtsol; send c.o.d., shikn oyf nokhtsol
cod, der dorsh
coddle, pankeven
cod-liver oil, der fishtron
coffee, di kave (R)
coffee-pot, der kavenik (R)
coffin, der orn (Jewish), dos shketele, di trune
cogwheel, di tseynrod
coil (n), di shpul
coin (gift or tip), di matbeye (H)
coin (gold), dos rendl
coin box (for charity), di pushke (R)
coins, klingers
cold (adj), kalt
cold (n), di kelt
cold (ailment) (n), di farkilung, der kater; "catch a cold", farkiln zikh
coleslaw, der kroytsalat
collapse (v), avekfaln, aynfaln, umfaln
collar (n), der kolner, der kragn
collect, klaybn, zamlen
collect dues, aynmonen, opmonen
collection, der tsunoyfnem, di zamlung
colloquial, shmuesdik
colloquial language, di shmuesshprakh
collusion, der tsunoyfred
colonel, der kolonel, der polkovnik (R)
colour (n), di farb, der kolir (R)
colt, der loshik (R)
comb (n), der kam, dos keml
Come now!, "gey gey"
"Come on", "nu zhe"
come (v), kumen; "Come home", aheymkumen
comfortable, bakvem, "Make yourself comfortable", "makh zikh bakvem"
comforter (bed), di perene (R)
coming (due), kumendik

command (n), der bafel, di komande
commemorate, batseykhnen dem
  ondenk fun
commend, nokhzogn a shvakh
commentary, der peyresh (H)
commercial (adj), komertsyel,
  sokhrish (H)
commercial (n), der anons
commit, bageyn, opton
commit (entrust), ibergebn
commit oneself, bindn zikh,
  miskhayev zayn zikh (H-Y)
common (average), prost
common (joint), beshutfesdik (H)
common (people), amkho (H)
  (Jewish), hamoynam (H)
common (usual), geveyntlekh
communal, klal, ko'olsh
community, der klal (H), dos koel (H)
  (Jewish), der tsiber
"Community of Israel", "der klal
  yisroel" (the Jewish people)
companion, der baleyter, der
  kompanyon
company (business), di firme
company (social), di gezelshaft
compare, farglaykhn, glaykhn
compared to, in farglaykh mit, legabe
  (H)
comparison, der farglaykh
complain, baklogn zikh, krekhtsn,
  taynen
complaint, di tayne (H)
complete (adj), fulshtendik, gants,
  gomur (H)
complete (v), dergantsn, farendikn
completely, beshleymes (H), far ful,
  gor, in gantsn
compliment (n), der kompliment, der
  shvakh
composition (written), der khiber
  (H)
comrade, der khaver (H), (f. di
  khaverte)
conceal, bahaltn, farshteln, tayen
concede, moyde zayn (H-Y)

conceive (mentally), banemen, maseg
  zayn (H-Y)
"It is conceivable", "es ken gemolt
  zayn"
concentrate (v), "kayen di bord"
  (chew one's beard), kontsentrirn,
  tsuleygn moyekh (H) (tsu)
concentration camp, der katset (R),
  der kontsentratsye lager (G)
concern oneself, arn, zorgn
concubine, der kepsvayb, di pilegesh
  (H)
condition, der bading, der tnay (H);
  "on condition that", bitnay az (H)
condition (state), der matsev (H), der
  tsushtand
conduct (n), di hanhoge (H), der oyffir
cone (of a tree), di shishke (R)
confer, bateyln mit, meyashev zayn zikh
  (H-Y)
confession, der moyde (H)
confession (deathbed), di vide (H)
confinement (birth), di kimpet
confuse, farplontern, tsedreyen,
  tsemishn
confused, tsedreyt, tsetumlt
confusion (mental), di behole (H),
  dos tsemishenish
congratulate, gratulirn, vintsheven
congratulate oneself, "patshn zikh in
  baykhl"
Congratulations!, "mazl-tov" (H)
congregation, di eyde (Jewish
  orthodox), di kehile (H)
conquer, aynnemen
conscription (n), dos muzdinst, di
  nemung, der priziv (R) (especially in
  Czarist Russia)
consecrate (v), aynheylikn, mekadesh
  zayn (H-Y)
consenting, maskem zayn (H-Y)
conservative (n), der konservator;
  (reactionary) der khnyok (R)
consider, baklern, barekhnen zikh,
  batrakhtn
considerably (coll), nishkoshedik
  (H-Y)

consort with, hobn tsu ton, khavern zikh mit

conspicuous (to be), onzen zikh, varfn zikh in di oygn

conspiracy, di farshverung, der yadakhes (H)

constipation, di farhaltung

construct, (oys)boyen

consultation, di barotung, der yishev-hada'as (H)

consume (swallow), farshlingen

consume (use up), farnitsn

container, der halter

contentious, makhloykesdik (H-Y)

continually, keseyder (H), rak (H), shtendik

contraceptive, der trog-farhiter

contradict, opfregn, soyser zayn (H)

contrary, farkert, heypekh (H); "on the contrary", leheypekh (H)

contribute, bayshtayern, gebn tsu shtayer

convent, der konvent

convert (to Christianity), der meshumed (H); (pl.) di meshumodim

convert (to Judaism), der ger (H), (pl.) di geyrim

converted (from Judaism), (ge)shmad (H)

cook (n), di kekhne (f), der kukher (m)

cook (v), kokhn, opkokhn

cookie(s), dos kikhl(ekh), dos lekekhl(ekh)

cooking (n), der kokhn

cooking pot, der top

cook up, farkokhn

cool (adj), kil, luftik

coop (chicken), der katukh (R)

cooper (barrel maker), der bodner

copper, dos kuper

copulate, baheftn zikh, porn zikh

cord (electric), der shnur

cord (string), der shpagat

cork (n), der korik, der propn

corkscrew, dos propn-tsier

corn, di kukuruze (R), der papshoy (R)

corn flakes, papshoy-shneyelekh

corn (toe), dos hineroyg

corned (adj), gepeklt; "corned beef", peklfleysh

corner, der ek, der vinkl; der rog (street)

corner (v), "farshtupn in a vinkl"

corny, hametne (R), umpikant

corpse, der bar-menen (H), der mes (H); (pl.) meysim

correct (adj), gerekht, rikhtik

correct (v), farrikhtn, korigirn

correction, di oysbeserung, der tikn-toes (H)

corrode, tse'esn, tsefresn

corrugated, gekhvalyet

corset, dos shnirlaybl

cosey, heymish, nuredik, shtubik

Cossack, der kozak (R)

cottage, dos baydl, di datshe (R), di hayzke, dos zumerhoyz

cottage (peasant's), di khate (R)

cottage cheese, der tsvorekh

cotton (n), der bavl

cotton batting, di vate

couch, di kanape, di kushetke

cough (n), der hust

cough (v), hustn

cough (while talking), unterhustn; "have a coughing fit", farhustn zikh

count (v), tseyln

countenance (n), dos gezikht, dos ponem (H)

country, dos land, di medine (H); "In the country", "oyf datshe"; "Old country", "di alte heym"; "Poor country", "dos oremland"

country (nation), di ume (H)

countryman, der landslayt, der landsman

couple (married), dos por-folk; (unmarried), dos porl

courage, der mut

course (way), der gang; golf course, der golfplats

courtesy, di eydlkeyt

court of justice, dos bes-din (H) (Jewish), dos gerikht

court yard, der hoyf
cousin, dos shvesterkind
covenant (re. "mile"), der bris (H)
cover (for book), der tovl
cover (paper wrapper), di hile
cover (for pot), dos dekl, dos shtertsl
cover (v), badekn; "to cover with a
  blanket", ayndekn; "to cover with a
  bedspread", farbetn
covering (n), der tsudek
coverlet (for the body to which
  "tsitses" are attached), dos layb-
  tsudekl
covet, glustn nokh
cow, di beheyme (H), di ku; (pl.) di ki
coward, der pakhdn (H)
coy, kloymersht shemevdik, lozn zikh
  betn
"Crack of dawn", der fartog, "ven got
  aleyn shloft nokh"
cracker, der biskvit, dos pletsl
cradle (n), di vig
craft (trade) (n), di melokhe (H);
  (vessel), di shif
craftiness, di khitrekeyt
craftsman, der bal-melokhe (H)
crafty, geshayt, khitre (R)
cramp (n), der kortsh, der kramp
cranberry, di brusnitse, di zhurekhline
  (R)
crash (n), der krakh, der trask (R)
crawl (v), krikhn
craze, dos meshugas (H), der shigoen
  (H)
crazy, meshuge (H), tsedreyt
creak (v), skripen, treshtshen
cream (sour), di shmetene (P), di
  smetene (P)
creator, der bashefer, der boyre (H)
cricket (insect), di gril, der tshirkun
  (R)
crime, der farbrekh, dos farbrekheray
crimson, pomsn
cripple (n), der bal-mum (H), der/di
  kalike
crisp, krukhle (R), merbik

criss-cross, durkhgekestlt, getseylemt
  (H)
croak (die) (v) (coll.), krepirn,
  peygern
crockery, der fayants (R), dos leymvarg
"crocodile tears", "tsibele trern"
crooked, krum
cross (n), der tseylem (H)
cross-eyed, kasoke (R), shikldik
crossroads, der sheydveg, der
  shnaydveg
crotchety person, der kvetsh
crowd (n), di mase, der oylem (H)
crowded, eng, gepakt, "kop oyf kop"
crude, goylemdik (H-Y), grob, prost
crummy (crushed), tsebrokhn,
  tsekrishlt
crumpled, tsekneytsht
crushed, tseknakt, tseshmetert
crust, der nit, di skore
crutch, di kulye (R)
cry (v), veynen
crying (wail) (n), di yelole (H)
cry out, oysshrayen
cuff (n), der manzhet (R)
cuff link, di shponke (R)
cup, der kos (H), der kubik, dos shelkhl
cupboard, di shafe (R)
cupping glass(es) (for drawing
  blood), di banke(s) (R)
curds and whey, di maslinke
cure (n), di refue (H)
cure (v), heyln
curious, naygerik, tshikave (R)
curl (n), dos grayzl, der lok
currant, dos vaymperl
curse (n), di klole (H)
curse (v), mekalel zayn (H-Y), shiltn,
  zidlen
curtain, der firhang
curtain (before the ark), der
  poroykhes (H) (Jewish)
cushion (n), der kishn, der yashik (R)
custom, der mineg (H)
customer, der koyfer, der koyne (H)
cut, der (ayn)shnit
cut (v), shnaydn

cutlery, makhshirim (H) (pl. only), dos meservarg

cutter (craftsman), der tsushnayder

D

dabble, amatoreven, madzhgen

daffodil, der geler nartsis

dairy (adj-re dietary laws), milkhik (Jewish)

dairyman, der milkhiker

daisy, di margeritke

damage (n), der hezek (H), der shodn

damage (v), kalye makhn, shedikn

"Damn him!", "a ruekh in zayn tatn arayn"

"I'll be damned", "take?"

damp, faykht, vilgotne

dance (n), der tants; Hasidic dance, der riked (H)

dance (v), tantsn

dandelion, dos luftl

dandruff, shupn

danger, di gefar, di sakone (H); "Danger to life" (when dietary laws are suspended), "der pikuekh-nefesh" (saving of a life) (H); "Mortal danger", "dos sakones-nefoshes" (H)

dangerous, mesukn (H), sakonedik (H)

dapper person, der khvat

dare (v), aroysfodern

dare (How dare you?), "vi kumstu?"

daring (adj), aynshtelerish, mutik

dark (adj), finster, tunkl

darkness, dos fintsternish, der khoyshekh (H)

darling, hartsenyu, neshomenyu lebn

darling (n), di lyuve

darn (v), fartsireven

dart, dos varfshpizl

date (appointment), di randke, di trefung, di ze'ung; (go on dates), geyn farbrengen, "randkeven zikh"

date (fruit), der teytl

date (time), di date

daughter, di tokhter; "lively, good-natured daughter", di shprintse; "only daughter", di bas-yekhide (H); "youngest daughter", di mizinke (H)

daughter-in-law, di shnur

dawn (n), der baginen, der fartog, der kayor

day, der tog; (pl.) di teg; "We haven't all day", "der tog shteyt nit"

dead (adj), (see intr.) geshtorbn, toyt

dead (n), der bar-menen, der mes (H); (pl.) mesim

deal, dos gesheft, der masematn (H), der opmakh; "A good deal" (many), "a hibsh bisl"; "Big deal", "a groyse metsie", "a tayere metsie"

dear (beloved, expensive) (adj), tayer; "I like you", "ikh hob dir holt"; "to hold dear", holt hobn

death, di ptire (H), der toyt; violent death, di mise meshune (H)

deathbed confession, di vide (H)

deathly, toyt (prefix)

debate (n), der vikuekh (H)

debate (v), misvakeyekh zayn (H-Y), shparn zikh

debauchee(er), der hultay, der noyef (H)

debauchery, di hultaystve, der nief (H), di oysgelasnkeyt, der znus (H)

debt, der khoyv (H)

deceive, firn in bod (lead to the bath) (humourous), opnarn

decent, laytish, mentshish, orntlekh

decide, bashlisn, bashtimen, paskenen (H), rashen (R)

decision, der bashlus, di hakhlote (H)

decision (judgement), der psak (H)

decree (n), der dekret, di farordenung, der prikaz (R); "Evil decree", di gzeyre (H)

decree (v), goyzer zayn (H-Y)

dedicated Talmud student, der masmid (H)

deduct, aroprekhnen

deed (good), di mitsve (H) (Jewish), di
   tu'ung
deep, tif
deer, der hirsh
defeat (n), di mapole (H), der opshnit
defecate, kakn
defect (in character), der khisorn (H)
defect (in the body) (n), der mum
   (H), der pgam (H), di pgime (H)
defiant, stirdish, tselokhesdik (H)
definitely, avade (H), bashtimik, zikher
deliberate (v), batrakhtn, meyashev
   zayn zikh (H-Y)
delicacy, der maykhl; (pl.) di
   maykholim (H)
delicious, batamt (H), geshmak,
   maykhldik (H)
delightful, mekhayedik (H),
   mekhayenefoshesdik (H)
delinquency, dos pasles (H)
deliver, opgebn, oysleyzn
delivery, der tsushtel
delude, farfirn, opnarn
"Self delusion", dos zikh-aynredenish
demand (v), fodern, monen
demon, di klipe (H), der ruekh (H), der
   shed (H)
den (room), der alker
denial, di hakkhoshe (H), di
   opleykenung
denounced, gemasert (H)
denouncer, der moyser (H)
dense, gedikht
dense (stupid), temp
dent (n), der aynshnit, der karb
dent (v), aynkarbn
deny (v), leyknen, makkhesh zayn
   (H-Y)
depart, opgeyn
depend; "it depends", "es vent zikh",
   "vi ven", "vi ver", "vi vos", "vi vu";
   "depend upon", farlozn zikh oyf,
   onkumen tsu
deposit (place on d.), aynleygn,
   deponirn
depressed (sad), farkhoyshekht (Y-H),
   farklemt

deprive, tsunemen; "Don't deprive me
   of the honour", "nem bay mir nit tsu
   dem koved"
derby (hat), der kapelyush (R) (also
   ladies' dressy hat)
derision, dos geshpet, der khoyzek (H),
   dos letsones (H)
derma (stuffed), di kishke (R)
descendant, dos eynikl, der
   opshtamling
desecrate, farshvekhn, farumverdikn,
   mekhalel zayn (H-Y)
desecration, der khilel (H)
deserted, farlozn, vist
deserted wife, di agune (H)
deserve, zayn vert kumen, zoykhe zayn
   (H-Y)
design (n), di kavone (H); "Have
   designs", "sharfn zikh di tseyner"
desire (n), der rotsn (H), di velung
desk, der shraybtish
desperate, fartsveyflt; "Be desperate",
   krikhn oyf glaykhe vent"
despise, faynt hobn
dessert, dos farbaysn
destination, der fortsil
destined, bashert
destitute, faroremt, orem; "Become
   destitute", "blaybn in eyn hemd"
destroy (v), aynleygn, farnikhtn
destroyed, fartilikt, khorev (H)
destruction, der khurbn (H), der tel
   (H)
detach, opknipn, opteyln
detail (n), der detal, di pitshevke; in
   detail, befroytret (H); "In great detail",
   "mit ale pitshevkes"
deter, ophaltn
detergent, dos loygvarg
deteriorate, farergern zikh
detract (from), minern
devil, der ruekh (H), der shed (H), der
   tayvl, der vatnmakher (see intr.)
devote, opgebn
devoted, getray, ibergegebn
dew, di rose, der toy
diabetes, di tsukerkrenk

diagram, dos gemel
diamond(s), der brilyant(n)
diaper, dos vikele, dos vindl
diarrhea, der loyzer mogn, der shilshl
(H)
dictionary, dos verterbukh
did (caused), ongemakht
die, shtarbn (see intr.)
die (dice), der toplshteyn, der verfl
die (re. animals), peygern (see intr.)
diet, di diete
diet (starvation d.) (v), unterhungern
dietary laws, dos kashres (H)
difference, der khilek (H), di nafkemine (H), der untersheyd
different (adj), farsheydene
different (adv), andersh
difficult, shver
difficulty, di shverikeyt; "With great
difficulty", "mit grine verem"
digest (v), fardayen
digestion, di fardayung
dignified, bekovedik, gehoybn,
statetshne (R)
dill, der krop
dill pickle, di zoyere ugerke
dim (v), optunklen
dime, dos tsenele; "Be a dime a dozen",
"valgern zikh in di gasn"
dimple(s), dos kheyn-gribele(kh)(H)
ding-dong, bim-bam, kling-klang
dingy, hekdeshdik (H), opgelozn
dinner, dos onbaysn, dos varmes; mid-
day, der mitog
dip (v), toyvlen (H) (Jewish), tunken
dip (depression), der aynkvetsh
dipper, der kokhlefl; "The Big Dipper",
der groyser ber
direct (show the way), vayzn dem veg
direct (a play) (v), rezhisirn
director (theatre), der rezhisor
dirt, di blote (R), dos shmuts; "dirt-
cheap", "bilik vi borsht"
dirty, shmutsik
dirty oneself (soil), aynrikhtn
disagreeable, prikre (R), umayngenem,
umsimpatish

disappear, farfaln vern, farshvundn
vern, nelm vern (H-Y)
disappointed, antoysht
disaster, der brokh, dos umglik
discomfort, di umbakvemkeyt
disconsolate, umetik
discontented, umtsufridn
discount store, di rabatkrom (R)
discourage, antmutikn, "leygn shteyner
oyfn hartsn", opmutikn, opredn
discover, khapn zikh, oyfdekn
discuss, arumredn
discussion, der arumred, di diskusye,
der shmues
disease, dos khalas (H), di krankeyt, di
krenk
disentangle, oysplontern
disgrace (n), der bizoyen (H), di bushe
(H), di kharpe (H)
disgrace (v), farshemen, mevayesh
zayn (H-Y)
disgraceful, shendlekh
disguise (n), di farshtelung
disguise (v), farshteln
disgust, der ekl, der migl
disgusting person, der parkh (R)
dish, di shisl, der teler
disheveled (hair), tsepatlt, tseshoybert
disheveled (shirt), tsekhrastet
dishonest, umerlekh, umorntlekh
dishonesty, di umerlekhkeyt
dishrag, di hantsherke, di stsirke
dishwasher, der keylim-vasher (H-Y)
dislike (v), faynt hobn, nit holt hobn
dismal, farumert, klogedik
disobey, nit folgn
dispensable, lavdafke (H)
dispense, oysteyln, tsegebn
dispense justice, oysmestn
dispense drugs, tsugreytn
disperse, tseshpreytn, tsetraybn,
tseyogn
display, aroysvayzn, oysshteln
displease, makhn umtsufridn, nit gefeln
displeasing person, der paskudnik (R)
dispose of, bazaytikn, poter vern fun
(H-Y)

disposition, dos gemit

disputation, der disput, der vikuekh (H)

dispute (v), misvakeyekh zayn zikh (H-Y), shparn zikh

disrespect (n), der umderkherets (Y-H)

disrupt, farshtern, tseshtern

dissatisfied, umtsufridn

dissolve, tsegeyn, tselozn, tserinen zikh

distance, di vaytkeyt; "This is some distance", "folg mikh a gang"

distant relative, "ferds fus podkeves an eynikl"

distinguish, mavdl zayn (H-Y), untersheydn

distinguished, khoshev (H), ongezen

distinguished ancestry, der yikhes (H)

distinguished man, der yakhsn (H)

distinguished woman, di yakhsnte (H)

distort, duren (R), farkrimen, tsedreyen

distraught, "arumgeyn on a kop", tsekhusht (tsekhisht), tsetraytlt, "zayn vi nit keyn higer" (to be like a foreigner)

disturbance, dos geruder, di shterung

ditch (n), der grovn, der rov, der shants

dive (n), der kopnshprung, di kopnurke

dive (v), "makhn a kopnurke", untertunken zikh

divide (v), teyln

division (arithmetic), der khilek (H)

division (part), der kheylek (H), der opteyl, der teyl

divorce (n), der get (H); (v) getn

divorcé (m), der goresh (H)

divorced, geget (H)

divorcée (f), di grushe (H)

do, makhn, ton, tuen; "This will not do", "dos toyg nit"

docile, nokhgibik, polgevdik

doctor, der dokter, der royfe (H)

dodge (v), aroysdreyen zikh fun, oysmaydn

dog, der hunt (hint), der kelev (H)

doghouse, di bude

dollar, der dolar, der doler, der tuler

dolt, der klots (col.), der shlimazl (H), der tipesh (H)

domineering woman, "a yidene a kozak"

done, opgepotert (Y-H); done in, farfaln

done with (that's that), poter (H)

donkey, der eyzl

doodle (v), blayern

door, di tir

doorstep, di shvel

dope (drug), dos fartoybekhts

dot, dos pintl, der punkt

dots, pintelekh (reference to Hebrew)

double (adj), topl, tsveyik

double bed, di porfolkbet

double-breasted, tsveybortik

doubt, der sofek (H), der tsveyfl

dough (flour), dos teyg

dough (money), klingers, mamtakim (H)

dove, di toyb

down (adj), anider, arop, arunter, nider; "Let down", aroplozn

down (n), der pukh

down (to go down), untergeyn

downhearted, dershlogn, "zayn vi unter der vant"

downpour, der shlaksregn

downstairs (place), untn; (direction), arop di trep

dowry, der nadn (H)

doze (v), dremlen (R)

doze off, ayndremlen

dozen, der tuts

drag (v), shlepn

drag out, oystsien

drake, der kotsher

drape (n), der gardin

draught (air), der tsug

draught (drink), der trunk

draught (military), di nemung

draught (plan), der proyekt

"Draw out the words", "shlepn far der tsung"

drawer (furniture), der shuflod; (desk/table drawer), dos tishkestl
draw out (drag), farshlepn
drayman, der balegole (H), der furman
dreadful, moyredik (H)
dream (n), der kholem (H), der troym (ideal)
dream (v), kholemen (H)
dreary, khmarne (R)
dress (n), dos kleyd
dress (v), onton
dress a wound (v), farbandazhirn
dress down, oyssheygetsn (Y-H)
dressed up, "in esik un in honik"
dresser, der kamod
dress up, oysputsn
dried up (out), ayngedart, ayngetriknt
drill (tool) (n), der boyer
drill (v), boyern
drink (n), der trunk
drink (v), trinken
drip (v), kapen (R), tripn
drive (n), der for, di yazde; (psychological) der yeytser (H)
drive (v), firn, forn, traybn
drive hard (goad), untertraybn; "Go for a drive", "forn shpatsirn"
driver (of a wagon), der balegole (H)
drive-in movie, der aynfor-kino
drive out (banish), aroystraybn
drone (n), di erbin, di vaserbin
drone (v), hudyen, zhuzhen
drool, farslinen zikh, gavern
drop (n), der kap, der tropn; "At the drop of a hat", "abi vos"
drop (v), aroplozn
drop in, araynkhapn zikh, iberkhapn zikh
dropsy, di vaserkrenk
drought, di trikenish
drown, dertrunken vern
drowsy, farshlofn, shleferik
drudge (toil) (v), horeven, matern zikh
drudgery, di horevanye, dos maternish
druggist, der apteyker (R)
drug store, di apteykkrom

drum (n), der baraban, di poyk
drum (v), barabaneven, payklen
drummer (tympany), der barabantshik, der paykler
drumstick, dos poykshtekl
drumstick (fowl), di polke (R)
drunk (adj), farshikert (Y-H), farshnoshket (humourous), ongeshikert (Y-H)
drunk (n), der shiker (H); "Get drunk", farshikern, onshikern
drunkard, der shiker (H)
drunkenness, dos shikres (H)
dry (adj), trukn
duck, di katshke (R)
dud, der pushtshak (R)
due (payable) (adj), felik
due (proper) (adj), geherik
dues, der optsol
dull (boring), nudne (R), skutshne (R)
dull (not sharp), temp
dull (not shiny), bleyz, mat, tunkl
dumb (mute), shtum
dumb (stupid), narish
dump (v), avekvarfn, oysshitn
dumpling(s), dos kneydl(ekh)
dun (v), monen
dung, dos mist
dupe (n), dos nebekhl, der yold
dupe (v), aroyffirn oyfn glitsh, "onhengen a lung-un-leber oyf der noz"
durable, gedayik, geverik, oyshalt(evd)ik
duration, der gedoyer, der meshekh (H)
dusk, der farnakht
dust, der porekh, der shtoyb
dustpan, dos shayvele
dwarf (n), der karlik, der monts, dos shretl
dwindle, ayngeshrumpn vern
dye (n), di farb
dye (v), farbn
dying, shtarbndik; "be dying", goysesn (H), haltn baym shtarbn; "be dying for", shtarbn far

dying person, der goyses (H)

E

each, yeder
each one, yeder eyner
eager (to be), shtark veln, yogn zikh
  nokh
eagle, der odler
ear, der oyer
earlock (hair), di peye (H)
early, fri
earn, fardinen; "Wage earner", der
  fardiner
earshot (within), "vi vayt der oyer
  greykht" (as far as the ear reaches)
earth, di erd; "To the end of the earth",
  "vu di velt hot an ek"
easel, dos bildgeshtel
east, mizrekh (H); "the Far East", der
  vayter mizrekh; "the Middle East", der
  mitler mizrekh; "the Near East", der
  no'enter mizrekh
Easter, der keysekh (R), di paskhe
easy, gring, laykht; "easy-going", gelasn,
  lagodne (R); "Take it easy", "hob
  tsayt", "khap nit"
easy task, dos shpileray
eat (v), esn
eating (finished e.), opgegesn
eat up, oyfesn
eavesdrop, unterhern zikh
echo (n), dos viderkol
eclipse (n), di like (H)
eclipse (lunar), di like-levone (H)
eclipse (solar), di like-khame (H)
economize, kargn, shporn, zhaleven
Eden (Garden of E.), der gan-eydn (H)
edge, der breg, der kant, der zoym
edgy, nervez
edible, esevdik, "khotsh, nem un es es"
educated (well e.), gebildet
educated man, der gelernter
eel, der venger

efface, farmekn, farvishn
efficient person, der/di berye (H)
effort, di bamiyung, di mi, di
  onshtrengung; "Make an effort",
  "bamiyen zikh"; "Make every effort",
  "leygn zikh in der leng un in der
  breyt" (to extend oneself in length
  and width); "Spare no effort",
  "avekleygn ale koykhes" (Y-H)
egg, dos ey; (pl.) di eyer
eggplant, der patlezhan (R)
eggwhite, dos vaysl
ego, der ikh
Egypt, dos mitsrayim (H)
eight, akht
eighteen, akhtsn
eightfold, kuflshmoynedik (H)
eighty, akhtsik
either (adj), oder der oder yener
either (or), oder . . . oder
eke out, dergantsn; "Eke out a living",
  "oysshlogn zikh dos bisl parnose"
elapse, farbaygeyn
elastic (adj), elastish, gibik
elastic (n), di gume, di gumelastik
elbow (n), der elnboygn
elect (v), oysklaybn, oysveyln
election(s), valn (pl.)
electric, elektrish
electricity, di elektrie
elephant, der helfand
elevator, di heybmashin
elevator (grain), der shpaykhler
elevator shaft, di shakhte (mine shaft)
eleven, elf
elk, der los
ell (measurement of length), di eyl
elm, der knupboym
else, anit; somewhere else, ergets
  andersh; what else, vos nokh
embankment, der onshit
ember, di holeveshke (R)
embezzle, baganvenen (Y-H),
  farshvindlen
embroider, oys'haftn, oysneyen
embroidery, di merezhe (R), dos
  oysneyekhts

emerald, der shmorak (R)
emergency, di emergents, der gvald
emotion, di emotsye, der patos (R)
employ (use) (v), banitsn
employ (work), basheftikn, onnemen
employee, der ongeshtelter
employer, der basheftiker
empty (adj), leydik, pust (R)
emulate, nokhton
encore, der bis; for an encore, oyf bis
encourage, mutikn
end (n), der ek, di end, der sof (H); "Stand on end", "shteyn kapoyer"; "Where the world has an end", "vu di shvartse fefer vakst"
end (v), ekn zikh, endikn
endlessly, bli-kets (H), on a sof (H)
endure, fartrogn, oys'haltn, oysshteyn
enema, di kane, der klistir
enemy, der soyne; (pl.) di sonim (H)
engage (hire) (v), dingen, onshteln
engage in, farnemen zikh mit, oysek zayn in (H-Y)
engage (marry), farknasn
engagement (wedding), di farknasung
England, dos england
English (adj), englishe
English (language), dos english
enjoy, genisn, hanoe hobn (H-Y)
enlarge, fargresern
enlightenment, di oyfklerung
Enlightenment, di haskole (H)
enough, genug; "Hardly enough", "klekn oyf a tson"; "More than enough", "iber genug"
enquire, fregn, nokhfregn, onfregn
enrage, oyfkokhn
enraged, oyfgebrakht; "to become enraged", aroysgeyn fun di keylim
enslave, farshklafn
enter, arayngeyn
enterprise, di unternemung
entertain, farvayln
enthusiastic (to become), nispoel vern (H-Y)
entrance, der arayngang
envelope, der konvert

envy (n), di kine (H)
envy (v), mekane zayn (H-Y), nit farginen
epidemic, di mageyfe (H), der untergang
equipment, di oysshtatung; ware, varg (suffix)
equivocate, "plontern mit der tsung"
era, di tkufe (H), di tsayt
erase, oysmekn
eraser, der meker
error, der feler, der grayz, der toes (H)
escalator, di vikltrep
escape (v), antloyfn
especially, bifrat (H), spetsyel
estate, der mayontik, di nakhle (H); real estate, dos grunt-eygns
esteem, der derkherets (H), der onzen
esteemed, khoshev (H)
estimate (n), der opshats
estimate (v), opshatsn
ethnic association, der landsmanshaft
eulogy, der hesped (H)
evaluate, opshatsn
evaporate, oysvepn zikh
evasion, der aroysdrey, di oysmaydung
eve (on the eve of), erev (H)
even (adj), azh (R), glat, glaykh
even (adv), afile (H)
even (get even), oprekhenen zikh
even (not odd), grod
evening, der ovnt
evening prayer, der mayrev (H) (Jewish)
eventually, mit der tsayt, "sof kol sof" (H)
ever, amol, eybik, tomed (H); "Ever bigger", "vos a mol greser"
evergreen, der nodlboym
every, ale, itlekher, yeder
everyone, ale, yeder eyner
everything, alts, altsding
everywhere, iberal, umetum
evidence, der bavayz, di raye (H)
evil (adj), beyz
evil (n), der shlak

evil eye (n), dos beyz oyg (Jewish), der eyn-ore (H) (Jewish)
evil person, der paskudnyak (paskudnik) (R)
evil spirit, di klipe (H)
evil thing, di roe (H)
exact (adj), genoy, pinktlekh
exactly, akurat, kakhabe (H), punkt
exaggerate, ibertraybn, makhn fun a vort a kvort (to make a quart from a word), megazem zayn (H)
exaggeration, di guzme (H)
examine (question), farhern
examine (scrutinize), iberkukn, unterzukhn
example, der bayshpil, der moshl (H); "For example", a shteyger, dehayne (H), ledugme (H), lemoshl (H), "tsum bayshpil",
exasperated, oyfgekokht
excavation(s), di oysgrobung(en)
excellent, oysgetseykhnt
excellent house, "a hoyz fun hayzerland"
except, akhuts (H), oyser; unless, saydn
exception, der oysnem
excess, iberik, oydefdik (H-Y), tsu fil; "Carry to excess", "ibertsien dos shtrikl"
exchange, oysbaytn
excitable person, der hitskop
excite (v), oyfregn, tsehitsn
excited (adj), oyfgehaytert, oyfgetrogn
excitement (n), dos geruder, di oyfregung
exciting, shpanendik
excrement, der kal, di tsoye (H)
excuse (n), der farentfer, der terets (H); (pl.) di terutsim; "make excuses", farentfern zikh
excuse (v), antshuldikn, moykhl zayn (H-Y); "Excuse me", antshuldikt (mir)
exempt, poter (H)
exercise (n), di genitung (gym)
exercise (v), genitn zikh (gym)
exert, onshtrengen
exert oneself, mien zikh (H-Y)

exhale, oysotemen
exhausted, "faln fun di fis" (fall off your feet), oysgematert, oysgemutshet
exhort, doykhek zayn (H-Y), fodern, tsuredn
exile, dos goles (H)
exist, eksistirn, zayn faran
existing, faran
exit (n), der aroysgang
exit (v), aroysgeyn
exodus, di yetsie (H); "The Exodus", yetsies-mitsrayim (H)
exonerate, reynvashn
exorbitant, "gor on a mos" (without measure), "nit tsu batsoln"
exorcise, opshprekhn
expect, rikhtn zikh
expectant mother, "di froy oyf der tsayt"
expectorate, shpayen
expense, di hetsoe (H)
expensive, tayer
experience, di genitshaft
experience (v), durkhmakhn, iberlebn
experienced, genit, ongelernt
expert (n), der meyvn (H), der mumkhe (H)
expert (proficient) (adj), bahavnt
explain, derklern; "Explain things in detail", "araynleygn a finger in moyl", "tseleygn oyf telerlekh"
explode, oyfraysn
expose, oysshteln
express (adj), befeyresh (H)
expressly, eygns
expressway, der gikhshtroz, der oytostrad
exquisite (adj), mehuderdik (H-Y); "something exquisite", an antik
extraordinary, oysergeveyntlekh, umgeveyntlekh
extremely, gor gor, shebe (H) (prefix); "extremely hot", heys shebeheys
eye, dos oyg; (pl.) di oygn
eyebrow(s), di brem(en)
eyeglasses, briln, glezer, shpakuln (R)
eyelash, di vie

eyelid, dos oygn-lepl
eyesight, di rie (H)

F

fabric, di shmate (coll.), der shtof, di
skhoyre (H)
face (n), dos gezikht, dos ponem (H),
di tsure (H); "Face-to-face", "oyg oyf
oyg", "ponem-al-ponem" (H); "Make
faces", "krimen zikh", "makhn piskes"
fact, der fakt (see intr.); as a matter of
fact, eygntlekh; in fact, aderabe (H),
faktish
factory, di fabrik, der zavod (R)
fade, farvelkn, opgeblyakevet vern (R-
Y)
fail, farfeln, farlozn
failed, nit gerotn
faint (squeamish) (adj), mlosne
faint (n), dos khaloshes (H)
faint (v), khaleshn (H)
fair (adj), hel; "Fair and square", kosher
veyosher (H); "Middling fair",
nishkoshedik
fair (n), der yarid (H)
fairness, der yoysher (H)
fairyland, dos ergetsland, dos fe'enland
fairytale, di bobe-mayse, dos maysele
faith, der bitokhn (H), di emune (H),
der gloybn
faithful, getray; the faithful, di gleybike
fall (v), faln
fall (season), der harbst, der osyen (R),
der yeshn (R)
fall into, araynfaln
false (not true), falsh
false (unfaithful), umgetray
falter, "plontern mit der tsung", vaklen
zikh
fame, di barimkeyt, der shem-dover (H)
family, di familye, di mishpokhe (H)
famous, barimt, bavust
fan (n), der fokher

fan (admirer), der onhenger
fanatic, der fanatiker, der kanoy (H)
fanatical, fanatish
fancy (adj), getsatsket
far, vayt
farewell, der gezegenung; "bid
farewell", gezegnen zikh
farmer, der poyer, der yeshuvnik (R)
farther, vayter
fast day, der tones (H); (pl.) di
tayneysim
fasten, aynmotseven, farfestikn
fastener (snap), di knopke (R)
fasten on (glue), onklepn
fat (adj), dik, grob
fat (n), dos fets, dos shmalts
fat (rendered), gribenes, grivn
father, der foter, der tate (R)
Father (our F.), ovinu (H) (Jewish)
father-in-law, der shver
faucet, der krant
favour (n), di toyve (H), di tsulibzakh
fawn (v), lashtshen zikh, unterlekn zikh
fear (n), di moyre (H), der pakhed (H),
der shrek
fearful, moyredik (H)
featherbed, dos iberbet, di perene (P)
fed up, zayn zat
feeble-minded, shvakhkepik, tamevate
(H)
feed (v), bashpayzn, kormen, shpayzn
feed poultry, shtopn
fellow, der feler (Yiddish jargon, lit.
defect), der khevre man (H-Y)
fellow, der khover (H) (fellowship
holder)
felt (n), dos filts, der poysht
feminine, feminin, froyish, vayberish,
vayblekh
fence (n), der ployt (R)
fender, der blote-fligl, dos shitsblekh
fern, dos federgroz
festive, shabesdik (H-Y), yontevdik (H-
Y)
fever, di hits, dos kadokhes (H)
few, bisl, getseylt, veynik, vintsik; "A
few", a bisl, etlekhe

fickle, baytevdik, plyaderdik
fiction (lit.), di beletristik (F-Y)
fiddle (n), der fidl; "Fiddlesticks", narishkeytn, "veys ikh vos!" (do I know?)
fiddle (v), fidlen
fidget, "nit kenen aynzitsn", "nit kenen zikh gefinen keyn ort" (not able to find oneself a place)
fifteen, fuftsn
fifty, fuftsik
fig, di fayg
fight (n), dos geshleg, der kamf
fight (v), bakemfn, shlogn zikh; "to fight over nothing", krign zikh iber a fasolkele (lit. fight over a little bean)
figure out, oysrekhnen
filbert, dos valdnisl
fill (v), filn; "Fill a tooth", "leygn a plombe", plombirn
filling (dental) (n), di plombe
filthy, blotik, paskudnye (R), shmutsik
fin, di flusfeder
finally, lesof (H)
find (v), gefinen; "Find one's way", "trefn tsu"
fine (adj), fayn
fine (minute), drobne (R)
fine (punishment) (n), der shtraf
fine arts, di sheyne kunstn
finest, faynste, shenste
finger (n), der finger
fingernail, der nogl; (pl.) di negl
fingernail water, negl-vaser (Jewish)
fingerprint, der fingerdruk
fingertip, der shpits finger
finish (v), farendikn, opton
finished, fartik
finish up, endikn, makhn a sof tsu (Y-H-Y)
finite, endlekh
fir (tree), di sosne (R), di yodle
fire (n), der fayer, di sreyfe (H); "Set fire to", ontsindn
fire engine, der lesh'oyto
fire extinguisher, der leshshprits
firefly, der glivorem

fireman, der fayerlesher
fireplace, der kamin
first, ersht; "At first", lekhatkhile (H), tsum ershtns; "First of all", koydem kol (H)
first aid, di gikhe hilf
fish, der fish
fish (v), fishn, khapn fish
fishing rod, di ventke (R)
fishy (odd), nit glat
fist, di foyst, der kulik
"Fits and starts", "ven nit ven"
five, finf
fixer, der makher
flabby, shlaberik
flag (n), di fon
flame, der flam
flap (n), di kliape; (table), der blat
flapper (girl), dos flampletsl
flash (n), der blishtsh (R), der blits
flashlight, di batereyke, dos lamterl
flask, der flakon
flat (adj), flakh, platshik (R)
flat (music) (n), der bemol (R)
flatiron, der pres
flatten out, oysplatshikn (Y-R)
flatter (v), khanfenen (H), "krikhn in di oygn", unterlekn zikh
flattery, di khnife (H)
flat tire, der pantsher
flavour (n), der aromat, der tam (H)
flavour (v), farpraven
flea, der floy; (pl.) fley
fleece (n), di fel
fleece (v), "shindn di hoyt"
fleet (naval), der flot
flesh, dos fleysh; (body flesh), di hoyt, dos layb; "Flesh and blood", "boser vedom" (ordinary man) (H)
flicker (v), tsanken
fling (have a fling), "a hulye ton"
flock (birds), di tshate (R)
flood, di farfleytsung, dos geviser, der mabl (H)
floor, di padloge (R), der dil
floor (parliament), dos vort; ask for the floor, betn a vort

floor (storey), der gorn, der shtok
flop (v), fokhn
flophouse, dos hegdesh (H)
flour, di mel
flow (v), fleytsn, flisn
flower (n), di blum, der kveyt (R)
flower (v), bliyen
flowerpot, der blumentop, der vazon (R)
flu, di influentsie
flue, di yushke (R)
fluffy, pukhik, vilne
flushed (face), farflamt, farreytlt (blushing)
fly (pants), der krok
fly (n), di flig
fly (v), flien
flying saucer, dos fli-telerl
foam, di pine, der shoym
foam rubber, di shoymgume
fog, der nepl
foil (metal), der leysh
fold, der falb, der kneytsh
fold (arms), farleygn, kneytshn; "Sit with legs folded", "zitsn oyf terkish" (sit Turkish-style)
folly, di narishkeyt (H-Y), shmontses
fondling, "dos kutsenyu-mutsenyu"
food, dos esn, di shpayz; "Forbidden food" (adj) (Jewish), treyf (H); "Forbidden food" (n), dos tarfes (H), di treyfe (H); "Room and board", di kest (Jewish)
fool (n), di beheyme (H), der nar (H); (pl.) di naronim; der shlemiel, der shoyte (H), der tipesh (H)
fool (v), narn, opnarn; "You're fooling", "gey, du narst"
foolish, narish
foolishness, di narishkeyt
foot, der fus; (pl.) di fis; small foot, dos fisl
footpath, di steshke (R)
footprint, der fusdruk, di shpur
footstep, der trot (trit); (pl.) di trit
for, far; (with object of fetching), nokh

forbid, farvern; (ritual), asern (H) (Jewish); "Forbidden to enter", "me tor nit arayngeyn"; "G-d forbid", "got zol op'hitn", "khas-vekholile" (H), "khas-vesholem" (H)
force (n), der koyekh (H), di kraft; "By force", bigvald; in force, in kraft
forecast (n), der foroyszog
forecast (v), foroyszogn
foreclose (exclude), oysshlisn
foreclose (mortgage), kasirn
forehead, der shtern
foreign, fremd
foreign countries, dos oysland
foreign minister, der oysland-minister
forelady, di oyfze'erin
forelock, di tshuprine
foreman, der oyfze'er
foremost, vikhtikst
foresight, di baklerikeyt
forest, der vald
forever, eybik, fareybik
forfeit (v), onvern
forgery, di felshung, di nokhmakhung
forget, "aroysgeyn fun zinen", fargesn
forget-me-not, dos fargesnitl
fork (table f.), der gopl
former, amolik, frierdik
fornicate, trenen (coll.)
forth ("Back and forth"), "ahin un aher"
forthcoming, kumendik, onkumendik
fortitude, di gvure (H)
fortress, di festung
fortunate, mazldik (H-Y)
fortune (luck), di marokhe (H), dos mazl (H); "To tell fortunes", "oysleygn kortn"
fortune (money) (n), dos ashires (H), der mayontik
fortune teller, der vorzoger
forty, fertsik
forward (adj), khutspedik (H-Y)
forward (adv), foroys
foundling, dos untergevorfne kind
four, fir
fourteen, fertsn

fracture (n), der brokh
fragrance, dos gerukh
fragrant, shmekedik
frame (n), di rem, di rom; "Frame of mind", dos gemit; "Frame of reference", di shaykhes-rem (H-Y)
France, dos frankraykh
frank, ofntlekh
frantic, panish, tirefdik (H)
freak, der kapriz
freak (monster), dos farze'enish
freckle(s), klayen (pl. only), dos zumershprenkl(en)
free (adj), fray
freedom, di frayheyt
freethinker, der fraydenker
freeze, aynfrirn, farfroyrn vern, frirn
freezing weather, der frost
French (adj), frantseyzish; (language), dos frantseyzish
French (person) (n), der frantsoyz
french toast, dos gefrishte broyt, der gefrishter koyletsh
frequent (adj), oft
frequently, "ale montik un donershtik" (hum.), ale vayle, a sakh mol, oftmol
fresh, frish, tsapldik
fret, grizhen zikh, varfn zikh
Friday, der fraytik
friend, di bakante (f), der bakanter (m), der fraynd, der guter bruder, der khaver (H) (m), di khaverte (H) (f); (pl.) di khaveyrim; "Boy friend", der khaver (H); "Girl friend", di khaverte (H)
friendship, di frayntshaft
fright (n), der shrek
frightened, dershrokn, tseshrokn; "Terribly frightened", "zikh antfaln der mames milkh"
frightening (adj), moyredik (H), shreklekh
frigid (sexually) (adj), frigid
frigid woman, di kalte kuznye (a cold forge)
frock coat, der khalat
frog, di frosh, di zhabe

from, fun
from (of it), derfun
front, der fornt; "in front of", far fornt
frosted glass, dos milkhgloz
frozen (adj), farfroyrn
frozen stiff, farshtart
frugal, shporevdik
fruit, di frukht, di peyre (H)
fruitless, aroysgevorfn, umfrukhtik; be fruitless, "oyslozn zikh a taykh fun" (to result in a river)
frustrate, farshtern, kalye makhn
fry, prazhen, preglen
frying pan, di fan, di skovrode (R); (small frying pan), dos fendl
fulfill, mekayem zayn (H-Y), oysfolgn
full, ful, mole (H); "full blast", mitn fuln bren; "Full to the brim", "ful vi an oyg", "oyf tish un oyf benk", "oyf vos di velt shteyt" (on what the world stands)
fumble (v), bobren zikh, tapn di vent
fume(s) (n), der roykh(n); carbon monoxide fumes, der tshad
fun, di hanoe; (ridicule), der khoyzek (H); "Have fun", farvayln zikh, hanoe hobn (H-Y); "In for fun", "oyf katoves"
fund (charity), der fond
fund-raising, shafn gelt
funeral, di levaye (H)
funnel (n), dos kreyndl, di leyke
funny, komish, shpasik, vitsik
funny (odd), modne
fur, der futer, der pelts
fur coat, der futer
fur hat (high, worn by Jews), der spodik (R)
fur hat (worn by Chasidic Jews), dos shtrayml
furious, oyser zikh, tsekokht
furniture, mebl
furrier, der kirzhner
further, vayter
fuss, der tareram, der tsimes (hum.); "make a fuss", makhn a tareram/tsimes, tareramen

futile, umzist; "Make futile attempts",
"krikhn oyf glate vent" (to climb on
straight walls); "To talk futilely", "redn
tsu der vant" (to talk to the walls)
future (n), der osed (H), di tsukunft

G

gab (v), ploydern
gabardine, der kaftn (worn by
observant Jews), di kapote (R)
gadget, der dzhimdzhik, di makherayke,
di tsatske (R)
gag (v), farkhlinyen zikh
gain weight, ontsern zikh
gale, di bure, der (yam-)shtorem
gall, di gal
gall (arrogance), di khutspe (H), dos
yandes
gallows, di tlie (H)
galore, lerov (H), "vifl s'harts glust" (as
much as the heart desires)
galoshes, kaloshn
gamble (n), der aynshtel, di rizike
gamble (v), shpiln oyf gelt
gambler, der rizikant
gander, der goner
gang, di bande, di shayke
gang (bunch of friends), di
khalyastre, di khevre (H)
gangrene, di brand, di gangren
gangster, der bandit
gap, der aynrays, der bloyz
garbage, dos mist, der opfal
garbage can, der mistkastn
garbage man, der mistler
garden, der gortn
Garden of Eden, der gan-eydn (H)
gargle (n), dos shvenkekhts
gargle (v), gorglen, shvenken
garlic, der knobl
garment, der beged (H), dos malbesh
(H)
garrulous, baredevdik

garter, di podishke (R), dos zokn-bendl;
"garter belt", podishkes
gasp (v), kaykhn, sapen
gate, der toyer; "field gate", di rogatke
gather, klaybn, zamlen
gathering, der tsunoyfkum
gathering (meeting), di farzamlung
gaudy, shrayik
gauge (n), di mos
gauge (v), mestn
gauze, di merle
gem, der eydlshteyn
generally, beklal (H), in algemeyn
generation, der dor (H); (pl.) di doyres
generous, breyt, breyt'hartsik
genitals, geshlekht-organen
genius (n), der goen (H), der ile (H);
"Like a genius", ge'oynish
genteel, eydl
gentile (f), di goye
gentile (m), der goy
gentile boy, der sheygets (H); (pl.) di
shkotsim
gentile girl, di shikse (H); (pl.) di
shikses
gentle, lind, mild, tsart
gentleman, der her; "Gentlemen!",
khosheve fraynd (H-Y), "raboysay!"
(H)
genuine, ekht, emesdik (H-Y)
germ, di germe
get, krign
get away with, opkumen, yoytse zayn
(H-Y)
get-together, der tsunoyftref, der
tsuzamen
get up, oyfheybn zikh, oyfshteyn
giant (n), der gigant, der riz
giddy, shvindldik; "I feel giddy", "es
shvindlt mir in kop"
gift (charitable), di nedove (H)
gift, di matone (H); (coin), di matbeye
(H)
giggle (v), khikhen, khikhikn
gimmick, der dzhimdzhik
gin, der dzhin; cotton gin, der bavl-
dresher

ginger, der ingber
ginger ale, der ingber-vaser
gingerbread, der ingberlekekh
girdle (n), der pas
girl (eligible spinster), di kale-moyd (H-Y)
girl (young), dos meydl, dos pultsl; "Little girl", meydele
give, gebn
give in, nokhgebn
give up, oplozn
glad, tsufridn
gladden, derfreyen
gladly, gern
glamour girl, dos blishtshmeydl (R-Y)
gland, di driz
glare (n), der bliask, der opshayn
glare (v), "oysshteln a por oygn", "raysn di oygn"
glass (adj), glezern
glass (pane), dos gloz, di shoyb; drinking glass, dos glezl, di gloz; small drinking glass, di glezele
glasses (spectacles), briln, shpakuln (R)
gleam (n), der glants
gleam (v), blanken, finklen, glantsn
glisten, shimerirn
gloat, kveln
globular, kaylekhdik
gloomy, kalemutne (R), umetik
glory, di gdule (H)
glove(s), di hentshke(s)
glue (n), der kley
glue (v), klepn, tsuklepn
glum, ongezolyet
glutton, der freser, der geshmaterhaldz (Y-H-Y) (converted throat)
gnarled, sukevate
gnash (teeth), farkritsn
gnat, di muk
gnaw, grizhen, khromtshen
go, geyn; "Go on!", "gey shoyn gey"; "Not know how to go about it", "nit visn mit vos men est es" (not to know with what one eats)

goal (practical), der takhles (H), der tsil
goal (sports), der toyer
goat (m), der bok, der tsap; (f) di tsig
go away, avekgeyn
go away (leave alone), optshepn zikh fun
go away (pain), ibergeyn
gobble up, aynshlingen, opfresn
goblet, der bekher
G-d, der got (see intr.)
godfather, der kvater (R)
god-fearing, gotsforkhtik, yerey shomayim/eloyhim (H)
G-d forbid, khas vekholile/vesholem (H)
godmother, di kvaterin (R)
goggles, kukers, vaserbriln, vintbriln
golden, gildn, goldn
gone, avek, farbay, gegangen, nito
good, gerotn, glaykh, gut, voyl; "As good as the next person", "a glaykher yakhtsn mit andere"; "Be good at", "zayn a berye" (Y-H); "Be very good at", "zayn a moydim" (Y-H); "Good for nothing", "toyg oyf kapores" (Y-H); "Good Luck!", "al dos guts", "in a mazldiker sho", "zol zayn mit glik/mazl"; "Good things of life", "di gutikeytn fun lebn"; "It's a good thing he came", "a marokhe (H) vos er iz gekumen"; "Not too good", "nit foygldik"; "Pretty good", "nishkoshe" (H); "What good is it?", "vos toyg es?"
good luck (n), dos mazl (H)
good-for-nothing (n), der bodyung, der gornit, di puste keyle (Y-H), der zhulik (R)
good-natured person, "a mentsh on a gal"
good (valid), giltik
good-will, der guter viln, di laytzelikeyt
goose, di ganz; (pl.) di genz
gooseberry, der agres (R) (same in pl.)
gooseflesh, di genzene hoyt
go out (eg. fire), oysgeyn

gorgeous, bildsheyn (pretty as a picture), hiderdik (H), prekhtik

gossip (n), dos barederay, di plyotke (R), di potsht, dos rekhiles (H); "Become the object of gossip", "araynfaln in laytishe mayler"

gossip (person) (n), der rekhiles-trayber (H-Y), der trayber

gourmand, der freser, der nasher (H)

gout, di podagre (R)

governess, di guvernantke, di nianye (R)

government, di regirung

governor, der gubernator

governor-general, der general-gubernator, der plats'halter

grab (n), der khap

grab (v), khapn

grace (n), di gnod, der khesed (H); "Say grace", bentshn

gracious (adj), gnedik, laytzelik

gradually, bislekhvayz

graft (n), der shtshep; bribe, der khabar, der shoykhed (H)

grain, di tvue (H)

grandeur, di gdule (H)

grandfather, der zeyde

grand larceny, di groys-ganeyve (Y-H)

grandmother, di bobe

grant (n), di bavilikung; (subsidy), der shtits, di subvents

grant (v), bavilikn, derloybn, nokhgebn

granulated, graypldik

granulated sugar, der melets

grape, di vayntroyb

grapevine, di pantofl-post

grasp (understanding) (n), der banem, der onkhap

grass, dos groz

grasshopper, der shpringer

grass widow, di agune (H), di shtroyene almone

grateful, dankbar

gratification, di tsufridnkeyt

gratify, bafridikn, tsufridn shteln

grave (adj), erntst

grave (n), der grub, der keyver (H), der keyver-yisroel (H) (Jewish); "grave clothes", takhrikhim (H); "grave of the fathers", di keyver-oves (H)

gravel, der zhvir

gravy, di brotyoykh

graze, pashen (R)

grease (n), dos fets, dos shmirekhts; "boot-black", dos dyegekhts, dos dzhegekhts

grease (v), onshmirn

great, groys

greatest, grestn

great-granddaughter, dos ureynikl

great-grandson, der/dos ureynikl

greatly, shtark, zeyer

greedy, girik, khaperish, loet (H), zhedne; "be greedy", hobn groyse oygn (have big eyes)

greedy person, der khazer (H), der nasher (H)

green, grin

greenhouse, di oranzherie

greenish, grinblekh

greet, bagrisn

greet (upon arrival), gebn sholem (H)

grey, gro, groy

greyhound, der khart

grieve, troyern

grill (n), di brot-reshotke

grim, farbisn

grimace (n), di havaye (H), der pisk

grimace (v), farkrimen zikh

grin (n), der breyter shmeykhl, der shmokh

grin (v), lakhn mit tseyner, shmokhn

grind (v), tsemoln

grindstone, der milshteyn, der shlayfshteyn

gritty, zemdldik

grocer, der shpayzkremer (Y-R)

grocery, di shpayzkrom (Y-R)

groin, der vinkl

groom, der basherter, der khosn (H)

groove (n), di gare

grope (v), matsen, nishtern, tapn

ground (basis), der grund, der smakh (H), der tam (H)
ground fog, der baydererdiker nepl
ground (soil) (n), di erd, der grunt
group (n), di grupe, di khevre (H), der tsiber (H)
grow (cultivate), hodeven; get bigger, vaksn; "Grow up", oysvaksn
growl (n), der vortsh
growl (v), vortshen
grudge (n), der faribl; "have a grudge again't", hobn a harts (oyf), hobn faribl oyf, trogn a harts (oyf)
gruff, rugzedik (H)
grumble (v), burtshen, mruken
grunt (n), der khruk
guard against, hitn zikh far
guarded speech, halbmoylik, "nit derzogndik"
guess (v), trefn
guest, der gast, der oyrekh; (pl.) di orkhim (H)
guffaw (v), khokhotshen
guilder, der guldn
guilder (Galician), der raynish
guilty, shuldik
guinea-pig, dos yam-khazerl (H); "Use as a guinea-pig", "lernen zikh shern oyf bord" (learn by cutting off one's beard)
gull, di meve
gulp (n), der zhlyok
gulp (v), zhlyoken
gum, di yasle
gums, dos tseynfleysh
gun, di biks (rifle), der harmat (cannon), der pistoyl (pistol), der revolver, der shpayer
gurgle, rizlen
gush (v), gisn zikh, plyukhen
gust (n), der plosh
gusto, der tshak; "With gusto", geshmak, tshakendik
gutsy (tear-jerker), shmaltsik
gutter, der rinshtok
guzzle, khliyeptshen, zoyfn

gymnasium, der sportzal; European school, di gimnazye
gypsy, der tsigayner

H

habit, di geveyntshaft, der hergl (H), di mide (H); "Break the habit", "opgeveynen zikh"; "Get into the habit", "ayngeveynen"
habitual, ayngeveynt, geveyntlekh
hackneyed, kazyone, shablonik
hag, di bobetse (R)
hail, der hogl
hail (greet) (v), bagrisn
hail (snow) (v), hoglen
hair, di hor
hairbrush, dos kopnbershtl
haircut (get a h.), opshern zikh
hairdo(s), der farkam(en), di frizur(n)
hairdresser, der frizirer
hairpin, di horshpilke
hairsplitter, der bal-makhloykes (H), der pilpl (H)
hairsplitting, pilpldik (H-Y)
half (adj), halb, khotsi (H)
half (n), di halb, di helft; "Be half dead", "fokhn mit der neshome"
half-wit, der tam (H)
halitosis, der moyl-reyekh (Y-H)
hall, der zal
ham, di shinke
Haman, homen (H)
hamburger, der kotlet
hammer (n), der hamer
hammer (v), hamern
hand, di hant; (pl.) hent; "Hand-and-glove", "knipl-beknipl"; "Hand out", "oysteyln"; "Hand over", "derlangen"; "Lend a hand", "untershteln a pleytse" (put a shoulder under); "Live from hand to mouth", "esn fun arbl" (eat from one's sleeve)
hand (clock), der vayzer

handful, der hoyfn, di zhmenye
handicap, di menie (H), der shter
handicapped (defect), mumik (H-Y);
   (be handicapped by), laydn fun, zayn
   gehamevet fun
handkerchief, dos noztikhl
handle (n), der tronik
handout, dos betlbroyt, di kitsve (H)
handsome man, der hadres-ponem
   (H)
hang, hengen, oyfhengen; "Hanged
   himself", "zikh oyfgehongen"
hanger-on, der shleper
hanging (death by hanging), di tlie
   (H)
hangman, der talyen (H)
hangover, der katsn-yomer
hang up, oyfhengen
happen, geshen, pasirn, trefn zikh
happen to, grod; "Things are
   happening", "es tut zikh maysim" (Y-
   H)
happy, freylekh, gliklekh, tsufridn;
   "Happy Birthday", "mit mazl geyert
   zikh"
harass, plogn
hard (difficult), shver (un biter);
   "Hard-earned", "farhorevet"; "Hard
   labour", "di shtrofarbet"; "Hard of
   hearing", "toyblekh"; "Hard to
   understand", "koshe" (H); "Very
   hard", "katorzhne"
hard (not soft), hart
hardly, kimat nit (H-Y), koym
hardship, di noyt
hardware, dos ayznvarg
hardware store, di ayznkrom
hare, der hoz
harlot, di gasnfroy, di zoyne (H)
harm (n), di roe (H), der shodn;
   "Harmless person", "nit tshepn keyn
   flig oyf der vant" (to not harm a fly on
   the wall); "There is no harm", "s'ken
   nit shatn" (v)
harsh, griltsik, shtreng
"Harum-scarum", "khap-lap (-tsap)",
   "vi a farsamte moyz"

harvest (n), dos geretenish, der shnit
harvest (v), aropnemen, shnaydn
has, hot
has been, iz geven
hash, dos hakfleysh
Hasid, der khosed; (pl.) di khsidim (H)
haste, dos ge'ayl, dos khapenish, dos
   yogenish
hasten, ayln
hastily, "oyf eyn fus"
hat, der hit, dos hitl, der hut; "Derby
   hat", der kapelyush (R); "Fur hat"
   (worn by Russian Jews), der spodik;
   "Talk through one's hat", "zoygn fun
   finger"
hate (v), faynt hobn, hasn, nit kenen
   onkukn
hatred, di sine (H)
hatter, der hitlmakher, der kirzhner
haughty, farrisn, gayvedik (H-Y)
have, hobn
havoc, der khurbn (H), der tel (H)
hawk (n), der falk
he, der, er
head, der kop; "at the head of the
   table", "oyvn on"; "Head over heels",
   "strom-halavoy"
headache, der kopveytik
headlight, der fonar
head off, farforn
headway, rirn zikh (make h.)
healing, di refue (H)
health, dos gezunt; "Drink to the health
   of", "trinken lekhayim" (Y-H)
healthy, gezunt
heap (n), der hoyfn, der koyp, di kupe
   (R)
heaping spoonful, "mit a shmits", "mit
   a verekh"
hear, hern; "Hear O Israel", "shma-
   yisroel" (H)
hearse, di agole (H) (Jewish)
heart, dos harts; "Heartbroken", fartsart
   (Y-H)
heartburn, "dos brenenish (untern
   hartsn)"
heartless, umberakhmonesdik (Y-H-Y)

hearty, geshmak, hartsik, munter
"Eat heartily", araynraybn
heat (n), di hits
heat (v), hitsn
heaven, der himl; "For heaven's sake", "gvald geshrign!"
heaviness (to have), drikn
heavy, shver
Hebrew (adj), hebreyish
Hebrew (language), dos hebreyish
heckler, der tsvishnrufer
heel (foot), di pyate
heel (shoe), der aptsas; "Take to one's heels", makhn vayivrekh (Y-H), "nemen di fis oyf di pleytses"
heifer, di telitse (R)
heir, der kadesh (H) (Jewish male, hum.), der yoyresh (H)
heiress, di yurshte (H)
hell, dos gehemen (H); "Hell has broken loose", "es tut zikh khoyshekh" (Y-H); "To hell", "tsu al di shvartse yor"
hello, "sholem-aleykhem" (H); the response is, "aleykhem-sholem" (H)
help (n), di hilf
help (v), helfn; "HELP!", "GVALD!", "SHMA-YISROEL!" (H)
helpful, nutsik
helpless, op'hentik
helter-skelter, khap-lap(-tsap) (R), shor-bor (H)
hem (n), der zoym
hem (v), ayntsamen, farzeymen; "Hem and haw", "dreyen mit der tsung"
hen, di hun; (pl.) di hiner
hence (therefore), deriber
henpecked, zayn untern pantofl
henpecked husband, der pantofl-man
her, ir, zi (accusative)
herb(s), dos kraytekhts(er)
here, do; "Here goes", "hayda!"; "Here kitty", "kits-kits-kits"
hereabouts, do ergets
hernia, der vinklbrokh
hero, der giber (H), der held
hesitant, kvenkldik

hesitate, kvenklen zikh, vaklen zikh; "I hesitate to say it", "ikh kvenkl zikh tsu zol ikh es zogn"
hiccup (n), der shlukerts
hiccup (v), shlukertsn
hick, der hekmentsh, der zhlob
hicktown, di hek
hide (v), bahaltn, fartayen
high, hoykh
higher, hekher
highest, hekhste
high school, di mitlshul; (European), di gimnazye
highstrung, ibershpirevdik, ongetsoygn
highway, der shosey, der shtroz, der trakt
hilarious, hiluledik (H-Y)
hill, dos bergl, der koyp
him, im
hindquarters, der okher (H)
hinge (n), der sharnir, di zavise
hinge upon, hengen oyf
hint (n), dos ontsuherenish, der remez (H)
hip, der klub, di lend
hire, dingen; "For hire", "tsum dingen"
his, zayn; "His own way", zaynike; "of his", "zayner a . . ."
hiss (v), siken, tsishen, zidn (vi a shlang)
historic, historish
hit (n), der klap, der zets; (goal), der traf
hit (v), shlogn
hoard (of savings), dos knipl, der matmen (H), der oytser (H)
hoarder, der matmenik (H-Y), der panisher onshporer
hoarse, heyzerik
hobo, der shleper
hodge-podge, der mish-mash, dos ongevorf, der shor-bor (H)
hoe (n), di sape
hoe (v), (arum) sapen
hogwash, di boykh svores (H), der umzinen

hoi-polloi, der layt
hold (v), haltn
holiday, der yontef (H. yomtov); (pl.)
di yontoyvim
holiday (adj), shabesdik (H-Y)
holiday (non-Jewish), di khoge (H)
holiness, di heylikeyt, di kedushe (H)
holocaust, der khurbm (H), di shoe
(H), der umkum
holy, heylik
home, di heym, di shtub; "At home",
aheym, bay zikh, in der heym, in shtub;
"Feel completely at home", "zayn vi a
fish in vaser" (be as a fish in water)
homebody, der heymblayber, der
shtubzitser
homeless, heymloz, onheymik
homeless (far from home), farvoglt;
"Be homeless", "valgern zikh"
homesick, farbenkt
homesickness, dos benkenish
homey (homely), heymish
homosexual (n), der homoseksualist
homosexuality, dos sdom (H)
honest, erlekh, orntlekh
"Honestly!", benemones (H), "khlebn"
(contraction of, "ikh zol azoy lebn"),
take
honesty, di erlekhkeyt, di orntlekhkeyt
honey, der honik (see intr.)
honeydew, di tsesarke
honeymoon, der honik-khoydesh (Y-
H), di khasene-nesie (H), di kushvokh
honour (n), der koved (H); "Word of
honour", dos ernvort
honour (v), opgebn koved (Y-H); "In
honour of", lekoved (H); "To honour
profusely", "arumtrogn oyf di hent";
"To honour with", mekhabed zayn mit
(H-Y)
honourable, bekovedik (H-Y)
hood, der kapishon
hook-and-eye, mendl-un-vaybl
hooligan, der bulvan, der buyan (R),
der trumbanik
hope (n), di hofenung
hope (v), hofn

hopscotch, klasn
hornet, di ferdbin
horror, di eyme (H), der groyl, der
shoyder
horse, dos ferd; "Beat a dead horse",
"raysn zikh in an ofener tir" (tear
oneself through an open door)
horse radish, der khreyn (R)
horseshoe, di potkeve (R)
hosiery, shtrimp, dos zoknvarg
hospitable, gastfrayndlekh
hospitable person, der makhnes-
oyrekh (H)
hospital, der shpitol
hospitality, di gastfrayndlekhkeyt; (to
offer hospitality), makhnes oyrekh
zayn (H-Y)
hostess, di baleboste (H), di
gastgeberin
hostile, kegnerish
hot, heys
hotcake(s), di latke(s) (R); "Sell like
hotcakes", "farkoyfn zikh vi matse-
vaser"
hotel, di akhsanye (H), der hotel
hothead, der gratsh
hour, di sho (H), di shtunde
hour-hand, der shoenvayzer
house, dos hoyz, di shtub
house (small), dos shtibl
housecoat, der khalat, der shlofrok
householder, der balebos (H)
household slops, di pamunitse
(pamoynitse) (R)
housewarming, der khanukes-habayes
(H)
how, vi, vi azoy; "How much?", "vifl?";
"How about that?", "vi gefelt dir di
mayse?"
hub, di bukshe
huckleberry, di tshernitse (R)
huddle (n), dos krentsl
huff (in a h.), ongedrudlt
hug (n), der arumnem, di haldzung
hug (v), arumkhapn (Y-R), arumnemen,
haldzn
huge, rizedik

hullaballoo, dos geruder, der hu-ha!
hum (n), der brum, der zhuzh
hum (v), zhuzhen
hum a song, brumen
humbug, di bliage, dos zhulikeray
humid, faykht, parne
humiliate oneself, "shvartsn zikh dos ponem" (Y-H)
humiliation, di bushe (H), di derniderikung
humour (n), der humor; "sense of humour", der humor
humour (v), dergodzhen
hump, der horb (R)
hunchback (n), der hoyker
hunchbacked (adj), horbate (R), hoykerdik
hundred, der hundert
hunger, der hunger
hunk, di luste, dos shtik
hunt (n), dos geyeg
hunt (v), "yogn zikh nokh"
hurl, valyen
hurry (n), dos aylenish, dos ge'ayl
hurry (v), (h)ayln; "What's the hurry?", "vu brent?" (where is something burning?)
hurt (adj), tsemazekt (Y-H)
hurt (n), der vey, der veytik
hurt (v), vey ton; "Hurt in a fight", "krign klep"; "My feet hurt", "di fis tuen mir vey"
husband, der man
Hush!, sha!
husky, kreftik
husky man, "a yung mit beyner"
hydrant, der leshplump
hydrophobia, di vasershrek
hypocrite, der tsvuak (H)
hypodermic (n), der shprits

I

I, ikh
ice skate(s), glitsher(s)
ice skating (n), dos glitshn zikh; "Go ice skating", "geyn oyf glitsh"
idea, der aynfal, der gedank, di hamtsoe (H), di ideye, der rayen (H); (pl.) rayoynes; "I don't have the slightest idea", "freg mikh bekheyrem/ bekhinem" (H), ikh hob nit keyn anung
idle (unoccupied), "shling-un-shlang"
idler, der leydik-geyer, der pustepashnik (R)
if, az, oyb, tomer, tsu (R)
if only, abi (R), boday, halevay (H), khotsh (R); "If even", "ma dokh"
ignite, ontsindn
ignoramus, der amorets (H); (pl.), di ameratsim
ignorant, ameratsish (H-Y)
ignore, hern vi dem koter (hum.), "makhn zikh nit visndik fun" (listen like a tomcat)
ill (slightly), "nit mit alemen"
illegitimate (child), onkdushendik (Y-H-Y), umgezetslekh
illiterate (adj), analfabetish, um'ivredik
illiterate (to be i.), "nit kenen keyn tseylem fun keyn aleph" (Jewish)
illiterate person, der analfabet, der um'ivrediker
illustrate (example) (v), opmoshlen (Y-H)
imagine, forshteln (zikh), moln zikh
imitate, nokhmakhn
immaculate, umbaflekt
immaterial, nit vikhtik; (be immaterial), nit shpiln keyn role
immediately, oyf der rege (Y-H), teykef (H)
immerse, ayntunken
imminent, ot-otik
immoral one, der hultay

immortalize, fareybikn
impair, farshẹdikn, kalye makhn
impartial, umparteyish, umtsdọdimdik (H)
impatient, umgeduldik; "To be impatient", "shpringen fun der hoyt"
imperfect, fẹlerdik
impersonate, nokhmakhn, ongebn zikh far
impertinence, dos azes (H), di khutspe (H)
importance, dos khshives (H), di vikhtikeyt
important, khoshev (H), vikhtik
important person, der ongeze'ener
impossible, ummeglekh; "Attempt the impossible", "geyn mitn kop durkh der vant", "krikhn oyf glate vent", "shlogn zikh kop in vant"
impotence, di menershvakhkeyt
impotent, "on koyekh" (Y-H)
impressed (adj), imponirt
impressed (be impressed by) (v), nispoel vern (H)
impression, der ayndruk, der royshem (H)
impression (copy) (n), der optsug
imprint, der opdruk
improbable, nit leygn zikh oyfn seykhl (Y-H)
impudence, dos azes (H), dos gehay, di ụmfarshẹmtkeyt
impudent (to be i.), umfarshemt
impulse, der shtoys, der shtup
impurity (moral), di tume (H)
in, arayn, in
incantation, der shprukh (shprokh)
in case, tomer
incense (n), der vayrekh
incense (v), dertsernen
incest, dos gile-aroyes (H) (Jewish)
incest, der intsest
inch, der tsol (same in pl.)
inclination, di netie (H), di neygung; "Evil inclination", "der yeytser-hore" (H); "Good inclination", "der yeytser-toyv" (H)

incoherent (he is i.), "es klept zikh bay im nit a vort tsu a vort"
incompatable, nit oysshtimlekh, "vi a lulev (H) mit an esreg" (H)
inconvienent, umbakvem
indeed, tạke
independence (n), di umop'hengikeyt, di zelbshtendikeyt
independent (adj), umop'hengik, zelbshtendik
indigestible, "nit tsu fardayen"
indignant, oyfgekokht
indispensable, neytik, umbageylekh
indulge, farginen
ineffective (void), botl (H)
inevitable, bashert, umfarmaydlekh
infect, onshtekn
infest, farfleytsn, farshertsn
inflection, der shtimbeyg
influence (n), der aynflus, di hashpoe (H)
influence (v), aynflusn, bavirkn, mashpie zayn oyf (H-Y)
influential man, der takef
informed (well i. in Talmud), der yadn (H)
informer, der moser (H)
ingenious, hamtsoedik (H-Y)
ingredient, der bashteyteyl
inherit, yarshenen (H)
in-law, di makhatẹniste (H) (f), der mekhụtn (m); (pl.), di makhatọnim
inn, di akhsanye (H), di kretshme (R)
innkeeper, der bal-akhsanye (H), der kretshmer (R)
innocent, umshuldik
insane, khoser deye (H), meshuge (H)
insane asylum, dos meshugoim-hoyz (H-Y)
insanity, dos meshugạs (H)
installment payment, di optsolung
installment plan, der oystsolplan
instruct, onvayzn, oyslernen
instrument, di keyle (H); (tool) der makhsher (H)
insult (n), di baleydikung
insult (v), baleydikn

insurance, di asekuratsie, di
farzikherung, di strakhirung
insure (insurance) (v), asekurirn,
farstrakhirn, farzikhern
insure (make sure), farzikhern zikh
intangible, nit ontsutapn
integrity, di orntlekhkeyt
intellectual (adj), gaystik, intelektuel
intellectual (n), der intelektual
intelligent (adj), bar-daasdik (H),
inteligent
intelligent person, der bar-daas (H)
intend, bedeye hobn (H-Y), mekhavn
zayn (H-Y)
intent, di kavone (H), der meyn
intercourse (sexual), seksuele
batsiungen, der tashmesh-hamite (H)
interest (money) (n), der protsent
interest-free loan, dos gmiles-khesed
(H)
interesting, interesant, tshikave
interfere, araynmishn zikh
interpret, fartaytshn
interpretation, di oystaytshung, der
peyresh (H); (pl.), perushim
interpretation of texts, der pshat (H)
(Jewish)
interrupt, araynfaln in di reyd, mafsek
zayn (H-Y)
intestine, gederem (H) (pl. only), di
kishke (R)
intimate (adj), intim, oysgebundn,
tsugelozt
intimate (v), gebn ontsuhern
into, in, in . . . arayn
intricate, farflokhtn, farviklt
introduce, bakenen, forshteln
introduce something, aynfirn
introduction, dos bakenen, dos
forshteln; (book), der araynfir
invention, dos oysgefins, der tsutrakht
inverse, farkert
inversely, kapoyer
invest (effort) (v), araynleygn
invest (v), investirn
invite, aynladn, farbetn

involved (to be i. in), shtekn in; "to be
involved with", hobn tsu ton mit
involvement, di arayngeflokhtnkeyt, di
arayngetsoygnkeyt
iodine, der yod
I.O.U., der veksl
I.Q., der inteligents-vifler
iron (n), dos ayzn
iron (pressing) (n), dos presayzn
iron (v), presn
ironing board, di presbret
irrelevant (to be i.), "klepn zikh vi
arbes in vant" (stick like peas to a
wall), nit shayekhdik (Y-H), nit tsu der
zakh
is, iz
island, der indzl
Israel, dos yisroel (H)
Israel (State of), di medines-yisroel
(H)
issue (edition) (n), der numer
issue (stocks) (n), der aroysloz
issue (question) (n), di frage, der
kamfpunkt
issue (v), aroyslozn
it, es
Italian (adj), italyenish
Italian (language), dos italyenish
Italian (person), der italyener
itch (n), dos baysenish
itch (v), baysn, gendzlen zikh, loptshn
it's, se
ivory, der helfandbeyn
ivy, kleterbleter

J

jackal, der shakal
jacket, di marinarke; (book jacket), di
hile, dos hemdl; (long jacket), di
bekeshe; (of a suit), dos rekl
jail, di tfise (H), di turme (R)
jalopy, di katerinke (R)

jam, dos ayngemakhts, di povidle (prune)(R), di varenye
jam (trouble) (n), dos gedrang, dos ge'eng, di tsore (H)
janitor, der kerer, der shveytsar, der strozh
Japanese (adj), yapanish
Japanese (language), dos yapanish
Japanese (person), der yapaner
jar (n), der sloy
jasmine, der yasmin
jaunty, khvatske (R)
jaw, der bordbeyn, der kayer
jealousy, di kine (H); (sexual), di eyferzukht
jeer at, hetsken, izdiyekeven zikh iber
jell (v), farglivern, farkiln
jelly, der galaret, der gliver
jerky, tsapldik
Jerusalem, dos yerushalayim (H)
jest (n), der katoves
jester, der badkhn (H), der lets (H), der marshelik
Jew, der yid
jewelry, dos tsirung
Jewess, di yidishe tokhter, di yidishke, dos yidish-kind
Jew's-harp, dos brum-ayzn
jingle (v), klimpern
jittery, oyf shpilkes (on tenterhooks)
job, di arbet, di shtele
jointly, beshutfes (H), in eynem
joke, di khokhme (H), der shpas, der vits; "As a joke", "oyf katoves"
joking, geshpas; "All joking aside", "dos gelekhter in a zayt"
journal (news), der zhurnal
journey (n), di nesie (H), di rayze
joy, dos fargenign, di freyd, di simkhe (H), der sosn (H)
joyful, freydik, mole simkhe (H)
joyous, freydik, sosnvesimkhedik (H)
joyous occasion, di simkhe (H)
jubilee, der yoyvl (H), der yubiley
judge (n), der meyvn (H) (connoisseur), der rikhter, der shoyfet (H)

judge (v), mishpetn (H)
judgement, di opshats(ung) (evaluation), der psak (H)(verdict)
jug, der karfin, der krug
juice, der zaft
juicy, zaftik
jump (n), der shprung; "Be one jump ahead", "haltn mit eyn trot vayter"
jump (v), shpringen
juniper, der yalovets
junk (n), der opfal
junk (inferior goods) (n), dos bovl, der ramsh
jurisdiction, di kompetents, der reshus (H)
just (adj), gerekht, yoysherdik (H)
just (exactly), punkt
just (now) (adv), grod, okersht, ot
just (only), bloyz, davke (H), nor
justice, di gerekhtikeyt, der tsedek (H), der yoysher (H)

K

kaftan, di kapote (R)
keep, haltn
keep away, "haltn (zikh) fun der vaytns"
keepsake, der ondenk
kerchief, di fatsheyle, di tukh
kerosene, der naft
kettle, der kesl
key, der shlisl
key (music), di tonatsye
key (piano, typewriter), der klavish
kick (n), der brik, der kope
kick (v), briken, kopen
kidnapped children in Czarist Russia forced into the army, poymene (R)
kidney, di nir
kill (v), hargenen (H), umbrengen
kind (adj), hartsik, lib

kind (n), der min (H), der shteyger, der zgal; "a kind of", aza; "All kinds of", alerley, kolerley (H-Y); "kind of", merveyniker

kindling (wood), der kin

kindness, di frayndlekhkeyt, di gut'hartsikeyt; "Loving kindness", der khesed (H)

king, der kinig, der meylekh (H)

kit and caboodle, kind-un-keyt

kiss (n), der kush

kiss (v), kushn; "cover with kisses", tsekushn

kitchen, di kikh

kitten, dos ketsl

knead, oysknetn

knee, der kni

kneel, kniyen

kneel for religious services, faln koyrim (Y-H)

knickers, aribergevorfene hoyzn

knife, der meser; (pocketknife), dos meserl; (slaughtering knife), der khalef (H) (Jewish); (small kitchen knife), der knipik

knit, shtrikn; "Knit one's brow", "farkneytshn dem shtern"; "Closely knit", geknipt un gebundn

knitting (n), dos shtrikeray

knock (v), klapn; "knock unconscious", dertshmelyen; "Knock on wood", "keyn eynore" (Y-H)

knot (n), dos knipl; (wood), der suk

knotty (wood), sukevate; (string), knipldik

know, kenen, visn; "I know", "ikh veys"; "Know by heart", "kenen oysnveynik"; "Know-it-all", der altsveyser; "What do you know", "herst a mayse!" (H), "te-te-te!"

know-how (n), dos yadones (H)

knowingly, visndik

knowledgeable person, der kener, der yadn (H)

knuckle, dos knekhl

L

label (n), di batseykhenung, der kleptsetl

label (v), batsetlen, batseykhenen

labour (n), di horevanye, dos maternish

labour (v), horeven, matern zikh; "be in labour", "geyn tsu kind"

lace (shoe) (n), dos shnirl; (pl.) di shnirlekh; "Ornamental lace", shpitsn

lace (v), (far)shnureven

lacemaker, der shmukler

lack (v), feln, opgeyn; "What does she lack?", "vos geyt ir op?"

lad, der bokher (H), der boytshik (anglicism with Russian suffix), der yat, der yung

ladder, der leyter

ladies' (adj), damske

lady, di dame; "Ladies!", "mayne damen!"

lady-bug, dos meshiekhl (H), "dos moyshe-rabeynes kiele"

lake, di ozere (R)

lamb, di lam, dos leml

lambskin, der shmoysh

lament, geveyn, di yelole (H)

lamentations, koyles (H); (pl. of "kol")

lamp, der lomp

lampoon(s), der pamflet(n)

land (country), dos land; (ground), di erd

land (plane) (v), landn; (passengers), aroyszetsn

landlady, di baleboste (H), di mises (anglicism)

landmark, der grenetsshteyn

landmark (event), der vendpunkt

landmark (historical), der ondenkpunkt

landowner, der porets (H); (pl.) di pritsim; der erd-farmoger

lane, der forveg, der shpalir, der shteg

language, dos loshn (H) (see intr.), di shprakh
lap, der shoys
lapel, der lats
large, groys
lark, dos trilerl
lash (n), di baytsh, der shmits
lash (v), kateven, shmaysn
last (adj), letst; "At last", "koym mit tsores" (H); "Last year's", farayorike
last (adv), tsu letst
last (n), der kapul
last (v), gedoyern, onhaltn; (suffice), stayen
latch (door), der ruker
late (adj), shpet
late (deceased), farstorbn, (Jewish female) olehasholem, (Jewish male) olevasholem
late (tardy), farshpetikt; "To be late", "farshpetikn zikh"
later, shpeter
latest, letst, nayst; "at the latest", "nit shpeter (vi)"
lathe, di tok
lather (foam), mulines, di pine
laugh, dos gelekhter, dos lakhn
laugh (v), lakhn; "Laugh at", "oplakhn fun"; "Laugh on the wrong side of the mouth", "lakhn mit yashtsherkes (lizards)"; "Laugh up one's sleeve", "lakhn in arbl"; "Laugh uproariously", khakhatuln; "Split one's side laughing", "tsezetst vern lakhendik"
laughing stock, der gelekhter; "Become the laughing stock", "vern tsu gelekhter"
laughter, gelekhter; "Roll with laughter", kayklen
laundry, dos vesh
law (n), dos gezets; (Jewish), der din (H); (the Jewish law), di toyre (H)
lawful (legal), gezetslekh
lawn, di lonke
Law of Judaism (rel.), di halokhe (H); "Oral Law", "di toyre shebalpe" (H)
Law of Moses, di toyres-moyshe (H)

lawsuit (Jewish Rabbinical Court), der din-toyre (H)
lawsuit, der protses
lawyer, der advokat
lax, opgelozn
lay (lie) (v), leygn; "Lay beneath", unterleygn; "Lay down", avekleygn; "Lay out", tseleygn
layer, der plast, di varsht
lazy, foyl
lead (adj), blayen
lead (n), dos blay; (pencil), der shtift
lead (v), firn
lead pencil, der blayer
leader, der firer, der tuer
leading, firndik
leaf, der blat
leak (n), der rin; "be leaky", "zayn tselekhtst"
leak (v), rinen
lean (adj), dar, moger
leap (n), der shprung; "Grow by leaps and bounds", "vaksn vi oyf heyvn" (grow as if with yeast)
leap (v), shpringen
leapfrog, "shpringen zhabke"
Leap Year, der iber-yor (H-Y)
learn (v), lernen
learned man, der gelernter
least (adj), klenst, mindst
least (adv), tsum veynikstn; "at least", khotsh (R), khotshbe, lekhol-hapokhes (H), veynikstns; "Not in the least", "oyf a hor nit"
leather (adj), ledern
leather (n), di leder
leave (v), farlozn ;(allow), lozn
leave behind, iberlozn
leave out, oysblaybn
leave over, iberblaybn
lecher, der noyef (H)
lecture (n), di lektsye, der referat
lecture (v), darshenen (H-Y) (Jewish), haltn a lektsye
lecture (chastize) (v), musern (H)
leech, di piavke
leek, di pore-tsibele

leer (v), "esn mit di oygn" (to eat with one's eyes)

left (adj), linke (also politically)

left-handed person, gelinkt

leftovers, shiraim (H)

leg, der fus; (pl.), di fis

leg (furniture), dos fisl

legacy, der izovn (H), der legat

legible, leynevdik

legitimate, gezetslekh, kdushndik (H) (child)

leisure, di fraytsayt

lemon, der tsitrin

length, di leng; "At length", barikhes (H); "Go to great lengths", "gor vayt", "shpringen fun der hoyt"

lengthen, farlengern

leopard, der lempert

leotard(s), der triko(en)

less, miner, veyniker, vintsiker

lesson, di lektsye; (in Talmud), der shier (H)

lest, "kedey . . . nit" (H-Y)

let, lozn; "Let go", oplozn, optshepen; "Let us", lomir (contr. of "lozn mir")

letter (correspondence), der briv; "Short letter", di brivele

letter(s) of the alphabet, der os(sing); (pl.), di oysyes (H)

lettuce, der salat, shalatn

level (adj), glaykh, oyf eyn heykh

level (n), di madreyge (H), der nivo (F)

Leviathan, der levyosn (H)

Levite, der leyvi (H)

liar, der ligner, der shakren (H)

library, di bibliotek

license, der derloyb, di litsents

license (poetic), di frayshaft

license (Rabbi's), di smikhe (H)

lick (v), lekn

licorice, der lakrets

lid, dos dekl; (of a pot), di pokrishke (R), dos shtertsl

lie (lay) (v), leygn

lie (n), der lign

lie (prevaricate) (v), laygn, zogn a lign

lie around, valgern zikh

lie down, avekleygn, lign

lie still, aynleygn

life, dos lebn; "Live the life of Riley", "lebn vi got in ades"; "To life", "lekhayim" (H)

lifetime, dos lebn, der meshekh (H); "Once in a lifetime", "eyn mol in a yoyvl" (Y-H)

lift (n), der heyb

lift (v), heybn, oyfheybn

lift up, oyfheybn

light (for a cigarette) (n), der fayer

light (in weight), gring, laykht

light (n), di likht

light (v), ontsindn

lighter (n), der ontsinder

lightning, der blits

like (as) (adv), vi

like (v), glaykhn (anglicism), holt hobn, lib hobn; "A likely storey", punkt!; "If you like", gezunterheyt

likeness, di enlekhkeyt, dos geshtalt

likewise, azoy, ilts; "Same to you", gamatem (H)

lilac, der bez, der may

lily, di lilye

limb (body), der eyver (H)

lime (fruit), di grine limene

lime (slaked), der kalkh, di vapne

limit, der grenets, der shier (H); "Without limit", "on a shier"

limp (v), hinken; "pretend to limp", unterhinken

line (cover) (v), baleygn

line (n), der pas; "In line with", kefi (H)

line (reading or writing), di shure (H)

line (rope) (n), der shnur

line (row) (n), di shure (H)

linen, di layvnt, dos vesh

lining (n), der untershlak

link (n), der bindrung, dos tsvishndl

link (v), keytlen zikh

linoleum, der linoley

lion, der leyb

lioness, di leybikhe
lip, di lefts, di lip
liquid (adj), flisik
liquid (n), di flisikeyt
liquor, der bronfn, di mashke (H), der shnaps
lisp (v), shepelyaven
listen, aynhern, hern, tsuhern zikh; "Listen attentively", "onshteln mol un oyern"
literally, mamesh (H) (meaning not literally, see intr.), os-beos (H)
Lithuania, di lite; (Lithuanian Jew), der litvak (m) (R), di litvitshke (f) (R)
Lithuanian (person), der litviner; (language), dos litvish
little (adj), kleyn
little (quantity), dos bisl, der kap
little bits, shtiklekh; "Little by little", bislekhvayz, shtiklekhvayz
live (reside), voynen
live (v), lebn
livelihood, di kheyune (H), di mikhye (H)
lively, lebedik, rirevdik, zhvave
liver, der leber
living (adj), lebedik
living creature, der bal-khay (H)
living (n), di kheyune (H), dos lebn, di parnose (H); "modern living", "der moderner shteyger"
living-room, di mitlshtub, der voyntsimer
lizard(s), di yashtsherke(s) (R)
load (n), di mase; "I got a load off my chest", "es iz mir arop a shteyn fun hartsn" (a stone was removed from my heart)
load (v), gruzen, lodn
loaf (bread), der labn, dos lebl; "Sugar loaf', dos hitl
loafer, der leydik-geyer (one who goes empty-handed), der pustepasnik, (f. di pustepasnitse)
loafer (shoe), der pantofl

loan (n), di antlayung, di halvoe (H); "Interest-free loan", dos gmiles-khesed (H)
loathsome, khaloshesdik (H), mies (H)
lobby (n), dos firhoyz, di peredne (R); (parliamentary), di shtadlonimshaft (H-Y)
lobby (for) (v), mishtadl zayn zikh (far) (H-Y)
lobbyist, der kuluarist, der shtadlen (H)
lobe (ear), dos lepl
lobster, der homar (F)
local (re: person), do'ik, hig
lock (n), der shlos
lock (sluice) (n), der shlyuz
lock (v), farshlisn; "lock in", "aynshlisn", "farshlisn"; "lock oneself in", "farshlisn zikh"; "lock out", "aroys shlisn"; "lock up", "farshlisn"
lock of hair, di lok
locker, dos shenkl
locket, der oyvl
locust, der heysherik
lodger, der kvartirant
loft, di boydemshtub
log, der klots
loiter, arumdreyen zikh
lollipop, dos lekerl, dos notshl
loneliness, di elnt, di elntkeyt
lonely, elnt, eynzam, smutne, umetik
long (adj), lang
long for, benken; "Long for desperately", "oyskukn zikh di oygn"
longer, lenger; "No longer", "mer nit", "shoyn nit"
longevity, dos arikhes-yomim (H)
longing, dos benkenish
long-lasting, gedoyerdik, langklekik
long-lived, arikhes-yomimdik (H)
look (n), der kuk
look (v), kukn; "Look here!", "her zikh ayn!"; "Look who's here", "skotsl kumt"; "To look around", "arumkukn zikh; "To look like", "hobn a ponem (H) fun"; "To take a good look", aynkukn zikh
loom (n), di vebshtul

loop (n), di petlie, der shleyf
loophole, di shislokh
loophole (figurative), dos shpeltl
loose (not tight), loyz
lord (n), der har, der porets (H), der srore (H)
lord (title), pani (panye) (R)
lose, derleygn, farlirn, onvern; (game), farshpiln
lose one's way, farblondzhen (R)
loss, der hezek (H), der onver; "Be at a loss", "nit visn vu ayn un vu oys", zayn tsetumlt
lost (adj), farblondzhet (R), farfaln, farloyrn, ongevorn; "To get lost", (far)blondzhen (R)
lot, der skhum
lot (a lot, a great deal), a fule, a sakh, a velt; "There is a lot", siz faran un faran
lot in life, di doyle, der goyrl (H)
lotion, dos aynraybekhts, dos shmirekhts
loud, hoykh; (colour), raysik
louder, hekher
lounge (n), der rutsimer
lounge (v), shlyondern (R)
love (n), di libe, di libshaft
love (v), lib hobn
lovely, kheynevdik (H-Y), sheyn
lover, der gelibter, der libhober
lover (of art), der moyker (H)
low, niderik
low (mood), koderdik
low- (suffix), . . . knap
"low-salt diet", "di zaltsknape diete"
low (vile), gemeyn
loyal, getray
loyalty, di getrayshaft
lozenge, di pastilke (R)
lucid, durkhbliklekh, durkhze'ik
luck, dos mazl (H)
luck (bad), dos shlimazl (G-H); "good luck", dos mazl (H); "Good Luck!", zol zayn mit glick/mazl; "Just my luck", "dos hot mir gefelt?"
lucky (adj), mazldik (H-Y)
ludicrous, khoyzekdik (H), shtusik (H)

ludicrous thing (n), der khoyzek (H)
luggage, der bagazh, tshemodanes (R)
lukewarm, leblekh
lullaby, dos viglid
lump (n), di hrude, der knoyl, di payde; (swelling), der bayl
lump together (v), oysmishn, tsunoyfmishn
lunch (n), dos onbaysn
lunch (v), esn onbaysn
lunchbox, dos shpayzrentsl
lung(s), di lung(en)
lure (n), dos farnarekhts, der khoykh
lure (v), farmanyen, farnadyen, tsutsien
lurk, lokern, tshateven
luscious, maydanimdik (H), tam gan-eydn (H)
lust (n), di tayve (H), di tshuke (H)
luxurious, luksusdik
luxury, der luksus, der voyltog
lye, der loyg

M

machine gun, der koyln-varfer, di mashinbiks
mad (angry), beyz, broygez (H)
mad (crazy), meshuge (H), vild
made, gemakht
magazine, der zhurnal
maggot, di mod
magic, der kishef (H)
magician, der kishef makher (H-Y), der kuntsnmakher, der magiker
magnifying glass, dos fargreser-gloz, di lupe
maid (servant), di dinst(meydl); "Old maid", "di alte moyd", di farzesene (moyd)
mainspring, di traybfeder
make (v), makhn; "make believe", "makhn dem onshtel"; "make good", "gut makhn"; "make into", "makhn fun"; "make sure", "farzikhern zikh"

make up (amends), iberbetn zikh

makeup (cosmetics), di shminke; "put on makeup", shminkeven

malleable, shmidevdik, shmidik

mammal, der zoyger

man, der mantsbil, der mentsh; "Lazy man", der akshn (H), der foylyak, (f. di foylyatshke); "Old man", der zokn (H); "Old woman", di zkeyne (H)

manage (direct), onfirn

manage (under difficult conditions) (v), oyskereven zikh, oyskumen

manager, der farvalter, der firer

mane, di grive

manger, der zholeb

manhole, di krikhlokh

manned, ekipirt, pilotirt

manner (way), der gang, der oyfn (H), der shteyger

manners (good), der derkherets (H), der manir(n); "Mind one's manners", "haltn zikh in der mayle (H)"

manoeuvre (military), der manever

manoeuvre (n), der lavir

manoeuvre (v), lavirn, manevrirn

mantle, der shleyer, der tsudek

mantlepiece, der kamingzims

manufacturer, der fabrikant

manufacturer (of homes), der khalupnik

manure, dos mist

many, a sakh; "As many", "azoy fil"

map, di karte, di mape

mar (v), farshtern, tseshedikn

marble (adj), mirmeln

marble (n), der marmer, der mirmlshteyn

marble (toy), dos bikl, dos reshl

mare, di kliatshe (R), di shkape (R)

margin, der gilyen (H), der grenets

marijuana, di marikhuane

marina, der yakhtbaseyn, der yampromenad

marinate, marinirn

mark, der simen (H), der tseykhn

mark (target), der tsil

mark (v), batseykhenen; "Hit the mark", "trefn in pintl"; "Mark time", "marshirn oyfn ort"; "Mark up (price)", oyfshlogn; "Mark up (soil)", bapatshken

market-place, der mark

maroon (colour), kestn broyn

marriage, di khasene (H)

marriage broker (f), di shadkhnte (H)

marriage broker (m), der shadkhn (H)

married, farheyrat (G), khasene-gehat (H-Y)

married couple, dos porfolk

married man, der bavaybter, der khasene gehater

married woman, di bamante, di khasene gehate

marrow, der kliok (R), der markh

marry, khasene hobn (H-Y)

marry off, oysgebn

mascot, dos mazele (H)

masculine (adj), mantsbilsh, menlekh

masculine man (strong) (n), der gvar (H)

mash (v), tsekvetshn

mashed potatoes, di kartofl-kashe

master (craftsman) (n), der mayster

master (owner) (n), der balebos (H)

masterpiece, dos maysterverk, der shedever

masturbate, onanirn

masturbation (n), der onanizm

mat, di rogozhe, der treter

match (betrothal) (n), der shidekh (H)

match (sulphur) (n), dos shvebele

match (v), porn, tsunoyfpasn

mate (mating) (n), der ziveg; (pl.), di zivugim (H)

material, der materyal

material (cloth), dos gevant, der shtof

maternity clothes, shvengerkleyder

maternity ward, di kimpet-palate

matrimony, dos man-un-vayb-lebn, di zivegshaft (H-Y)

matron, di madam, di matrone

matter (substance) (n)   **mere**

---

matter (substance) (n), di materye

matter (thing), der inyen (H); "No matter", "alts eynts"; "No matter how good", "vi gut es zol nit zayn"; "No matter what", "ove-tove"; "What's the matter?", "vos iz der mer?"

may (allowed) (v), megn

May (month), der may

maybe, efsher (H), ken zayn

may not, torn nit

maze, di blondzheray, der labirint

me, ikh, mir

meadow, di lonke (R)

meal (festive only), di sude (H)

meal, der moltsayt ("mol" is never used by itself as "meal")

mean (average) (adj), durkhshnitlekh

mean (low) (adj), beyz, hintish, shlekht

mean (n), der durkhshnit

mean (v), bataytn, meynen

meander, shlenglen zikh

meaning (n), der batayt, der taytsh

means (n), dos mitl, di takhbule (H); "By all means", "avade" (H), nit andersh, umbadingt; "By no means", "beshum-oyfn" (H), "far keyn fal . . . nit"; "By what means?", "vi azoy?"

meant, gemeynt

meanwhile, beshas-mayse (H), dervayl

measles, mozlen; German measles, di kushulye; "have the measles", opmozlen

measure (n), dos mestl, di mos

measure (step) (n), dos mosmitl; "to take measures", "onnemen mitlen"

measure (v), mestn; "Made to measure", "gemakht oyf mos"

measurement (n), di mestung, di mos; "take measurement", "(arop) nemen a mos"

meat (adj) (re: Jewish dietary laws), fleyshik

meat (n), dos fleysh

meatloaf, der klops

meddle, araynmishn zikh, krikhn, shtekn zikh (in)

meddler, der kokhlefl

mediate, "araynleygn zikh in sholem (H)", farmitlen

medley, dos gemish, der popuri (F)

meek person, der nikhne (H), der onev (H)

meet (v), bagegenen, trefn

meet (unexpectedly), ongegenen

meeting (n), di asife (H), dos bagegenish, di zitsung

melancholy (adj), farmore-shkhoyret, melankholish

melancholy (n), di more-shkhoyre (H)

mellow, zenftik

melody (n), di melodye

melody (Jewish music), der nign (H)

melon, di dinye (R)

melt, tsegeyn, tseshmeltsn

member (limb), dos glid

member (of an organization), der mitglid

membership, di mitglidershaft

membrane (n), dos haytl

memento, dos ondenkl

memorize, aynkhazern (Y-H), "oyslernen oyf oysnveynik"

memory, der zikorn (H); "Good memory", "der ayzerner zikorn"; "In memory of . . . ", lezikorn (H)

mend, farrikhtn

mendicant, der shnorer

menstruate, hobn di tsayt

menstruation, di tsayt

mental, gaystik

mention (n), di dermonung

mention (v), dermonen; "Don't mention it", "nito far vos"

merchandise (n), di skhoyre (H)

merchant, der hendler, der soykher (H)

merciless, umberakhmonesdik (H)

mercy, rakhmim (H), dos rakhmones (H); "Quality of mercy", dos rakhmones (H)

mere, bloyz; "A mere hint", "nit mer vi an onvunk"

merge, tsunoyfgisn

merriment, di freylekhkeyt, di khukhe-tlule (H); "There is merriment", "zayn layehudim" (Y-H)

merry (adj), freylekh; "Make merry", "mesameyekh zayn zikh" (H-Y)

mesh, di nets

mess (n), der balagan (H), dos khazeray (H), dos patshkeray; "Make a mess of", farpartatsheven; "Make a mess of things", "farkokhn a kashe"

message (n), der onzog, di yedie (H)

messenger, der meshulekh (H), der shikyingl (gofer)

Messiah, der meshiekh (H)

method, der gang, der metod, di shite (H)

mew (v), miyauken

middle (adj), mitl, mitlst; "middle-aged", "in di mitele yorn"; "middle-ages", "der mitl-elter"

middle (n), di mit, der mitn; "in the middle", "in mitn";

midst; "In our midst", "tsvishn undz"; "in the midst", in mitn; "In the midst of everything", "in mitn derinen", (in mitske derinen)

midget, der karlik, der liliput

midnight, di halbe nakht

midwife, di akusherke (R), di heyvam

mild, lagodne (R), lind, mild; "To put it mildly", "eydl geret"

mildew, der shiml

milk, di milkh; "Milk pail", di dinitse (R)

milk (v), (oys) melkn

milkman, der milkhiker

millinery, dos hutnputseray

million(s), der milyon(en)

millionaire, der milyoner

Milquetoast (Caspar), der/di lemishke (R)

mimic (v), nokhkrimen

mincemeat, dos kreplfleysh; "Make mincemeat of", "makhn ash un blote fun"

mind, der moyekh (H); "make up one's mind", "bashlisn bay zikh"; "Make up your mind", "nu shoyn! ahin oder aher!"; "Never mind", "meyle!", loz tsu ru; "I don't mind", "fun maynet vegn"

mine (possesive), mayn; "of mine", mayner a . . .

mine (shaft) (n), di shakhte

miner, der berger

minute (adj), montshink, pitsink

minute (time) (n), di minut

miracle, der moyfes (H); (pl.), di mofsim; der nes (H); (pl.), di nisim

miracle man, der bal-hanes (H), der balmoyfes

"Miracle upon miracle", "nisim veniflo'es" (H)

mirror, der shpigl

miscarriage, di maplung (H)

miscellaneous (n), farsheydene

mischief (harm) (n), der shodn; (bad ways), shlekhte drokhim (Y-H), dos shtiferay

mischievous boy, der mazek (H), der shtifer

miserable, klogedik, nebekhdik; "Make life miserable", "farshvartsn di yorn"

misery, tsores (H)

misfortune, dos umglik

mishap, di sibe (H), der tsufal, der umglikfal

mislay, farleygn

mislead, farfirn

miss (be late) (v), farzamen

miss (long for) (v), benken nokh, feln, zhaleven (R)

miss (not hit) (v), farbayshisn

Miss (title), fraylin, khaverte (H)

mist, der nepl, der tuman (R)

mistake (n), der feler, der grayz, der toes (H); "Make a mistake", a toes hobn (H-Y), makhn a feler

Mister (title), mister (see Mr.)

mistress, di baleboste (H)

mistress (love), di metrese

mistrust (n), der umtsutroy

mistrust (v), nit getroyen

misty, nepldik
mitten, dos kulikl
mix, mishn; "Mixed up", oysgemisht; (confused), tsedreyt, tsemisht
mixing bowl, di makrete (R)
moan (v), der yenk
moan (v), "okhtsn un krekhtsn", yenken
mock (v), khoyzek makhn (H-Y)
mocker, der lets (H)
mockery, der khoyzek (H), dos letsones (H)
model, der afir
moderate (adj), basheydn, lagodne (R)
modern, hayntik, hayntveltik, modern, naytsaytish
modernize, farhayntikn, modernizirn
modest (adj), anivesdik (H), basheydn
modest (person) (n), der onev (H)
mohair, di more
moist, faykht, naslekh
moisten, aynnetsn
molasses, di patike (R)
mold (form) (n), der furem
mold (form) (v), (oys)furemen
mold (growth), der shiml
moldy, farshimlt; "grow moldy", farshimlt vern
moment, di rege (H); "a moment ago", okersht
momentum, der impet; "gather momentum (in running)", "onloyfn zikh"
Monday, der montik
money, dos gelt
money-changer, der khalfn (H)
monk, der monakh
monkey (n), di malpe; "make a monkey out of", "makhn tsum nar"; "Monkey-business", "der kunkl-munkl"
month, der khoydesh; (pl.) di khadoshim (H); der monat
moo (v), muken
moon (n), di levone (H); "new moon", der moyled (H)
moral (adj), moralish

moral (n), di moral
moral (story) (n), der muser-haskl (H)
morality, di moral
morbid, krenklekh
more, mer, nokh; "No more", "mer nit"; "More and more beautiful", "vos vayter alts shener"
moreover, akhuts dem (H-Y), dertsu
moron, der balvan, di beheyme (H)
morose, atsvesdik (H), ongekhmuret
mortgage (n), di hipotek (R)
mortgage (v), farmashkenen (Y-H)
Moses, moyshe (H)
mosquito, der komar
most (adj), merste
most (adv), tsum merstn; "at the most", maksimum, "nit mer vi"
moth(s), der mol(n) (R)
mother, di mame, di muter
mother-in-law, di shviger
mother tongue, dos mame-loshn (Y-H)
motion (n), der baveg; (parliamentary m.), der forshlog
motion picture, der film, dos kino-bild
motive, der motiv, der tam (H)
mountain, der barg; (pl.), di berg; "Make a mountain of a mole-hill", "makhn fun a flig a helfand" (to make an elephant of a fly), "makhn fun a vort a kvort"
mourn (v), baveynen, troyern
mourner, der ovl (H); (pl.), di aveylim
mourning (n), der troyer; "To wear mourning", "geyn in klog"
moustache, vontses, (vontsn)
mouth, dos moyl, der pisk (of animal) (R); (of a river), di leftsung
mouthwash, dos shvenkekhts
move (game) (n), der gang
move (household) (n), der ibertsi
move (movement) (n), der baveg, der ker, der makh
move (v), rirn (zikh)
move (game) (v), geyn

move (household) (v), ibertsien zikh;
"Move heaven and earth", "aynleygn
veltn"

Mr. (title), her; (pl.), hern, khaveyrim
(H), (Jewish), reb (H), reb yid

Mrs. (title), froy, madam

much, a fule, a sakh; "as much as",
"azoy fil vi"; "how much", "vifl";
"Make much of", "makhn a tsimes
fun"; "not much of", "oykh mir a . . . ";
"very much so", graylekh

muck (n), dos gemoyzekhts

mucus, der shlaym

mud, di blote

muddy, blotik (R)

muff (n), di mufte

mug (face), der partsef (H)

mug (jug) (n), der kufl

mug (v), bafaln

mugger, der bafaler

mugging (n), di bafalung, der bafel

mum, sha!; "Keep mum", "shvaygn vi
yorkes hunt"; "Mum's the word",
"pasekh shin sha"

mumble (v), beben, "redn unter der
noz" (to talk under the nose)

mumbo-jumbo, dos geprepl

murder (n), der mord

murder (v), derhargenen (H),
(der)mordn

muscle (n), der muskl

mushroom, dos shveml, der shvoym

musician, der klezmer (H) (Jewish);
(pl.) di klezmorim, der muziker; (less
respectful), der muzikant

mustard, di gortshitse (R), der zeneft

mute, shtum

mutter (v), burtshen, preplen

myrtle, di mirt

myrtle branch, der hodes (H)

mysterious, misteryez, soydesdik (H)

mystery, di misterye, der sod (H)

myth, der mitos

N

nag (v), derkutshen, grizhen, totshen,
yaden

nagging fault-finding woman, di
arure (H)

nail (finger or toe), der nogl; (pl.), di
negl

nail (large), der tshvok; (pl.) di
tshvekes

nail (small) (n), dos tshvekl

nail (v), noglen, tsuklapn

naive, "keyn tsvey nit kenen tseyln" (be
unable to count to two), tmimesdik
(H)

name (n), der nomen

name (v), heysn; "Be named after",
"zayn a nomen nokh"; "By the name
of", "vos heyst"; "What's the name
of?", "vi heyst?"

namesake, "khaver tsum nomen"

nap (of cloth), di barve

nap (sleep) (n), der dreml

nap (v), khapn a dreml (catch forty
winks)

nape (neck), di patilnitse (R)

napkin, di servetke (R)

narration, di dertseylung

narrow, eng, shmol

narrow-minded, shmolkepik

nasty, bridke, paskudne (R)

nation, dos folk, dos land, di ume (H)

native (n), der ayngeboyrener, der hi-
geboyrener

natural, beteve (H), natirlekh

naturally, farshteyt zikh, geveyntlekh

nature (n), di natur

nature (of something), di teve (H)

naughty, umdertsoygn; "Naughty
child", "der shtifer"; "To be naughty",
"komandeven", "nit folgn"

nausea, dos khaloshes (H), der migl, di
nit-gutkeyt

nauseating, khaloshesdik (H), migldik

navel, der nopl, der pupik (R)

near (adj, adv), noent
near (prep), bay, lebn (nebn)
nearby (adj), derbayik, noent
nearby (adv), derbay, in der noent
nearly, kimat (H)
neat, tsikhtik
necessarily, dafke (H); "Not necessarily", lavdafke (H)
necessary, neytik; "If necessary", far noyt
neck, dos genik, der haldz un (n)akn, der kark; (of a bottle), dos heldzl
necktie, der shnips
need (n), di noyt
need (v), darfn; "Not needed at all", "darfn oyf kapores (H)"; "Not need to", "farshporn"; "That's all I need", "mer felt mir nit"
needle, di nodl; "knitting needle", dos shpizl; "Look for a needle in a haystack", "zukhn a shpilke in a vogn hey"
ne'er-do-well, der loy-yutslekh (H), der shlimazl (G-H)
neglected filthy place, dos hekdesh (H)
neighbour, der shokhn (H); (pl.) di shkheynim; "Female neighbour", di shokhnte (H)
neighbourhood, der gegnt, der kvartal
nephew, der plimenik
nerve(s), der nerv(n)
nerve (gall), dos gehay, di khutspe (H), dos yandes
nervous, nerveyish, nervez
nestle (v), lashtshen zikh, tulyen
neutral food (re: Jewish dietary laws), parev (H)
never, keyn mol nit
nevertheless, fort, fundestvegn
new, nay; "What's new?", "vos hert zikh?"; "Brand new", "shpoglnay"
news, nayes; "Local news", di khronik; "Good news", di bsure (H)
newspaper, dos blat; (pl.) di bleter; di tsaytung
newsstand, der kiosk

New Year, der nay yor
New Year (Jewish), der rosheshone (H)
New Year's eve, der silvester-ovnt
next (adj), kumendik, nekste, noentst
next (adv), vayter; "what's next", "vos vayter"
next door, "a tir lebn a tir", "mit a tir vayter"
nibble (n), dos nasheray (coll., nash)
nibble (v), grizhen, nashn, shtshipen
niche, di framuge (R), di nishe
nickel (metal), der nikl
nickel (money), dos finfele, der nikl
nickname, der tsunomen
niece, di plimenitse
night, di nakht; "Spend the night", ibernekhtikn
night cap, der kolpik (R)
nightingale, der solovey (R)
nightmare, der koshmar (F)
nimble, luftik, shmaydik
nincompoop, yukl fayvish
nine, nayn
nineteen, nayntsn
ninety, nayntsik
nipple, der opl
nit-wit, der glomp, der lekish
no (none), keyn
no (not yes), neyn; "none", keyn; "No one", keyner nit
noble (adj), eydl
nobleman, der adlman
noblewoman, di adlfroy
noise, dos gepilder, der liarem, der tuml
non-believer (doubter) in Judaism, der apikoyres (H)
non-committal, "mit halbn moyl"
nondescript thing, "nit dos nit yents"
non-existent, nit-eksistirndik; (humorous), nit-geshtoygn nit-gefloygn

nonsense, dos meshugas (H), di narishkeyt, shmokhtes, shmontses, der shtus (H), der umzinen, "Nonsense!", "blote!"; "To talk nonsense", "hakn a tshaynik (R)" (to bang on a teapot), "redn fun hits"

noodle(s), der loksh(n)

nook, dos vinkele

noose, di petlie (R), der vergshleyf

north, der tsofn (H)

nose, di noz

nostril, di nozlokh; (pl.) di nozlekher

not, keyn, nit, (nisht); "Is that not so?", "ayo?"; "Not at all!", "gor!"

notable, barimt, merkverdik

notch, der shtsherb

notch (v), aynshtsherbn (R)

note (short letter), dos brivl, dos kvitl, der tsetl

nothing, gornit, keyn zakh nit; "For nothing", umzist (uselessly); "Nothing of the kind", "a nekhtiker tog; "To be nothing compared to", "zayn a hunt antkegn"

notice (n), di akht, der bamerk; (newspaper), der anons, di medoe (H), di meldung, di notits; "Take notice", leygn akht oyf

notice (v), bamerkn

noticeable, (ba)merklekh, onze'evdik

notify, gebn tsu visn, onzogn

notion (idea), der aynfal, der bagrif

notions (goods), der tselnik

novel (adj), umgeveyntlekh

novel (n), der roman (F)

novelty, der khidesh (H), dos nays

now, atsind, atsinder, itst, itster, yetst; "Every now and then", "ale vayle"; "Just now", "nor vos" ; "Now and then", "fun tsayt tsu tsayt"; "Now ... Now", do ... do, dos ... dos, ot ... ot

now (floating participle), " ... zhe" (R) ("zhe" is not used by itself)

nowhere, in ergets nit; "be nowhere near", nit kumen tsu

nude (adj), naket

nude (art) (n), der akt

nudge, "a shturkh ton"

nuisance, dos tsutshepenish

nuisance (person) (n), der nudnik (R), (coll., der nudzh); "Make a nuisance of oneself", "krikhn in di oygn"

null (n), der nul; "null and void" (adj), botl umvutl (H)

numb, geleymt

number (quantity, figure) (n), di tsol; (designation), der numer; (digit), der tsifer

number (v), tseyln; (mark), numerirn

numbered, getseylt

numerous, filtsolik

nun, di monashke (R)

nurse (n), di krankn-shvester, di nianye (R); (male), der sanitar

nurse (v), niatshen (R)

nurse (suckle), zeygn

nursing home, der moyshev-zkeynim (H)

nut (for bolt), di muterke

nut (fruit), der nus; (pl.) di nisn

"Nuts!", "bobkes!"

nutrition, di dernerung, di shpayzung

O

oaf, der nar, der tipesh (H)

oak (adj), dembn

oak tree, der demb (der domb)

oar, der ruder, di vesle

oath, der neder (H), di shvue (H); "administer an oath", "mashbie zayn" (H-Y); "take an oath", "gebn a shvue"

oatmeal, der hobergritz

oats, der hober

obedience (n), di folgevdikeyt, dos folgn

obedient, folgevdik, horkhik

obeisance, faln koyrim (Y-H) (Jewish)

obey, folgn, horkhn

object (aim) (n), der kheyfets (H), der tsil; "Money is no object", "a rendl aroyf a rendl arop"

object (v), aynvendn, hobn kegn

oblique, kose

oblivion, dos fargesenish

oblong, lenglekh

obnoxious, dervider(dik)

obscene person, der grobyan

obsequious (to be), unterlekn, untertantsn

observe (obey), observirn; (holidays), op'hitn

obstacle, di menie (H)

obstinacy, dos akshones (H)

obtain, bakumen, krign

obvious, bashaymperlekh, klor vi der tog; "belabour the obvious", "brekhn zikh in an ofener tir" (break into an open door)

occasion (n), di gelegnheyt; "have occasion to", "oyskumen tsu"; "on the occasion of", lekoved (H)

occasionally, "ven nit ven"

occupied (busy), farnumen

occupation, der fakh, di melokhe (H)

occupation (military), di okupatsye

occupy oneself (with), mesasek zayn zikh (H-Y), oysek zayn in (H-Y)

occur (to happen), geshen, pasirn, trefn

occur (to think of), dakhtn zikh, kumen oyfn zinen

occurence, di pasirung, der traf

ocean, der okean

oddball, der tshudak (R)

odious, moes (H)

odour (n), der reyekh (H); "bad odour", der aver (H), der ipesh (H), der shmukht

of, fun

off, arop, avek, op; "Off and on", "vi a mol"; "Offhand", "oyf eyn fus"; "take some time off", "bafrayen zikh a bisl"; "We're off", "hayda!"

offence (n), di baleydikung; (crime), der ibershprayz; "to take offence", "onblozn zikh " (oyf)

offend (v), baleydikn, fartshepen

offended, broygez (H), ongeshtoysn; "To be offended", "hobn faribl oyf"

office (n), der amt, dos byuro (F)

official (adj), amtik, ofitsyel

official (n), der ba'amter, der funktsyonar

officialdom, natshalstve (R) (hum)

offspring, der nokhkumling; (coll.) der nokhvuks, der zoymen (H)

OH!, oy!, "oy vey" (woe is me); (really), take?

oil, der eyl

oil (edible) (n), der boyml

oil (fuel), der naft

oilcloth, di tserate (R)

oil well, der naftkval

ointment, di zalb

Okay!, gepoyelt, gut, s'geyt

old, alt

old age, di elter

Old Age Home, der moyshev-zkeynim (H)

"old and wrinkled", oysgetrukent

older, elter

Old Folks Home, der moyshev-zkeynim (H)

old maid, di alte moyd

old man, der zokn (H)

"old story", a mayse (H) mit a bord

old-time, amolik

olive(s), der eylbert(n), di masline(s) (H)

omelette, der faynkukhn

omit, iberhipn

on, oyf

once (adv), eyn mol; "At once" (in one time), "oyf eyn mol"; "once and for all", "eyn mol far ale mol"; "once in a blue moon", "eyn mol in a yoyvl (H)"; "Once upon a time", eyn mol

one, eyn, eynts; "One and only", "eyn un eyntsiker"; "One-way street", di ahingas; "One-way ticket", der ahin-bilet
one (pronoun), me, men
one time, eyn mol
onion, di tsibele (R)
only (adj), eyntsik
only (adv), bloyz, nor
only (as recently as), ersht (hersh)
only (necessarily), davke (H)
opaque, mat
open (adj), ofn
open (v), efnen, oyfmakhn
opinion, meynung, svore (H); "Expert opinion", dos mevines (H)
opposite (adj), antkegndik, farkert
opposite (adv), antkegn, kapoyer
opposite (n), der heypekh (H)
oppress, badrikn, gnoteven
optimist, der bal-bitokhn (H)
optimistic, optimistish
or, oder
orange (adj), oranzh
orange (n), der marants
orator, der orator, der redner
orchard, der sod; (pl.) seder
order (arrangement) (n), di ordenung
order (by mail) (v), oysshraybn
order (command) (n), der bafel; "Bring into order", "makhn a tolk"; "In order to", "kedey tsu" (H-Y); "In regular order", "keseyder" (H); "Out of order", "nit in ordenung"
order (command) (v), heysn
order (to be delivered) (v), bashteln
ordinary, prost (R)
organ, der organ
organ (pipe organ), der orgl; "Barrel-organ", di katerinke (R)
organ-grinder, der katerinshtshik (R)
oriental (adj), mizrekhdik (H)
ornament, der per (H), di tsatske, der tsir
ornate, getsasket, tsatskedik

orphan, der yosem (H); (pl.), di yesoymim
orthodox (religion), frum, ortodoksish
ostrich, der shtroys
other (the), ander; "the other day", anumlt
otherwise, andersh, anit
otter, di vidre (R)
ought (to be), darfn, volt gedarft, zoln
our, undzer
out, aroys, oys; "out-of-date", fareltert; "Out of doors", in droysn; "Out of the question", "zayn opgeret fun"
outbid, oyskonkurirn
outdo, aribershtaygn, "farshtekn in gartl" (hum.)
outer, oysveynikst
outhouse (privy), der optret
outlast, iberlebn
outright, direkt, umfarmitlt
outside, in droysn
outspoken, ofntlekh
outstanding, boylet (H), ongezen, oysgetseykhnt
outwit, iberkhitreven, iberklign
ovary, der eyershtok
oven, der oyvn
over (above), ariber
over (gone) (adj), farbay, oys
over (prep), iber; "all over . . . ", "iber . . . "; "Over and done with", farfaln; "over and over", "vider un vider"
overcharge (v), baraysn, iberrekhnen
overcoat, der mantl, der paltn
overcome (adj), gerirt; "He was overcome by the heat", "er iz gefaln a korbm fun der hits"
overcome (transitive), baykumen
overcrowded, farpropt, ibergepakt
overdo, "ibertsien dos shtrikl" (overpull the string)
overflow (n), der iberfleyts
overflow (v), aribergisn, ibergeyn
overgrown (person), ibergevaksn
overgrown (surface), bavaksn
overhaul (v), remontirn

overhead (adj), stelye
overhead (adv), oyvn
overhead (n), generale hetsoes (H)
overhear, unterhern
overlook (look down), aropkukn oyf
overlook (not see) (v), farkukn
overly, iberik
overnight (adj), ibernakhtik
overnight (stay) (v), (iber)nekhtikn
overpay, ibertsoln
overprotective, iberbashitserish
overripe, ibertsaytik
overrule, anulirn, iberpaskenen
oversight, der farze
oversleep, farshlofn
overtake, iberyogn
overturn, iberkern
overwhelm, pritshmelyen (R)
owe, kumen, shuldik zayn; "He owes me
  . . .", "er iz mir shuldik"
owl, di sove
own (adj), eygn
own (v), farmogn, hobn an eygn
owner, der balebos (m), di baleboste
  (f), der farmoger
ox, der oks; small oxen, di ekslekh
oxygen, der zoyershtof

P

pace (length) (n), der shpan
pace (rate), der temp
pace (v), arumshpanen
pace off, opmestn oyfn shpan
pacifier, dos mizyukl, der smotshik (R)
pacify, baruikn
pack (n), der pak
pack (cards), der pash, dos peshl
pack (wolves), di staye, di tshate
pack (v), (ayn)pakn; "pack up", farpakn
  (zikh)
package (n), dos pekl
package (v), aynpakn
pack-carrier, der pakntroger

packing (n), dos aynpakn
paddle (n), di lopete (R)
page (of a book), di zayt; (pl.) di zaytn
page (of Talmud), der daf (H)
paid up, oysgetsolt
pail, der emer, der kibl
pain (n), der vey, der veytik, yesurim
  (H)
paint (n), di farb
paint (v), moln, oysmoln
painter (artist), der moler
painter (house), der malyer
pair (n), di por
pair (v), tsunoyfporn
pale, blas
palm (hand), di dlonye (R)
palm branch (for Succoth), der lulev
  (H) (Jewish)
palm tree, di palme
palsy-walsy, knipl-beknipl
pamper, baleven, kekhlen, koshken (R)
pan (n), di fan, dos fendl, di skovrode
  (R)
pancake, di latke (R); (cheese p.), di
  blintse (R)
pane, di shoyb
panel, der tovl
pang, der shtokh, der tsup
pansy, "dos khaneles eygele", dos
  shtifmuterl
pant (v), sopen
pantry, di shpayzarnye
pants (trousers), hoyzn
paper (adj), papirn
paper (n), dos papir
parable, der moshl (H); (pl.) di
  moshlim
paradise, der gan-eydn (H), der oylem-
  habe (H)
parakeet, der langekiker popugay (Y-R)
paralyze, opnemen
parasite, der parazit
parasite (human), der shnorer
pardon, di bagnedikung, di mekhile; "I
  beg your pardon", "hob keyn faribl
  nit", "zayt mir moykhl"; "Pardon me",
  "antshuldik" (mir)

pare (v), opsheyln
parents, eltern, tate-mame
park (n), der shtotgortn
park (small), dos sedl
park (v), parkirn
parlor, di zal
parrot (n), der popugay (R)
parsley, di petrishke (R)
parsnips, der pasternak (R)
part (n), der kheylek (H), der teyl
part (in hair), der shrunt
part (participation) (n), der aynteyl, der onteyl, di role
part (leave) (v), gezegenen zikh
partial, teylvayz
particle (of dust), dos shtaybl
particularly, bifrat (H), der hoypt
parting, di gezegenung, di tsesheydung
partition, di tseteylung; (Jewish, in synagogue, separating men and women), di mekhitse (H)
partner, der shutef (H); "In partnership", shutfesdik (H-Y)
partridge, di kuropate (R)
party (participant), der tsad (H); "Fun party", der farbrengens, di simkhe (H); "Going away party", der tseyskho-lesholem (H); "Political party", di partey (H);
pass (permit) (n), der pasir-tsetl
pass (route) (n), der durkhgang
pass (hand over) (v), derlangen; "Come to pass", pasirn, "trefn zikh"
pass (overtake) (v), iberyogn
passable, nishkoshedik (H)
pass away, fargeyn, oysgeyn
pass by (time), farbrengen
passé, oysgeshpilt
passing, farbaygeyendik
passion, di laydnshaft; "To be passionate", "hobn heys blut"
Passover, der peysekh (H)
Passover unleavened bread, di matse (H)
past (adj), amolik, gevezn; "For some time past", "a shtik tsayt shoyn"

past, di fargangenheyt, der over (H); "half past two", halb nokh tsvey
paste (n), der pap, di paste
paste (v), klepn; "paste on", onklepn, tsuklepn
pastime, di farvaylung
pasture, di toleke (R)
pat (n), dos klepl, dos petshele (R); "a pat on the back", a knip in bekl (fig.) (a pinch on the cheek)
pat (v), a klepl ton, a petshl ton
patch (n), di late (R)
patch (v), farlatn
pathetic, klogedik, rirndik
patience, di geduld; "He lost his patience", "di geduld hot im geplatst"
patient (adj), geduldik
patient (n), der khoyle (H)
patient person, der savlen (H)
Patriarchs (The), di oves (H)
patronize (customer), zayn a shtendiker koyne (H)
patronize (look down), "kukn fun oybn arop oyf"
paunch, der trelbukh
pauper, der dalfn, der evyen, der kabtsn, der oni (all H); "Cheerful pauper", der kasril (H)
pause (n), di poyze
pause (v), zikh opshteln
pavement, der forveg
pavement (cobblestone walk), der bruk
pavement (sidewalk), der tretar (F)
paw, di lape (R); (small paw) dos fisl
pawn (chess), der pion
pawn (v), farmashkenen (H)
pawnbroker, der lombardir
pawnshop, der lombard
pay (v), batsoln
pay attention, aynhern zikh
pay out, oysgebn; "Pay off a debt", silekn
pea(s), der arbes (same in pl.)
peace, der sholem (H); "At peace", besholem (H)
peach, di fershke

peacock, di pave (H)
peanut, dos rebe-nisl, di stashke (R)
peanut-butter, di stashkeshmir
pear, di bar (barne)
peasant, der khlop, der muzhik (R), der poyer (R)
peck (v), dzhoben zikh
peculiar, modne
pedal (n), der tretl
pedal (v), tretlen
peddler, der pedler
pedigree, der yikhes (H)
peek (n), dos kukele
peek (v), unterkukn zikh
peel (n), di sholekhts
peel (v), sheyln
peephole, dos eygl, dos lekhl, dos oyg
peevish, kaprizne (R)
peg (n), dos flekl
pelvis, der bekn
pen, di feder
penalty, di pen, di shtrof
penance, di tshuve (H)
pencil, der blayer
pencil sharpener, der shnitser
penetrate, durkhdringen
peninsula, der halbindzl
penis, der menlekher eyver (Y-H), dos pepl, dos shmekl
penitence, di tshuve (H)
penitent (adj), tshuve ton (H-Y)
penitent (n), der bal-tshuve (H)
pen name, der psevdonim (R)
penny, der groshn (R), di prute (H)
pentagon, der finfek (five corners)
Pentateuch, der khumesh (five books of Moses) (H)
penthouse, di dakh-dire
people, layt, mentshn
people (nation), dos folk, di ume (H)
pep, dos heybekhts
pepper (n), der fefer
perceptible, merklekh
percolate, durkhrinen
percolater, der bulbler
perfect (adj), perfekt, shleymesdik (H)
perforate, durkhlekhlen

perform, forshteln
perform (ceremony), oprikhtn
perhaps, efsher (H), ken zayn, tomer (H)
period (age, time), der zman (H)
period (punctuation), dos pintl
perishable, kalye-verevdik (R)
perk up, oyfmintern zikh
permanent (adj), blaybik, shtendik
permissible, derloybt
permissible (Jewish religious), muter (H)
permission (n), dos derloybenish
permission (to have p.), megn
permissive (be), nokhgebn
permit (v), derloybn, derlozn
perpetrate, opton
perpetual, doyresdik (H), eybik
person, der parshoyn, di perzon
perspiration, der shveys
perspire (v), shvitsn
perspiring, farshvitst
persuade, aynredn
pest(erer), der nudnik, (coll.) der nudzh, dos tsutshepenish, di zlidne (R)
pester (v), "dergeyn di yorn", duln a kop
pestilence, di mageyfe (H)
pet (animal) (n), der gletling
pet (v), gletn, koskhen
petite, drovne (R)
petition (n), di petitsye
petition (v), petitsyonirn
pew, di kloysterbank
pewter (adj), tsinern
pewter (n), dos englishe tsin
pharmacy (store), di apteyk (R)
Pharoah, der pare (H)
pheasant, der fazan (R)
philacteries, boksn, tfiln (H)
philander (v), "shpiln a libe"
philanthropist, der bal-tsdoke (H), der nadven (H)
philosopher, der filosof
pick (v), oysklaybn
pickle (dill), di zoyere ugerke

pickled, marinirt, zoyer
pickle juice (brine), der rosl
pick up (v), oyfheybn
picture (n), dos bild; "take a picture", fotografirn, nemen a bild
picture (v), oysmoln zikh
piece (n), dos shtik, dos shtikl
pig, der khazer (H)
piggy bank, di shporpushke
pigsty, di khazer-shtal (H-Y)
pile (n), der koyp, di kupe (R)
pile (v), onkoypn
pill, di pil
pinch (n), der knip
pinch (snuff) (n), der shmek tabik; "Do you have a pinch of snuff?", "host a shmek tabik?"
pinch (v), knaypn, kvetshn
pine tree, di sosne (R)
pious, frum; "Pious man" (Jewish), der frumer yid, der khosid (H), der tsadek (H)
pitcher (jug) (n), der krug; (baseball), der varfer
pity (n), der fardros, der shod; "It's a pity", a fardros, a shod; "what a pity", sara shod
pity (v), merakhem zayn zikh (H-Y), rakhmones hobn (H-Y)
pivot, der dreypunkt
place (n), der ort
place (v), (avek) leygn
place under, untershteln
plague (n), di mageyfe (H)
plague (v), matern, plogn
plain (adj), eynfakh, poshet (H), prost
plaintiff, der onkloger
plane (tool) (n), der huvl
plane (v), huvlen
plant (botanical) (n), dos geviks
plant (factory), di fabrik, der zavod
plant (v), farflantsn
plaster (n), der tink
plaster (v), oystinkeven
plate (dinner), der teler (same in pl.)
platter, der palumesik (R), di tats
play (game) (n), di shpil

play (theatre) (n), di forshtelung, di pyese
play (v), shpiln, shtifn
playboy, der lebyung
playmate, der mitshpiler
plea (n), di bakoshe (H); (court), der entfer
plead (v), taynen (H)
plead for, farteydikn, zayn der firshprekher far
pleasant, ayngenem(en), simpatish, voyl
please (excuse me), antshuldik(t)
please (request), bite, ikh bet aykn, zayt azoy gut
please (v), gefeln
pleasurable, fargenigik
pleasure (n), der maykhl (H); (pl.), di maykholim, dos fargenign, di hanoe (H), di mekhaye (H), der tayneg (H); "Derive pleasure", "hanoe hobn" (H-Y); "For pleasure", "fun hanoe vegn" (H-Y)
pleat (n), der falb
pledge (n), di havtokhe (H), der tsuzog
pledge (v), menader zayn (H-Y)
plentiful, beshefe
plenty, a mase, genug
plenty (n), di shefe (H)
pliers, di drottsvang
plod, toptshen
plot (against) (v), "grobn a grub oyf"
plough (n), der aker
plough (v), akern
pluck (feathers), flikn, tsupn
plug (electric), der gopl
plug (n), dos farshtekl, der tsapn
plug (v), farshtekn, farshtopn
plug in, araynshtekn
plumber, der instalator
plumbing, dos vasergerer
plump, oysgepashet
plunder (v), avekgazlen (Y-H)
plunge (v), araynvarfn zikh
plywood (adj), dikhtn
plywood (n), der dikht
poached eggs, farloyrene eyer

pocket (n), di keshene
pock-marked, geshtuplt
poem, dos lid, di poeme, der shir (H)
poet, der dikhter, der poet
point (issue) (n), di frage, di zakh; "be on the point", haltn derbay; "that is the point", dos iz di zakh; "to the point", tsu der zakh
point (tip) (n), der shpits
point out, aroys'heybn, onvayzn
poise (n), der statik
poison (n), der sam (H)
poison (v), farsamen
poke (v), titshen
poker (cards), der poker
poker (tool), di kotshere (R)
Poland, dos poyln
pole (n), der drong, di shtabe, der slup, der stoyp
police, di politsey (R); (policeman) (sing.) der politsiant
police commissioner (in Czarist Russia), der pristav (R)
police officer, der strazhnik (R)
police station, der utshastok (R)
Polish, poylish
polish (buff), frotirn
polish (glass) (v), opshlayfn
polish (shoe) (n), der shuvaks
polish (shoes) (v), opputsn
polite, heflekh
politician (active in public life), der askn (H), der politikant, der politishn
pollen, der blumenshtoyb
pollute, farpestikn
pomegranate, der milgroym
pond, di sazhlke (R)
pony-tail, dos loshik-ekl
pool (game), der bilyard
pool (puddle), di (ka)luzhe (R)
pool (swimming), der baseyn
poor, orem; "Poor child", "nebekh, az okh un vey iz dem kind"; "Poor thing", nebekh
poor country, dos oremland
poorhouse, dos hegdesh (H)

poor man, der dalfn (H), der evyen (H), der kabtsn (H), der oni (H), der oreman
popcorn, kokoshes
pope, der apifyur (H), der poyps
poplar, di topolye (R)
poppy seeds, der mon
popular (peoples'), folkish; (beloved), balibt, populer; "Become popular", "arayngeyn in shustergas" (enter into the street of the cobblers)
porch, der ganik
porcupine, der shtekhl-khazer (Y-H)
porridge, di kashe (R), di lemishke (R)
portion, der kheylek (H); (pl.) di khalokim, di portsye
position, di lage
position (job), der postn, di shtele
positive (affirmative), pozitiv
positive (confident), ibergetsaygt, zikher
positive (definite) (adj), befeyresh (H)
positively, durkhoys, nit andersh
possess, farmogn, hobn an eygn
possession (n), dos farmogn
possessions, dos eygns, dos farmegn, der farmog; "Take possession", bazetsn
possessive (greedy), khaperish
possible, meglekh, miglekh; "As fast as possible", "vos gikher"
possibility, di meglekhkeyt, di miglekhkeyt
post (n), der slup, der stoyp
postage, der porto, dos postgelt
postage stamp(s), di marke(s)
poster, der plakat
post-mortem, der palmes; "make a post-mortem", palmesn
post-office, der postamt
postpaid, franko
postpone, opleygn
posture (n), dos haltn zikh
pot (cooking), der top; (small pot), dos tepl; (poker), der kon
potato, di bulbe (R), der kartofl; "sweet potato", di batate

pot-hole (in road)   **present (v)**

---

pot-hole (in road), dos tinterl
pot roast, dos roslfleysh, dos top-
gebrotns
potter, der teper
pottery (craft), dos teperay; (dish,
etc.), dos tepervarg
pouch, di tash, dos zekl
poultry, oyfes (H)
pound (n), der funt
pound (v), shmidn, tseshtoyshn
pour, shitn
pout (v), farshartsn zikh, makhn lupes
poverty, der dales (H), di oremkeyt
powder (explosive), der pulver
powder (n), der proshik (R);
(cosmetic), der puder
powder (v), baproshen; (cosmetic),
bapudern
power, der koyekh (H), di kraft (G),
der reshus (H); "the powers that be",
di makht
practice (experience) (n), di praktik;
(custom), der fir
practice (v), genitn zikh; "Get into
practice", ayngenitn zikh
praise (n), di loyb
praise (v), loybn
prank, der optu, dos shpitsl
prankster, der kundes, der lets (H)
pray (v), davnen (H); (orn, obs.); "Pray
for someone", mekayekh zayn (H-Y)
"Afternoon prayer", di minkhe (H)
(Jewish)
"Closing prayer of Yom Kippur", di
nile (H) (Jewish)
"Evening prayer", der mayrev (H)
(Jewish)
"House of prayer", der beys-tfile (H)
(Jewish)
"Midnight prayer", der khtsos (H)
(Jewish)
"Morning prayers", der shakhres (H)
"Penitential prayer", di slikhe (H)
(Jewish)
"Prayer for health", der mishebeyrekh
(H) (Jewish)

"Prayer for the dead", der kadesh (H)
(Jewish)
"Sabbath and holy days prayers", der
musef (H) (Jewish)
"To complete prayers", opdavnen
prayer, di tfile (H)
praying shawl, der tales (H)
preach, darshenen (H-Y) (Jewish),
preydikn
preacher (itinerant), der preydiker
preacher (Jewish), der bal-darshn (H),
der maged (H)
precede, geyn afrier, kumen afrier
precious, tayer; "Be precious", zayn a
rendl; "something precious", an antik
precious (metal) (adj), eydl
predicament, di klem
predict (v), foroyszogn, "zayn a novi
az" (Y-H)
prediction, der foroyszog
predominate, hershn
preferable, bilkher, ongeleygter
pregnancy, di shvangershaft, dos trogn
pregnant, muberes (H), shvanger,
trogedik; "To be pregnant", shvangern,
trogn
prejudiced, hobn a forurtl
premature, fritsaytik
premises, der lokal
premises (on the p.), "oyfn ort"
premonition, dos forgefil; "I have a
premonition", "dos harts zogt mir"
(the heart tells me)
preoccupied, farhavet, fartoret
prepare, greytn, tsugreytn
prepared, greyt, tsugegreyt; "Finished
preparing", fartik
prescription (medical), der retsept
presence, dos bayzayn; "presence of
mind", di oryentirung; "divive
presence", di shkhine (H) (Jewish)
present (adj), hayntik, itstik
present (in attendance), bayzayik, do,
faran
present (n), di matone (H)
present (v), shenken (a present);
forshteln (introduce)

presentable, "nit hobn mit vos zikh tsu shemen" (nothing to be embarrassed about), shtaltik

preserves (n), dos ayngemakhts

president, der nosi (H) (Jewish-of Israel), der prezident

president (of the Synagogue), der gabe; (wife of the president), di gabete

press (pressure) (v), kvetshn; "I am badly pressed for time", "di hoyt brent oyf mir" (my skin is burning)

pressure, der ondrik; "high-pressure", der hoykhdruk; "High-pressure salesman", der khoykhe

prestige, dos khshives (H), der onzen, der shem (H)

presume, mekhtikn zikh (make bold), meshaer zayn (H-Y)

presumptuous, hozedik (H)

pretend, makhn an onshtel, makhn zikh; "Pretend not to hear", "makhn zikh nit herndik"

pretense, der onshtel, di oysgebung; "Under false pretenses", "unter falshe oysgebungen"

pretext, der oysred, der terets (H)

pretty (adj), sheyn

pretty (adv), gants

prevalent, breyt farshpreyt

prevaricate, lignen

prevent, farhitn, farmaydn

preview (n), di foroysike vayzung

preview (v), vayzn/zen in foroys

previous, frierdik

price (n), der mekekh (H), der prayz; "At a fair price", "in glaykhn gelt"

priceless, "on a shats"

prickle (v), shtekhlen

pride (n), der shtolts; "Pride oneself", "greysn zikh", shtoltsirn

priest (Jewish), der koyen (H)

priest (non-Jewish), der galekh (H)

prim, shtayf

primrose, der priml

prince, der ben-melekh (H), der prints

princess, di bas-malke (H), di printsesn

principal (money), der kern; (school), der direktor, der printsipal

principle, der iker (H); "in principle", in printsip

print (copy), di kopye

print (fine) (n), oysyes (H)

print (v), opdrukn

prison, di tfise (H), di turme

privacy, di aleynkeyt

privilege, di skhie (H); "privileged person", der yakhsn (H)

prize (n), dos gevins, di premye

prize (v), tayer haltn

probable, "kenen gring gemolt zayn"; "Most probably", "gikher far alts"

probably, "a ponem" (H), mashmoes (H), minastam (H), mistome (H)

problem, di oyfgabe (task), di problem

proceed, geyn foroys

proceeds (n), di leyzung

process, der gang, der protses; "In the process", "in gang"

proclamation, di hakhroze (H), der kolkoyre (H), der kruz (H)

procrastinate, balemutshn

procreation, "di frukhperung un merung"

prod, untershtupn

prodigy, der ile (H), dos vunderkind

produce (n), produktn

produce (v), oysarbetn; (a play), oyffirn, shteln

producer, der oyffirer

profane, vokhedik

profanity, di grobkeyt

profession, der fakh

professional (adj), fakhmenish, profesyonel

profit (n), der revekh (H)

profit (v), genisn

profound, omek (H), tif

progress (n), der gang, di pule (H)

progress (v), progresirn; "To make progress", "rukn zikh fun ort"

prohibit, farvern; (Jewish), osern (H)

prolong, farlengern, mayrekh zayn (H-Y)

prominent, bavust

promiscuous, mufkerdik (H), "seksuel nit iberklayberish"

promise (n), der tsuzog, dos vort

promise (v), gebn a vort, tsuzogn

promoter, der tsureder

promotion (person), di hekherung; (cause), di protezhirung; (products), di tsuredung

prompt (adj), baytsaytik, pinktlekh

prompt (adv), baldik

prompt (v), untersuflirn; "To prompt furtively", unterzogn

promptly, bald, punkt

pronounce, aroysredn; "Have trouble pronouncing", "brekhn di tseyn", "brekhn zikh di tsung"

proof (n), der dervayz; (print), di korekte; "Rain-proof", "regn-bavornt"

proper, geherik, laytish, rekht

prophet, der novi (H)

proposal, der forshlog, der onshlog (marriage)

prop up, untershparn

proselyte to Judaism, der ger (H)

prospect (n), der oysblik, der oyskuk

prosper, gedayen, matsliekh zayn (H-Y)

prosperous, bliendik; "Become prosperous", oyfgerikht vern

prostitute (n), di kurve, di nafke (R), di prostitutke, di zoyne (H)

protect, bashitsn, oys'hitn

protection, dos shitsmitl

protector, der bashitser

protest (n), der protest

protest (v), protestirn

protester, der protestir

protractor, der vinkl-mester

protrude, aroysshtekn

proud, shtolts; "To be proud", shtoltsirn (mit)

prove, aroysvayzn zikh far, dervayzn

proverb, dos shprikhvort, dos veltsvertl

provide, bazorgn, farzorgn

providence, di hashgokhe (H)

provider, der shpayzer

province, di provints; "Russian province", di gubernie (R)

provoke, "aroysbrengen fun geduld", tsebeyzern

prow, der shnobl

prowl, shlaykhn zikh

pry into, araynshmekn in

P.S. (postscript), I.S. (iker-shokhakhti) (H), SH.N.F. (shier nit fargesn)

psalm, dos kapitl tilim (Y-H)

Psalms (book of), der tilim (H)

pub, di shenk

public (adj), efntlekh; "Public affairs", "kolishe inyonim" (H); "Public at large", der klal (H)

public (n), der oylem (H); (Jewish), dos ko'ol

publicity, der pirsem (H), di reklame

publicly, bifresye (H)

publisher, der farleger

pucker up, makhn a vaynshl fun di lipn

pudding, der kugl, dos teygekhts

puddle, di (ka)luzhe (R)

pudgy, pukhke (R)

puff (on a pipe), pipken, tsien fun

puff (pant) (n), der praykh, der sope

puff (pant) (v), praykhn

puff out, oyspoyshn zikh

pull (n), der shlep, der tsi

pull (v), raysn, shlepn, tsien

pulley, der blok, der trits

pulpit, di bime (H), der shtender

pulpit (Jewish), der omed (H)

pulse (n), der deyfek (H), der puls

pump (n), der plump, di pompe

pump (v), pompen

pumpkin, di dinye (R), der kirbes

pun, der kalambur (F), di vertershpil

punch (blow) (n), der zets

punch (drink), der puntsh

punch (v), gebn a zets, zetsn

puncture (n), der durkhshtokh, dos lekhl

puncture (v), aynshtekhn

punish, shtrofn

punish (physically), shlogn

punishment, der oynesh (H), der psak (H), di shtraf (di shtrof) (R)
pup, dos hintl, der tsutsik (R)
puppet, di lyalke (R), di maryonet
purchase (n), der aynkoyf, di knie (H)
purchase (v), aynhandlen, koyfn
pure, gole, hoyl, reyn
purge oneself of guilt (charges), opshuldikn zikh
purification (of a dead body), di ta'are (H) (Jewish)
Purim, der purim (H)
Purim presents, der shalakhmones (H)
purpose, der takhles (H), der tsil, der tsvek; "On purpose", bekivn (H), umishne (H); "To no purpose", umzist
purposeless, glat azoy
purr, mruken
purse, dos baytl, der tayster
pus, der eyter
push (n), der ruk, der shtoys, der shtup
push (v), shparn, shtupn
pushbutton, di knopke
"To be a pushover", "zayn gring vi a hor fun milkh"
pussy, dos ketsele
pussycat (term of endearment), di kotinke (R)
put, avekleygn, shteln
put down, avekshteln
put in, araynleygn
put on (wear), onton; "He is putting it on" (pretending), "er makht zikh"
put out (extinguish), oysleshn
put up at, farforn
puzzle (n), di geduldshpil, der plef; "To be puzzled", "oysshteln a por oygn"; "To look puzzled", "brekhn zikh dem kop"
puzzle (v), (far)intrigirn

Q

quack (n), der flekl-dokter, der znakher
quack (v), kvaken
quail, der vakhtl
quaint, altfrenkish
quality, di eygnkeyt, dos eykhes (H)
qualm, der ibertrakht, der khshash (H)
quantity, dos kames (H); (amount), der skhum (H)
quarrel (n), di krig, dos krigeray, dos makhloykes (H)
quarrel (v), krign zikh, raysn zikh
quarter (fourth), dos fertl; (lodgings), di kvartir; (money), der kvoder; (of a city), der kvartal
quarter (v), tsefertlen
queen, di malke (H)
queer, meshune, modne (R); "queer person", der tshudak (R)
quench, shtiln
"Qu'est-que c'est?", "staytsh?" (Contraction of: "vi heyst es oyf taytsh?" "What's the translation?")
question (n), di frage, di kashe (H), di shayle (H); "perplexing question", di klots-kashe (G-H); "be a question of", geyn in; "be out of the question", nit kumen in batrakht
question (v), fregn; (interrogate), oysfregn
questionable, sofekdik (H), unter a fregtseykhn (under a question mark)
question mark, der fregtseykhn
queue (n), di rey
queue up, shteln zikh in rey
quick, gikh (gekh), shnel (G); "Touch to the quick", "nemen di leber"
quickly, geshvind, oyf der gikh
quiet (adj), ruik, shtil; "Be quiet!", "sha!", zol zayn sha
quiet (n), di ru, di shtil(keyt)
quiet (v), aynshtiln, baruikn
quietly, in der shtil, shtilerheyt
quilt (n), di koldre (R)

quilt (v), tsushtepn
quit, oyfhern
quite, gor, hipsh; "Quite a few", "a hipshe bisl"
quiver (v), drozhen, tsaplen, tsitern
quiz (n), der oysfreg
quiz (v), oysfregn
quiz programme, "der her-un-tref"
quorum, der minyen (H) (for Jewish prayers), der misper (H)
quotation, der tsitat
quotation marks, fremdtseykhns, gendzn-fislekh (duck-feet)
quote (v), tsitirn; (refer to), farrufn zikh oyf; "put in quotes", aynfislen
quotient, der vifler

R

rabbi, rebe (in direct address) (H), der rov (H); "Rabbi's wife", di rebetsn
rabbinate (office), dos rabones (H)
rabbi's associate, der dayen (H)
rabbi's license, di smikhe (H)
rabbit, dos kinigl
rabid, meshuge (H), meturef (H)
raccoon, der shop
race (n), di rase, der shtam
race (contest), dos geyeg
racetrack, di yogeray, der yogveg
rack (n), dos geshtel
rack (as in torture) (v), paynikn; "Rack one's brains", "brekhn zikh dem kop"
racket (noise), dos gepilder, koyles (H), der tuml
racket (sports), di rakete
racketeer, der shvindler
racy (story), gevirtsik, gezaltsn
radiate, oysshtraln
radish, der retekh; horse radish, der khreyn (R); "Red radish", dos (resh-)khoydesh-retekhl (H-Y)
raffle, der plet

raffle (off) (v), (oys)pletn
raft, der plit
rafter, der balkn, di krokve (R)
rag, di shmate (R); "In rags and tatters", "krue-blue", "opgerisn un opgeshlisn"; "rags and tatters", lakhmanes
rage (n), der yirgozn (H)
rage (v), busheven, vildeven
ragged, shmatedik (R), tseflikt
rail (n), der rels (R)
railroad, di ayznban (G)
railway station, der vokzal (R) (see I.O.)
rain (n), der regn
rain (v), regnen; "Light rain" (drizzle, shower), dos regndl; 'Rain cats and dogs", khlyapen, plyukhen (R)
raise (in wages) (n), di hesofe (H)
raise (bring up) (v), dertsien, hodeven (R), megadl zayn (H-Y)
raisin(s), di rozhinke(s) (R)
rake (n), di grablie
rake (v), grablyeven, sharn
ram (n), der baran (R)
ramble, arumshlyondern
rancid, yelke (R)
rankle, "a bri ton"
ransack, durkhnishtern
rape (n), di fargvaldikung
rape (v), fargvaldikn
rapid, bistre, gikh (gekh), shnel
rapidly, geshvind
rapids, di shtromshvel
rare (not thick), shiter
rare (uncommon), zeltn
rarity, der antik, dos yekar-hamtsies (H), di zeltnkeyt
rascal, der ganef (H), der yungatsh
rascally, gneyvish
rash (adj), hastik, hitsik
rash (med.), der oysshit
raspberry, di malene (R)
rat, der rats, der shtshur
rate (of exchange) (n), der kurs; (of speed), di gikhkeyt, der tempo; "At any rate", al kol ponem (H)
rates (n), der tarif

rather (more likely), ender
rather (preferable), libersht
rather (quite), gants
rather than, eyder
ration (n), der payọk (R)
ratrace, di gratshke
rattle (sound), dos grageray, der khorkhl
rattle (toy), der grager, di kalekotke (R)
rattle (v), gragern, klapern
rattlesnake, di klapershlang
rave (v), bredyen, "redn fun hits"; "rave about", "loybn in himl arayn", "nit kenen zikh oploybn fun"
raven (n), der voron (R)
ravine, der bargshpalt, di shlukht, der yar
raw, roy; "completely raw", kiz roy
ray, der shtral
rayon (adj), kunstzaydn
rayon (n), di kunstzayd
razor, der golmeser
reach (n), der greykh; "Out of reach", "nit tsu dergreykhn"; "within reach", in greykh
reach (a goal) (v), dergreykhn
reach (destination) (v), derflien, derforn
read (v), leyenen
read (from Torah), lezn
read aloud, forleyenen
reader in the synagogue, der bal-koyre (H) (Jewish)
reader of the prayers, der bal-tefile (H) (Jewish)
ready, greyt; "get ready", makhn (zikh) greyt, (on)greytn (zikh)
real, ekht, emes (H), faktish
real estate, dos grunteygns
really, take (R)
rear (adj), hinter
rear (n), der hinterteyl, der hintn
rear (v), hodeven (R)

reason (n), der farvọs, der tam (H); "For no good reason", "glat azoy", "glat in der velt arayn", stam azoy (H-Y); "It stands to reason", "der seykhl trogt oys"
reasonable, lagodne (R), seykhldik (H); "To be reasonable", "lozn zikh hern"
reason with, redn al-pi seykhl (H)
reassure, baruikn
rebel(s) (n), der oyfshtendler(s)
rebel (v), bunteven zikh, rebelirn
rebellion, der bunt (R), di meride (H), der oyfshtand
rebound (v), opbạlemen zikh
recede, opgeyn
receipt (as in a note), di kabole (H), der kvit
receipt (receiving) (n), dos krign
receive (guests), oyfnemen
receive (v), bakumen, krign
receiver (n), der oyfnemer
receiver (telephone), dos traybl
recently, anumlt, nit lang
reception, dos kaboles-ponem (H), der oyfnem
receptionist (n), der/di oyfnemer(in) (m & f)
recipient, der bakumer, "der/di vos bakumt"; (of a prize), der premirter
recite, dertseyln
recline, onlenen zikh, zitsn ongelent
reconciled (to be r.), iberbetn zikh (mit), mushve vern (H-Y), sholem makhn (H-Y)
reconsider, iberklern
record (n), dos fartseykhenish; (achievement, feets), der rekọrd; (minutes), der protokol
record (music) (n), der disk, di plate
record (v), farshraybn; (music), rekordirn; "break a record", "shlogn rekord"
recourse, di breyre (H), der oysveg; "have recourse to", onkumen tsu
recover, tsurikkrign; (health), genezn vern, kumen tsu zikh

recovery (health), di genezung; (retrieval), der opzukh
recruit (n), der rekrut
recruit (v), rekrutirn, verbirn
rectangle, der grodek
rectum, di grode kishke
recuperate, farrikhtn zikh, kumen tsu zikh
red, royt
redeem, derleyzn, oyskoyfn
redemption (of the Jews), di ge'ule (H)
redouble, fartoplen
reduce (lessen), minern
reduce (price), aroplozn
reed, der ror (H)
reek, smukhtn mit
refer (v), farrufn zikh (oyf); "refer to", zayn negeye (Y-H), zayn shayekh tsu (Y-H-Y)
referee, der shoyfet (H)
refine, laytern, oyseydlen
refined (person), eydl
reflect (optics), opshpiglen; (consider), fartrakhtn zikh, ibertrakhtn
reflection (optics), di opshpiglung
reflection (thought), di ibertrakhtung
reforestation, di (krik)bavaldung
refrain (n), der refren, der tsuzung
refrain (v), tsurik'haltn zikh
refresh (v), derfrishn, opfrishn
refreshment (n), di derkvikung, dos iberbaysn, di lobung, traktamentn
refreshments (to visitors), der kibed (H)
refrigerator, der frizhider, der kelterer
refund (n), der kriktsol
refund (v), kriktsoln, umkern
regarding (about), vegn
regardless, alts eynts ver/vos
regards (n), der grus; "send regards", grisn
regiment (n), der polk (R), der regiment
region, der gegnt, der kant

register (n), der register; (cash-r.), di (opkling-)kase
register (v), farshraybn
regret (n), di kharote (H)
regret (v), kharote hobn oyf/az (H); "Regret bitterly", "oyfesn zikh far dem vos"
regular, geveyntlekh
regulate, onshteln
reign (n), di hershaft, di memshole (H)
reign (v), hershn, kinign
rein(s) (n), di leytse(s) (R)
reincarnated (v), megulgl vern (H-Y)
reincarnation, der gilgl (H)
reindeer, der renifer
reject (v), farbrakirn, opvarfn
rejoice, freyen zikh
rejuvenate, faryingern
relate, dertseyln (recount)
relative (put in relation), farbindn
relative (n), der korev (H)
relative (by marriage) (n), der mekhutn; (pl.) di makhatonim (H)
relax, opruen (zikh), opshpanen (zikh)
release (n), der aroysloz, di bafrayung; (news), di meldung
release (v), bafrayen, oplozn
relent, nokhlozn
relentless, farbisn
relevant, bataytik
reliable, farlozlekh
reliance, der tsutroy
relief, di kitsve (H); "Sigh with relief", "opotemen"; "What a relief", a mekhaye (H), "arop a shteyn fun hartsn"
relish (n), dos zoyers
relish (v), posmakeven zikh
reluctant (be r.), breklen zikh, nit hobn keyn kheyshek (H)
reluctantly, on kheyshekh (H); "To give reluctantly", zhaleven (R)
remain, (far)blaybn; (be left over), iberblaybn
remedy (medical), di zgule (H)

remember, gedenken; (recollect), dermonen zikh; "To remember suddenly", khapn zikh

remembrance, di dermonung, der zeykher (H)

remind, dermonen

reminder, der dermon, di dermonung

remnant, dos iberblaybs, der resht; "remnants of a disaster", di sheyres-hapleyte (H)

remorse, di kharote (H)

remote, opgelegn, vayt

removal, di bazaytikung

remove, tsunemen

renew, banayen

renounce, farleykenen, mevater zayn oyf (Y-H-Y), opzogn zikh fun

renown, der shem (H), der shem-dover (H)

rent (n), dos dire-gelt (H-Y)

rent (from) (v), dingen

rent (to) (v), fardingen

repair (n), di reparatur, dos tsurekhtmakhn

repair (v), farikhtn, reparirn

repay, tsuriktsoln

repeat, nokhzogn; "repeat oneself over and over", malegeyren (H) (chew the cud)

repel, opshtupn

repent, "shlogn zikh alkhet" (H)

repetition, di iberkhazerung (H)

replace, farbaytn

reply (n), der entfer

reply (v), entfern

report (account), der barikht

report (noise), der knal, der shos

report (shot), der shos

report (account) (v), opgebn a barikht fun; (present oneself), meldn zikh

repress, farshtikn

reproof (sermon of r.), der muser (H)

repulsive, khaloshesdik (H), opshtoysndik; "Utterly repulsive", khulshe-khaloshes (H)

reputable, onshtendik

reputation, der shem (H) (see intr.)

request (n), di bakoshe (H), di bite

request (v), betn, farlangen

requirement, dos baderfenish, di foderung

rescue (n), der ratunik

rescue (v), rateven (R)

resemblance, di enlekhkeyt, di gerotnkeyt

resemble, zayn enlekh tsu, "zayn gerotn in"

resent, fardrisn, hobn faribl oyf

reside, voynen

resign oneself, sholem makhn mit (H-Y)

resist, kegnshteln zikh, oys'haltn

resistance, di kegnshtelikeyt

resonance, der opklung

resort (n), der kurort (R)

resort to (v), onkumen tsu

resound (v), opklingen

respect (n), der derkh-erets (H), der koved (H), der opshay; "With respect to", benegeye (H)

respectable, orntlekh; "Respectfully yours", "mit groys derkh-erets" (H); "To look respectable", "hobn a ponem" (H)

responsibility, dos akhrayes (H), di farantvortlekhkeyt

responsible (reliable), farantvortlekh; "be responsible", trogn dos akhrayes (H)

rest (n), di menukhe (H), di ru; (remnants), di iberike, der resht

rest (v), ruen

restaurant, der restoran

restless, "nit kenen aynzitsn", umruik

restrained, ayngehaltn

restrict, bagrenetsn; "restrict oneself", metsamtsem zayn zikh (H-Y-Y)

rest room, der optret

result, der rezultat, der takhles (H)

result (v), aroyskumen

resurrection of the dead, der tkhies-hameysim (H)

resuscitate, opmintern

retail (adj)   **robe (n)**

---

retail (adj), entsl; (at retail), oyf entsl;
"sell retail", farkoyfn oyf entsl
retire (from employment) (v),
pensyonirn (zikh)
retired, emeritirt, oysgedint, pensyonirt
retroactive, krikvirkik
return (give back) (n), di krikgebung;
(come back), der tsurikker
return (give back), krikgebn; "Many
happy returns", "biz hundert un
tsvantsik"
revel (revel in) (v), hulyen, kveln fun
revere, akhpern
revenge (n), di nekome (H)
revenge (v), noykem zayn (H-Y),
oprekhenen zikh
reverse (adj), farkert
reverse (n), der heypekh (H); "in
reverse", farkert; (rearward),
hintervaylekhts
reverse (v), iberdreyen
revile, "shlogn kapores mit" (Y-H),
"zidlen un shnidlen"
revive, oyflebn
revolve, arumdreyen
revolving door, di dreytir
reward (n), di baloynung, der skhar,
(pl.) di skhires (H)
reward (v), baloynen
rhinoceros, der noz'horn
rhyme, der gram; "Without rhyme or
reason", "on a tam un on a ram"
rhyme (v), gramen zikh
rib, di rip
ribbon, di band (pl. di bender), di
lente, di stenge, di tashme
rice, der rayz
rich, raykh; "Strike it rich", "araynfaln in
a shmaltsgrub"
riches, dos ashires (H), di gvirshaft, dos
negides (H)
rich gentile, der porets (H) (coll.)
rich man, der gvir (H), der noged (H);
(rich man's wife), di negidiste (H);
"Very rich man", der gvir adir (H)
rid (get rid of), oppotern (H), poter
vern fun (H-Y)

riddle (n), dos retenish
ride (n), der for, di yazde (R)
ride (v), forn
ridge, der bargrukn
ridicule (v), khoyzek makhn fun (H-Y-
Y), oyslakhn
right (adj), rekht; "To the right", rekhts
right (correct), rikhtik; "Right away!",
glaykh, "ot!" (R); "Right here!",
"otado" (R)
right (entitlement) (n), dos rekht
right (political) (n), "di rekhte"
rigid, shtayf
rigmarole, der pizmen (H), dos
ployderay
rim, der kant, der rand
ring (for finger), dos fingerl
ring (v), klingen
rinse (action) (n), der shvenk
rinse (v), oysshvenken
riot (n), di mehume (H)
riot (v), makhn a mehume (H)
rip (n), der ris; "Rip apart", tseraysn;
"Rip open", oyftrenen; "Rip out",
oysraysn
ripe, tsaytik
ripen, oyfkumen, tsaytik vern
ripple (n), di khvalke, dos krayzl
ripple (v), krayzlen zikh, runtslen zikh
rise (get up), oyfheybn zikh
rise (sun), oyfgeyn
risk (n), der aynshtel; "Risk (one's
life)", aynshteln (dos lebn)
river, der taykh
rivet (n), di nite
rivet (v), tsuniteven
road, der veg; (dirt road), der shlyakh
(R)
roadhouse, der traktir
roar (n), der bril, der brum
roar (v), briln, brumen, ritshen
roast (n), dos gebrotns
roast (v), opbrotn, oysbrotn
rob (an object), tsuganvenen (H)
rob (by theft), baganvenen (H)
robber, der gazlen (H)
robe (n), der khalat; (Jewish), der kitl

robin, dos royt'heldzl
robot, der goylemat (H)
robust, "gezunt vi a poyer" (healthy as a peasant), koyekhdik
rock (n), der feldz, der shteyn
rock (v), shoklen, vign zikh; "to rock to sleep", aynlyulyen
rod, dos drengl, di rut, di shtabe
roe (deer), di sarne (R); (fish), der royg
rogue, der ma-yaysenik (H), der zhulik (R)
roll (bread), der bulke, der zeml; (flat roll), dos pletsl
roll (v), katshen, kayklen; (eyes), farglotsn
roller, der val
roller skate (n), der redlshukh
roller skate (v), redlen zikh
rolling pin, dos valgerholts
roll up, oyfviklen, viklen
roof, der dakh
room (of a house), der kheyder (H), der tsimer
room and board, di kest (Jewish)
rooster, der hon
root (n), der vortsl
root (take r.) (v), shlogn, vortslen
rope (n), der shnur, der shtrik; "To know the ropes", "visn vi a tir efnt zikh" (to know how a door opens)
rose (n), di royz
rosin, di kanfolye (R)
rot (n), dos foylekhts
rot (v), farfoylt vern
rotten (rotted), farfoylt, tsefoylt; (person), hintish, paskudne (R)
rouge, dos baknreytl, di shminke (G)
rough, ratsik, roy; "Make a rough guess", "trefn oyfn oyg"
roughly, be'erekh (H), mer-veyniker, oyfn oyg
round (adj), kaylekhik (kaylekhdik); "All year round", "a kaylekhik yor"
round off (v), farkaylekhn
row (n), di rey, di shure (H)
row (v), rudern

rowdy (adj), tumldik
rowdy (n), der bodyung, der khuligan
rub (There's the rub), "do ligt der hunt bagrobn" (there lies the dog buried)
rub (v), raybn; "To rub it in", "shitn zalts oyf di vundn"
rubber, di gume(lastik)
rubber band, di gumke
rubbish, dos mist
"Rubbish (nonsense)", "a bobe mayse", "umzinen"
ruble, dos kerbl, der rubl
ruby, der rubin
rude, grob; "Rude person", der amorets (H); (pl.), di ameratsim, der grobyan
ruffian, der grober-yung
ruffle (v), tsepudlen
rug, der divan, der kilyem, der tepekh
ruin (v), makhn a tel fun (Y-H-Y), patern
rule (law) (n), der khok (H)
rule (lead) (v), bahershn
ruler (leader), der hersher
ruler (measuring tool), di vire; "Straight as a ruler", "glaykh vi a strune" (lit. straight as an instrument string)
rummage (v), nishtern
rumour (n), dos gliml, der klang
rump, der tul
run (n), der loyf
run (v), loyfn, yogn; "Give the runaround", "shikn nokh a suke-sher (H-Y)" (lit. send someone after a tabernacle shears); "Have a run in one's stockings", "farlirn an eygl in zok"; "In the long run", "frier oder shpeter", sof kol sof (H); "Run away", antloyfn, optrogn zikh
rung, der shtapl
run-in, di stitshke
run over, iberforn
runway, der impetveg
rupture (n), di kile, der ris; (hernia), der vinklbrokh
rush (hurry) (n), dos ge'ayl, dos geyog

rush (the plant) (n)   **satisfy**

---

rush (the plant) (n), der kamish
rush (v), ayln, yogn zikh
rush hour, di ayl-sho (G-H)
Russia, dos rusland
Russian (adj), rusish; of Russia,
  ruslendish
Russian (language), der rus, der
  rusish
Russian (pertaining to Russia), dos
  ruslendish
Russian (n), der rus (R)
rust (n), der zhaver
rust (v), farzhavert vern
rustle (n), der shorkh
rustle (v), shorkhn
rut, di redershpur
rye, der korn

S

Sabbath, der shabes (H)
Sabbath meal (third), der shaleshudes
  (Hebrew, shalosh-se'udot)
sack (bag) (n), der zak
sack (beggar's), di torbe (R)
sackcloth (sacking), dos zaklayvnt
sacred, heylik
sacrifice (n), der korbm (H), der oper
sacrifice (v), makrev zayn (H-Y)
sacrilege, der khilel-hakoydesh (H),
  der khilel-hashem (H)
sad, troyerik, umetik
saddle (n), der zotl
safe (adj), zikher
safe (n), di fayer-kase, der seyf
safety pin, di agrafke (F)
sagacity, dos kharifes (H)
sage (wise man), der khokhem (H);
  (pl.), di khakhomim
sail (n), der zegl
sail (v), zeglen
sailboat, di zeglshif
sailor, der matros (R)

saint (Jewish), der tsadek (H) (coll.
  smart aleck)
sake (for the sake of), leshem (H),
  tsulib; "For my sake", "fun maynet
  vegn"
salami, der vursht
salary, dos getsolt, (dos) skhires (H)
sale (clearance), der oysfarkoyf
salesgirl, di farkoyferin
salesman, der farkoyfer
salesman (travelling), der
  komivoyazhor (R), der moykher (H)
saliva, dos shpayekhts
salmon (smoked), der laks (G)
saloon, di shenk
saloonkeeper, der shenker
salt (n), di zalts
salt (v), (ba)zaltsn
salt shaker, dos zeltserl
salty, gezaltsn
salute (military) (n), der salut
same, zelber (zelbiker); "All the same",
  "alts eynts"; "Same to you", gamatem
  (H)
sample (n), der muster, dos pruvl
sample (v), farzukhn
sanctification, der kidesh (H) (Friday
  p.m.) (Jewish)
sanctify (v), farheylikn, mekadesh zayn
  (H-Y) (Jewish)
sanctimonious, frumakish
sanctimonious person, der frumak
sand, dos zamd
sandwich (n), di shnitke
sanitary napkin, der damen-bandazh
sapling, dos shprotsl
sapphire, der shafir
sash, di sharf
Satan, der sotn (H)
satchel, dos rentsl
satin (adj), atlesn
satin (n), der atles
satisfaction, dos nakhes (H), di
  tsufridnkeyt; "derive satisfaction",
  klaybn nakhes (H), shepn nakhes (H)
satisfied, tsufridn
satisfy, bafridikn, tsufridn shteln

Saturday, der shabes (H)
Saturday lunch, der shalashudes (H)
 (Jewish, third Sabbath meal)
sauce, der sos; "brown sauce", der
 aynbren
saucer, der spodik (R), dos telerl; (pl.)
 di telerlekh, dos tetsl
sausage, der vursht (G)
save (economize), farshporn
save (put away), opshporn
save (rescue), matsl zayn (H-Y),
 rateven (R)
saw (n), di zeg
saw (v), zegn; "saw in two", iberzegn
sawdust, palevines, dos zegekhts
say, zogn; "I say!", "her nor!"; "You
 don't say?", "azoy gor?"
saying (n), dos vertl
scab (blemish), der strup
scald (v), farbrien
scale (of fish), di shup
scale (weigh), di vogshol
scamp, der yungatsh
scamper, karapken zikh
scandal, der skandal
scapegoat, dos kapore-hindl (H-Y), der
 soer-lazozl (H)
scar (n), der heft, der shtrom
scarce, zeltn
scarcely, kimat nit (H-Y), koym
scare (v), dershrekn, ibershrekn; "He is
 scared", "di hoyt tsitert oyf im" (his
 flesh is quivering); "To be scared",
 moyre hobn (H-Y)
scarecrow, der shrekfoygl, di strashidle
 (R)
scarf, di shal, di sharf
scatter, tseloyfn zikh, tseshitn; "Widely
 scattered", tsezeyt un tseshpreyt
scatterbrain, der flaterkop
schedule (n), der (tsayt)plan
schedule (v), bashtimen
scholar, der gelernter
scholar (Jewish), der ben-toyre (H),
 der lamdn (H), der talmed-khokhem
 (H)

scholar of unusual brilliance, der
 goen (H)
scholarship, di stipendye
school, di shul, di shule; "Elementary
 school" (Jewish), di talmetoyre (H);
 "High school", di gimnazye
 (European) (R), di mitlshul
scissors, dos sherl
scoff (v), yekn
scold, zidlen
scoop (n), der shufl
scoop (v), shepn; "News-scoop", der
 oyskhap
scorch (v), opbrenen
score (account) (n), der khezhbm (H)
score (in a game) (n), der vifl-ver;
 "What's the score?", "vu halt di shpil?"
score (a victory) (v), ophaltn
scorn (n), di farakhtung
scorn (v), farakhtn, "makhn ash un
 blote fun"
scotch (drink), der bronfn
scoundrel, der dover-akher (H), der
 oysvorf, der yemakh-shmoynik (H)
scour, oysshayern
scowl (n), dos fintstere (krume)
 ponem (Y-H)
scowl (v), "onkhmuren dos ponem"
 (H)
scramble (v), grablen/karapken zikh;
 "Scrambled eggs", di prezhenitse (R),
 di yayshnitse (P)
scrap (n), dos brekl
scrap (junk) (n), dos brekh
scrape (v), shkroben
scrape together, tsunoyfkratsn
scratch (n), der krats
scratch (v), kratsn; "Start from scratch",
 "onheybn fun der alef" (H)
scrawl (n), "kotsheres mit lopetes" (lit.
 pokers and shovels)
scrawl (v), patshken mit der pen
scream (n), dos geshrey, der kvitsh
scream (v), kvitshen, shrayen
screen (n), di shirme; (TV screen), der
 ekran (F)

screw (n), der shroyf; "He has a screw loose", "es felt im a klepke"
screwdriver, der shroyfn-tsier
scribe (n), der shrayber, der soyfer (of Torah) (H)
scroll (door post), di mezuze (H) (Jewish)
scrotum, der kis (H)
scrounger, der shnorer
scuff (v), frotirn
scuffle (n), dos geshleg
scythe, di kose (R)
sea, der yam (H); "At sea", oyfn yam; "Red sea", der yam suf (H)
sea gull, di meve
seal (n), der khoysem (H)
seal (animal), der yam-hunt (H-Y)
seal (v), farklepn
seam (n), di not
seamstress, di neyterke, di neytorin
search (n), der opzukh, dos zukhn
search (v), zukhn
seashell, dos meyerkepl, dos yam-multerl
seat (n), dos zitsl, der zitsort
seat (v), bazetsn
seating of the bride, dos bazetsns (Jewish)
seaweed, dos yam-groz
second (adj), tsveyt
second (time) (n), di sekunde
second (a motion) (v), shtitsn
secret (n), der sod (H)
secretly, besod (H), bishtike (H)
section (n), der kheylek (H), der opteyl; (of Talmud), di mesekhte (H) (Jewish)
secular, veltlekh
sedate, gelasn
sedative, dos aynshtilekhts
see (v), zen; "I see", "Aha!"; "You see?", farshteyst?
seed (n), der zoymen
seed (v), bazoymenen
seek, zukhn
seek out, oyszukhn

seem, dakhtn zikh; (appear), oyszen; "It seems", es dakht zikh, es zet oys, lekhoyre (H)
seemingly, a ponem (H)
seen, gezen
seldom, zeltn
select, opklaybn, oysklaybn
self (by oneself), aleyn, zikh
self-defence, di zikh-farteydikung
self-evident, farshtendlekh fun zikh, opgeret
self-explanatory, mimeyle (H), redn far zikh aleyn
selfsame, di dozike (f), der doziker (m), dos zelbe
self-satisfied, "patshn zikh in baykhl" (pat one's own belly), tsufridn mit zikh
sell, farkoyfn
seller, der farkoyfer, der moykher (H)
semester, der zman (H)
send, shikn, tsushikn
send word, lozn visn
sensation, dos gefil; "cause a sensation", maresh-oylem zayn (H-Y)
sense (judgement) (n), der seykhl (H)
sense (n), derfiln
sense (to make s.), hobn a zinen
sensible, oysgerekhnt
sensitive, honerove (hum.), shpirevdik; "To be sensitive", "nemen zikh tsum hartsn"
sentence (grammar) (n), der zats
sentence (verdict), di shtrof
sentence (v), farmishpetn (H)
separate (adj), bazunder
separate (v), tsesheydn, tseteyln
separated, tsesheyt
separated (man & wife), funandergegangen
separation, di havdole (H) (at Sabbath end, marking beginning of week) (Jewish), di tsesheydung
sequence, di nokhanandkeyt, der seyder (H)
serious, erntst

sermon, di droshe (H) (Jewish)
sermon (n), di preydik
servant, der diner (m), di dinst (f), der meshores (H)
servant girl, di dinst meydl
set (n), der skhum (H)
set (down) (v), anidershteln; (watch), onshteln
set out (things), oysleygn; "Set the table", "greytn tsum tish"
settle (a country), bazetsn
settle (a question), farentfern
settle down, aynordenen zikh, vern a mentsh
settlement (n), der heskem (H), der oysglaykh
settlement (community), der yishev (H)
settle with, oprekhenen
set up (a buisness) (v), aynordnen, oyfshteln
seven, zibn
seventeen, zibitsn
seventh (adj), zibet
seventh (n), dos zibetl
seventy, zibetsik
several, etlekhe
severe, shtreng
sew, neyen
sew up, farneyen
sex (n), dos geshlekht, der min (H)
sexton, der shames (H) (Jewish); (pl.), di shamosim
shabby, opgelozn
shade, der shotn
shadow, der shotn
shady, shotndik
shady (sinister), tunkl
shake (n), der shokl
shake (v), shoklen, treyslen
shake hands, drikn/gebn di hant
shaken up, tsetreyslt
shaky, "oyf hinershe fis" (on chicken's feet), vakldik
shall (future), vel
shall (obligation), darf, zol
shallow, platshik

shame (n), di bushe (H), di kharpe (H), di shand, der shod
shame (v), farshemen, "mevayesh zayn" (H-Y); "Shame and disgrace", "mies un moes" (H); "Shame on you", "shem zikh in vaytn haldz arayn" (be ashamed deep down in your throat)
shampoo (n), dos tsvogvaser
shampoo (v), tsvogn
shape (n), dos geshtalt
share (n), der kheylek (H); (stock), di aktsye
share (v), teyln zikh mit . . . mit
shark, der hayfish
sharp, sharf
sharp (cunning), farshpitst
sharp (music), der dyez (R)
sharp (on time), punkt
shave (n), di golung; "have a close shave", "koym-koym aroysgeyn"
shave (v), goln
shaver, der goler
shawl, di fatsheyle; (praying s.), der tales (H) (Jewish)
she, zi
sheaf, der snop
sheep, der sheps, di shof
sheet (bed), der laylekh
sheet (paper), der blat, der boygn
shelf, di politse (R)
shell (explosive) (grenade) (n), der granat
shell (peel) (n), di shol(ekhts)
shell (bomb) (v), bombardirn
shell (peel) (v), sheyln
shepherd, der pastekh (R)
sherbert (sherbet), dos frukhtayz
shiftless man, der batlen (H)
shine (n), der blishtsh (R), der glants
shine (v), blishtshen (R), glantsn, shaynen
shingle (roof) (n), di dakhlke
shiny, glantsik
ship (n), di shif
ship (v), ekspedirn, ibershikn
shirt, dos hemd
shirt front, dos harts

shiver (n), der tsiter
shiver (v), tsitern
shock (n), der klap, der shok
shock (v), shokirn, untertrogn
shocked, oyfgetreyslt
shoe (n), der shukh; (pl.) di shikh
shoe (v), bashukhn; (a horse), untershmidn
shoehorn, der shukhlefl
shoelace, dos shukhbendl
shoemaker, der shuster; (wife), di shusterke
Sholem Aleichem's mythical village, "Boyberik" (Back of the beyond)
shoot (v), shisn
shop (n), di kleyt (R), di krom (R)
shop (v), aynkoyfn
shore (n), der breg (R)
short, kurts; "Be short of", feln, nit hobn genug; "In short", bekitser (H); "In short order", "eynts-tsvey"
shorten, farkirtsn
shortening (n), dos geshmilts
shorts, kurtskes
short-tempered man, der kaysn (H)
shorty, kutsepindrik
shot (n), der shos; "Not by a long shot", "vayt nit azoy"
shoulder, der aksl, di pleytse; "Give the cold shoulder", "oysdreyen zikh mit der pleytse tsu"
shoulder blade, di lopetke
shout (n), dos geshrey
shout (v), shrayen
shove (n), der ruk, der shtup
shove (v), rukn, shtupn
shovel (n), di lopete
shovel (v), shuflen
show (n), di forshtelung
show (v), dervayzn, vayzn; "Show off" (n), der oysfayner; "Show off" (v), "krikhn in di oygn" (crawl in one's eyes)
shred (v), tsepitslen
shrew, di arure (H), di klavte (H), di klipe (H)
shriek (n), der g(e)vald, der kvitsh

shriek (v), g(e)valdeven, kvitshen
shrimp, dos rakl, der shnek (fig.)
shrink, ayntsien
shrivel, ayngedart vern
shrouds, takhrikhim (H) (Jewish)
shrub, der kshak
"Shrug one's shoulders", "kvetshn mit di pleytses"
shrunken, ayngeshrumpn
shudder (n), der groyl
shudder (v), groyln, tsitern; "A shudder went through me", "es iz mir ibergergangen a groyl (kelt)"
shuffle (v), dreptshen
shuffle (cards) (v), tashn
shun, oysmaydn
shut (v), farmakhn, tsumakhn; "Keep your mouth shut", "halt s'moyl"; "Shut one's eyes to", "kukn durkh di finger oyf"; "Shut up!", "shvayg!"
shutter (camera), dos ledl
shutter (window), der lodn
shuttle (n), dos vebshifl
shuttle (v), pompediklen
shy (adj), shemevdik; "Be shy", shemen zikh
shy person, der bayshn (H)
siblings, di geshvister (G)
sick (adj), krank
sick (to be), krenken; "be sick of", deresn vern
sick man, der khoyle (H)
sickness, di krenk
side (n), di zayt; (dispute), der tsad; (pl.), di tsdodim (H); "To be on the side of", haltn mit
sideburns (whiskers), bakn berd, di peye(s) (H) (Jewish)
sidewalk, di lave, di tretar (F)
siege (n), di balegerung
siege (v), balegern
sieve, di reshete, di zip
sift, durkhzayen
sigh (n), der zifts
sigh (v), ziftsn
sight (vision), di rie (H)
sight-see (v), onkukn tshikavesn

sign (n), der simen; (pl.), di simonim (H)

sign (signature) (v), untershraybn

signature, di khsime (H), di untershrift

signboard, der shild

significance, der batayt

significant, bataytik

signify, bataytn, meynen

sign language, dos shtum-loshn (Y-H)

sign up, farshraybn

silence, di shtilkeyt

silent, shtil; "To be silent", shvaygn; "To fall silent", "onnemen a moyl mit vaser" (take on a mouthful of water)

silk, di zayd, dos zaydns

silken, zaydn

silly, narish

silver, dos zilber

similar, enlekh, gerotn in

similarity, di enlekhkeyt

simile, di farglaykhung

simmer, unterzidn

simple, poshet (H), prost (R)

simple-minded, narishevate, yoldish

simple person, der pashtn (H); (pl.), di pashtonim

simpleton, der tam (H)

simply, poshet (H), stam (H)

sin (n), di aveyre (H) (Jewish), di zind

sin (v), zindikn

since (adv), "fun demolt on"

since (prep), zint

since even, ma dokh

sincere, hartsik

sincerity, di ofn-hartsikeyt

sinful, zindik

sinful Jew, der poshe-yisroel (H)

sinful woman, di bal-tayvenitse (H)

sing, zingen

singe (v), smalyen

single, eyntsik

single (not married), frayleydik, nit khasene gehat" (Y-H-Y)

single-handed, eyner aleyn

singly, eyntsikvayz

sink (n), der opgos

sink (v), aynzinken

sink (a ship) (v), untergeyn

sinner, der bal-aveyre (H), der bal-tayve (H), der zindiker

sip (n), der zup

sip (v), zupn; "sip loudly", khlyeptshen

sir (title), mayn her (G), pani (panye) (R)

sirloin, di ledvitse (R)

sissy, dos nebekhl, dos nyunkele

sister, di shvester

sister-in-law, di shvegerin

sit, zitsn; "sit down", zetsn zikh; "sit up", oyfzetsn zikh

situated, gefinen zikh

six, zeks

sixteen, zekhtsn

sixty, zekhtsik; (three-score), der shok

sizable, hipsh; "Sizable amount", hipsh bisl

size, di greys; (of clothing, shoes), der numer; (of a book), der format

sizzle, zidn

skate (ice) (n), der glitsher; (roller skate), der redlshukh

skate (ice) (v), glitshn zikh; (roller skate), redlen zikh

skeleton, dos gebeyn

sketch (n), di skitse

sketch (v), onvarfn, skitsirn

ski (n), di narte

ski (v), nartlen zikh

skiing (n), dos nartleray; "down-hill skiing", dos arop-barg nartleray

skim milk (n), di opgeshepte milkh

skim (milk) (v), opshepn

skin (n), di hoyt; "by the skin of one's teeth", koym-koym; "Get under your skin", "farkrikhn unter di neygl"; "to skin alive", shindn

skinny, dar, "hoyt un beyner", moger

skip (v), iberhipern, shpringlen

skipping rope, der shpring shnur

skirt (n), dos halbekleydl, dos rekl

skull, der sharbn

skull cap, di yarmlke (Jewish)

skunk, der tkhoyer

sky, der himl; "Out of a clear sky", "fun heler hoyt" (from fair skin), "plutsem in a mitvokh" (suddenly on a Wednesday)

skyscraper, der volkn-kratser

slack (adj), loyz

slacks, pludern

slander-monger, der rekhilesnik (H)

slant (n), der onbeyg, der ukos

slant (v), shteln kose

slap (n), der patsh; (in the face), der frask (R)

slap (v), patshn (R)

slattern, di shlumperke, di tshukht

slaughter (n), di kaylung; (Jewish), di shkhite (H)

slaughter (Jewish), koylen, shekhtn (H)

slaughter (v), tsekayln

slaughter (mass) (v), oysshekhtn (H)

"Ritual slaughterer" (Jewish), der shoykhet (H); (f) di shoykhetke (wife of ritual slaughterer)

slave, der shklaf

sleep (n), der shlof

sleep (v), pofn (coll.), shlofn; "get enough sleep", oysshlofn zikh

sleep in, aynshlofn

sleeping pill, di shlefpil

sleepless, on shlof

sleepy, farshlofn, shleferik

sleet, der graypl-regn

sleeve, der arbl (same in pl.); "laugh in one's sleeve", lakhn in arbl, lakhn in di foystn; "up one's sleeve", bahaltn

sleigh (n), der shlitn

sleigh (v), shlitlen zikh

slice (n), der penets, dos reftl

slice (v), tsepenetsn

slide (v), glitshn

slide down, aropglitshn

slip (petticoat), dos unterkleyd

slip (slide), der oysglitsh

slip (fall) (v), oysglitshn zikh

slipcover, der tshekhol

slipper, der latsh

slippery, glitshik

slob, di dravke, der/di murze

slope (on land) (n), der bargarop (downward); der bargaroyf (upward)

sloppy person, der shlump

slow(ly), pamelekh (R), pavolye (R)

slow down (v), farpamelekhn zikh

slow motion, di krikhgikhkeyt

slowpoke, der marudnik (R)

slum (n), dos dales-hoyz (H-Y), di mapoyles (H)

slush, di sliote (R)

sly, khitre (R)

smack (powerful) (n), der frask

small, kleyn; "small talk", dos geploysh

smaller, klener

smallest, klenst

smart, klug

smart aleck, der beserveyser, der sheygets (H)

smash (v), tseshmetern

"Have a smattering of", "kenen oyf shpits meser"

smear (a name) (v), bashmutsn

smear (spread) (v), shmirn

smell (n), der reyekh (coll.) (H)

smell (v), shmekn

smell bad, hern zikh

smelt (fish), di shtinke

smile (n), der shmeykhl

smile (v), shmeykhlen

smirk (n), dos shpetshmeykhele

smock, der khalat

smog, der tshadnepl

smoke (n), der roykh

smoke (v), roykhern (reykhern)

smokestack, der koymen

smooth, glat

smoothly, glat; "very smoothly", vi geshmirt

smooth over, fargletn

smother, dershtikn

snack (n), dos iberbaysn, dos nash (coll.), dos nasheray

snack (v), iberbaysn, nashn

snail, di poyle-royle

snap (sound), der knak

snap (break) (v), tsebrekhn

snap (click) (v), a knak ton
snapdragon, dos leybnmoyl
snapped up, tsekhapt
snatch (n), der khap
snatch (v), khapn (R)
sneak (v), shlaykhn zikh
sneak in, arayganvenen zikh (Y-H-Y)
sneak up on, unterganvenen zikh (Y-H-Y)
sneeze (n), der nos
sneeze (v), nisn
snicker (v), khikhen, "lakhn in arbl"
sniff (n), der shmek
sniff (v), nyukhen
snivel (v), "rinen fun noz", "tsien mit der noz"
snore (v), khropen (R), shnorkhtsn
snort (v), forshken, smoren
snout, der pisk; (trunk), der shnuk
snow (n), der shney
snow (v), shneyen
snowball, di shneykoyl
snowdrift, der farshney
snowflake, dos shneyele
snow storm, der shneyshturem
snub-nosed, karnose
snuff (n), der shmektabik; "Snuff a candle", arumshnaytsn
snug (cozy), nuredik
snug (fit), shlisik, shtilne
snuggle, tsunuren
snuggle up, tsunuren zikh
so, azoy; "Is that so?", azoy (gor)?, take?; "So and so", "aza un aza", "azoyner un azelkher"; "So as to", "kedey tsu" (H-Y); "So be it", "zol zayn azoy"; "So do (am) I", "ikh oykh"; "So there", "zest!"; "So what?", "iz vos?"
soak, durkhveykn
soap (n), di zeyf; "Soap opera", di zeyf-opere
soap (v), aynzeyfn
sob (n), der khlip (R)
sob (v), heshen, khlipen
sober, nikhter
sober up (v), oysnikhtern
sociable, gezelshaftik

social security, di sotsyal-farzikherung
society, di gezelshaft, di khevre (H); "Burial society", di khevre kedishe (H) (Jewish); "High society", "di hoykhe fentster"
sock(s) (n), der skarpet(n), der zok(n)
sodium, der natroym
Sodom, dos sdom (H) (Any form of evil)
soft, veykh
soft-boiled, loyz
softness, di veykhkeyt
soil (n), der grunt
soil oneself, aynmakhn, aynrikhtn
soldier, der soldat, der zelner; (Russian soldiers), di yevonim; (sing.), der yovn (R)
sole (adj), (eyn-un-)eyntsik
sole (fish), di yam-tsung (H-Y)
sole (foot), di pyate
sole (shoe), di padeshve
solitary, bazunder
solution (to a problem), der farentfer, di farentferung
solve, basheydn, farentfern
somehow, vi es iz
someone, emetser
someone else, anderer
somersault (n), der kozhelik
somersault (v), iberkulyen zikh
something, epes; "something of a", a shtikl
sometime (adj), gevezt; (adv), a mol
sometimes, a mol, oft mol; "Sometimes one way, sometimes another", "vi a mol"
somewhat, a bisl, epes
somewhere, ergets; "somewhere else", ergets vu
son, der zun; (pl.), di zin; "Only son", der ben-yokhed (H)
song, dos lid; (Sabbath songs), zmires (H)
son-in-law, der eydem (H)
sonny, zunenyu
sonorously (to talk s.), fonfen
soon, bald

soothsayer, der vorzoger

sore (adj), veytikdik

sore (n), di vund

sorrow, di leyd, der troyer, der tsar (H); "Be sorry", fardrisn; "Be sorry for", "rakhmones hobn oyf' (H-Y-Y); "So sorry!", "zayt moykhl" (H)

sort (n), der min (H), der zgal; "All sorts of", alerley; "Sort of", epes

so-so, nishkoshe (H)

soul, dos nefesh (H), di neshome (H)

sound (n), der klang; "Make a sound", "aroysgebn a klang"; "Not make a sound", "keyn pips nit ton"

soup, di yoykh (R), di zup; (ambrosia), di yaykhl (R)

sour, zoyer (zovr)

source, der moker (H); (pl.), di mekoyrim

sour cream, di shmetene (R), di smetene (R)

sour milk, di zoyermilkh

south, der dorem (H)

southward, oyf dorem

souvenir, der ondenk

sovereign (adj), suveren

sovereign (n), der hersher

soy beans, di soye

spank (n), der shmits

spank (v), opshmaysn

spare (economize) (v), zhaleven

spare (exempt), farshporn

spark (n), der funk, der nitsets (H)

sparkle (n), der finkl

sparkle (v), blishtshen (R), finklen

sparkler, der kalter fayer

sparrow, der shperl

spatula, der shpatl

speak, redn

spear (n), di shpiz

special, bazunder, spetsyel

species, der zgal (H)

specific, spetsifish

specify, dermonen befeyresh (H), spetsifitsirn

specimen, der muster

speck, dos shprenkl

spectacles, briln, glezer, shpakuln (R)

spectre, dos derze'enish, der shed (H)

speculate, spekulirn

speculate (ponder), ibertrakhtn

speech (language), reyd; (discourse), di rede; "make a speech", "haltn a rede"

speechless (n), on loshn

speed (n), di gikh (keyt); "At full speed", "hendem-pendem"; "Speed limit", "di maksimale gikhkeyt"

speed (v), yogn

speedy, geshvind

spell (incantation) (n), der kishef (H)

spell (period) (n), der meshekh (H), dos tsaytl; "cold spell", di kelt; "hot spell", di hits

spell (v), oysleygn, zogn di oysyes (H) fun

spend, oysgebn

spent (tired), oysgeshept

sperm, di sperme, di zere (H)

sphere, di koyl

spice (n), dos gevirts

spick-and-span, "finkldik un fekhldik"

spider, di shpin

spider web, dos shpin-geveb

spike (n), der relsn-nogl

spinach, der shpinat

spinach borsht, der shtshav (R)

spine, der ruknbeyn

spineless person, der/di lemishke (R) (porridge)

spinning wheel, di shpinrod

spinster (eligible), di kale-moyd (H-Y)

spiral staircase, di shvindltrep

spirit, der gayst; "Divine spirit", der ruekh-hakoydesh (H); "Evil spirit", der dibek (H) (Jewish), di klipe (H); "To be in low spirits", "zayn ongezolyet oyfn hartsn"

spit (saliva), dos shpayekhts; (skewer), di brotshpiz

spit (v), shpayen

spite, der lehakhes (H), der tselokhes (H)

spite (for) (in spite of), oyf tselokhes (from "lehakh'is" (H), "to anger")

spiteful person, der lehakhesnik (H)

spit out, oysshpayen

spittle, di sline

splash (n), der pluntsh, der plyukh

splash (v), plyukhen, shpritsn

splashdown (spacecraft), der aroppluntsh

spleen, di milts

splendid, "hakndik un tshakndik", prakhtik

splinter (n), di skabke

split (as with an axe) (v), tseshpaltn; "to split hairs", griblen zikh, pilplen zikh (H-Y)

spoil, iberfirn zikh, kalye makhn, patern (H)

spoil (child), tsebaleven

spoiled (as a child), kalyedik; "act spoiled", festen zikh

sponge (n), der shvom

spool, dos kletsl

spoon (small), dos lefele; (table s.), der lefl (same in pl.)

spot (n), der flek

spot (place) (n), der ort

spot (notice) (v), derzen

spot (soil) (v), baflekn

spotless, "on a flek"

spout (n), der shnobl

sprain (n), der lunk

sprain (v), oyslinken zikh

sprawl (v), tseleygn zikh; "urban sprawl", der shtot'oystsi

spray (n), der shprits

spray (v), bashpritsn

spread (n), dos bashmirekhts

spread (v), tseshpreytn

spread butter, tseshmirn

spread out, farshpreytn

spread out (lay out), oysleygn, tseleygn

spree, di hulyanke; "go on a spree", zikh lozn voylgeyn

spring (on a vehicle), der resor

spring (season), der friling, di vesne (R); "in the spring", frilingtsayt

spring (source) (n), der kval

spring (well), di krenitse

springy, federdik

sprout (n), der shprots

sprout (v), shprotsn

spruce tree, der tenenboym, di yodle (R)

sputter (v), shprudlen; (engine), unterhustn

spy (n), der shpion

spy (v), shpionirn

squander, tsetrentslen

squandered, ongevorn

squanderer, der pazren (H)

square (adj), kvadratish

square (n), der kvadrat

square dance, der kvadrattants

squarehead, der grober kop

squash (vegetable), der kabak (R)

squash (v), tsekvetshn

squat (v), "zitsn oyf di pyates"

squeak (n), der pishtsh, der skrip

squeak (v), pishtshen, skripen

squeamish, migldik, mlosne (R); "Feel squeamish", "gendzlen in boykh"

squeeze (n), der kvetsh

squeeze (v), kvetshn

squid, der tintfish (no pl.)

squint (v), farzhmuren di oygn, kukn kose

squirm, tsaplen

squirrel, di veverke (R); "grey squirrel", der fey

squirt (n), der shprits

squirt (v), shpritsn

stab (n), der shtokh

stab (v), shtekhn

stab to death (v), dershtekhn

stage (n), di bine, di stsene (R)

stage (v), opshpiln

stagger, pritshmelyen, unterhakn di fis

stagnant, fardumpn

stain (n), der flek, di plyame (R)

stain (for colouring), der beyts

stain (v), baflekn

stainless, zhaver-bavornt
stair (n), dos trepl; "flight of stairs", (di) trep
stale (air), dumpik
stale (food), yelke; (become s.), oysblezlen zikh, oysvepn zikh (lose effervescence)
stalk (n), dos shtengl
stalk (v), optshateven
stall (booth) (n), di shtel
stall (stable) (n), di shtal
stall (delay) (v), makhn shies (Y-H)
stallion, der oger
stamen, der shtoybfodem
stamina, di kegnshtelikeyt, der oys'halt-koyekh (Y-H)
stammer (v), keketsn
stamp(s) (postage), di marke(s)
stampede, di mehume (H)
stamp out, oysshtampn
stand (position) (n), di shtelung
stand (v), shteyn
stand out, "varfn zikh in di oygn"
staple (fastener), dos dretl
star(s), der shtern (same in pl.)
starch (n), der krokhml
stare (v), glotsn, "oystarashtshen di oygn"
start (beginning) (n), der onfang, der onheyb
start (shock) (n), der tsiter
start (to begin) (v), onfangen, onheybn
startle, dershrekn
starve, oys'hungern
starve (voluntarily), unterhungern
state (condition) (n), der matsev (H), der tsushtand
state (nation) (n), di melukhe (H)
state (province) (n), der shtat; "United States", di fareynikte shtatn
state (v), derklern, festshteln
statement, di derklerung; (of account), der (konte-)oystsug
station (railway), di stantsye (R), der vokzal (R)
status, der matsev (H), di shtelung

stay (v), blaybn, iberzayn
steady, fest, shtendik; "Go steady", zayn a porl (mit)
steal (v), (tsu)ganvenen (H)
steal across the border, ganvenen dem grenets (H-Y)
steam (n), der damf (G), di pare (R)
steamer, der damfer, der parakhod (R)
steer (v), firn
steering wheel, der kerever
stench, der ipesh (H)
step (n), der trit (same in pl.), der trot (pl. trit)
step (stair) (n), dos trepl; "A step away (from)", a katsnshprung (fun)
step (v), tretn
stepbrother, der shtifbruder
step-mother, di shtifmuter
stew (n), (meat) dos gedishekhts, (fruit, vegetable) der tsimes
stew (v), dempn, dishen
stick, dos shtekl, der shtekn; "out in the sticks", ergets in a hek
stick (glue) (v), tsuklepn
stick in (v), araynshtekn
sticky, klepedik
stiff, shtayf; "have a stiff leg", hobn a shtayfkeyt in fus
still (adv), alts, nokh, nokh alts
still (nevertheless), fort, fundestvegn
stinging nettles, di kropeve (no pl.), shtekhavkes (Y-R)
stingy (adj), karg
stingy (to be s.), kargn
stingy person, der kamtsn (H), der karger
stink (n), dos geshtank, der ipesh (H)
stink (v), shtinken
stinker, der shtinkern
stinking, farshtunken
stink up, farsarkhenen (Y-H-Y), farshtinken
stipulate, oysnemen
stir (n), dos geruder, der oyfrir, der tuml; (mix), der kokh; "create a stir", onmakhn a kokh/tuml
stir (mix), durkhmishn, mishn

stir (to whip), tsekloytsen
stitch (n), der shtokh; (knitting s.), dos
 eygl
stitch (v), neyen, shtepn
stock (financial) (n), di aktsye(s)(R)
stock-broker, der berze-mekler (F-Y)
stock-exchange, di berze (F)
stockings, shtrimp, der zok(n)
stomach (n), der boykh, der mogn;
 "On an empty stomach", "oyfn
 nikhtern hartsn" (on an empty heart)
stone, der shteyn; (pit), dos kerl; "Leave
 no stone unturned", "arbetn maysim"
 (H), "zukhn mit likht"
stone-deaf, "toyb vi di vant"
stooped, ayngeboygn
stop (v), op'haltn, oyfhern
stop-gap, der eyder-vos-ven
store (n), di krom (R)
storekeeper, der kremer, der soykher
 (H)
storey, der gorn
stories (a three-storey-
 high building), der draygornik
stork, der bushl
storm (n), der shturem
story (tale), di geshikhte, di mayse (H)
stout (adj), balaybt
stove, der eyvl; (cooking), der oyvn
straddle, "ayngoplen mit di fis"
straight, glaykh
straight jacket, dos meshugoyim-hemdl
 (H-Y)
strain (sift) (v), zayen
strand of hair, dos herele
strange, fremd, meshune (H), modne
 (R)
stranger, der fremder
straw, di shtroy; "The last straw", "dos
 reshtl tsu di tsores" (H)
strawberry, di truskafke; (wild) di
 pozemke (R)
stray (adj), hefker (H)
stray (deviate) (v), farblondzhen (Y-R)
street, di gas
streetcar, der tramvay (R)
streetwalker, di gasnfroy, di kurve (H)

strength, der koyekh (koykhes)(H), di
 shtarkeyt; "on the strength of", oyfn
 smakh (H) fun; "With all one's
 strength", "mit ale koykhes"
stress (n), der druk; "Stress and strain",
 "der drik-un-shtik"
stress (v), untershtraykhn
stretch (n), der tsi; (distance), der
 mehalekh (H)
stretch (v), oystsien, tsien
stretch out, tseleygn zikh
stride (v), shpanen; "In one's stride",
 "mir-nit dir-nit"
string bean(s), di grine fasolye(s), dos
 lopetkele(kh)
strip (v), oyston zikh naket
striped, gepasikt, geshtrayft
striptease, der bleyztants
stroke (medical), der onfal, der shlak
stroke (v), gletn
stoll (n), der shpatsir
stroll (v), shpatsirn
strong, kraftik, shtark
stubborn, ayngeshpart, farakshnt (H)
stud horse, der zavod
student, der talmed (H); "High school
 student", der shiler; "University
 student", der student
student of Yeshiva, der yeshive bokher
 (H) (Jewish)
studio, der atelye (F)
study (n), di forshung, der limed (H)
study (secular) (v), shtudirn
stuff (n), der shtof
stuff (v), onfiln, shtopn
stuffed (adj), ongeshtopt; (food) gefilt
stuffing (n), dos gefilekhts
stuffy, farshtikt; (person), onshtlerish;
 "to be stuffy", blozn zikh
stump (n), der kortsh, der stotshik
stun (v), farduln, pritshmelyen
stupid, narish; "Stupid!", khokhem
 eyner!
stupid question, di klots-kashe (G-H)
 (also perplexing question)
sturgeon, der balik
stutter (v), farhiken zikh, shtamlen

stutterer, der shtamler

sty (eye), der gersht

style, di mode; "in style", "in der mode"; "Live in great style", "firn a groysn shtat"

subconscious (n), di untervisikeyt

subject (of instruction) (n), der limed (H)

subject (topic) (n), di teme

submerge (dunk), untertunken

submit (an application) (v), ayngebn

submit (propose) (v), firleygn

submit to (v), untervarfn

subway, di sobvey, di unterban

succeed (v), matsliekh zayn (H-Y)

success (n), der baglik, di hatslokhe (H)

successful (to be), matsliekh zayn (H-Y)

succession, der nokhanand; "in succession", keseyder (H)

Succoth festival booth (Tabernacle), di suke (H)

such, aza; "as such", etsem (H); "such and such", der un der

such as, dehayne (H)

suck (v)zoygn; (candy), smoktshen

sudden, plutsemdik, plutslingdik; "all of a sudden", "in mitn derinen"

suddenly, plutsem, plutsling, raptem

suds, mulines

suffer, krepirn (humans only), laydn

suffering (n), laydn, dos opkumenish, di payn, yesurim (H); "mental suffering", dos agmes-nefesh (H), (dos ages-neyfesh)

sufficient, genug(ik)

sufficient (to suffice), stayen (R)

sugar, der tsuker

sugar bowl, di tsukernitse

suicide (n), der zelbstmord (der aleynmord); "commit suicide", "nemen zikh dos lebn", "zikh onton a mayse" (H)

suit (cards) (n), der mast

suit (clothes) (n), der garniter

suit (law) (n), der protses

suit (v), pasn; "not suit", "pasn vi a khazer (H) a zotl" (like a saddle on a pig)

sulky (adj), broygez (H), ongedrodlt

sullen, farbeyzt

sum (n), der batref, der sakhakl (H), di sume; "in sum", a klal (H)

summer, der zumer

summery, zumerdik

sum up, farsakhaklen (H), sumirn

sun, di zun

Sunday, der zuntik

sundry, kolerley (H), mine (H)

sunflower seed(s), di semitshke(s)

superficial, oyvnoyfik

superfluous, iberik

superstition, dos ayngleybenish

supper, di vetshere (R); "Wedding supper", di khupe vetshere (H-R) (Jewish)

support (physical) (n), der onshpar; (aid), di untershtitsung

support (a cause) (v), solidarizirn

support (financially) (v), mefarnes zayn (H-Y), oys'haltn

support (morally) (v), unterhaltn

support (physically) (v), untershparn

suppose (v), meshaer zayn (H-Y), onnemen; "How am I supposed to know?", "fun vanen zol ikh visn?", gey veys; "suppose (that)", lomir zogn az, loz zayn az

suppository, dos tsepl

sure, gevis, zikher; "Sure enough", "farshteyt zikh", "voden!"

surface (n), di eyberflakh; "On the surface", oybn oyf

surmise (n), der onshtoys, di svore (H)

surmise (v), (on)shtoysn zikh

surprise (feeling) (n), der khidesh (H); (object), der surpriz

surprised, nishtoymen (H), nispoel (H)

surrender (n), di kapitulirung

surrender (v), ibergebn, opgebn, untergebn zikh

surround, arumringlen

survive, iberkumen, nitsl vern (H-Y)
suspect (n), der khoshed (H); (pl.),
  khshudim
suspect (v), khoyshed zayn (H-Y)
suspenders, shleykes (R)
suspense, di shpanung
suspicion, der khshad (H);
  (apprehension), der khshash (H)
suture, di not
swaddling clothes, vikelekh
swallow (bird), di shvalb
swallow (n), der shlung
swallow (v), aynshlingen
swallowed up, dervorgn
swarm (n), der shvorem
swarm (v), "shviblen un griblen"
swear, shvern
swear (curse), zidlen zikh
sweat (n), der shveys
sweat, shvitsn
sweep (v), kern, oyskern
sweet, zis
sweetheart, der gelibter (m), di gelibte
  (f); "Sweetheart!", dushenyu (R),
  "hartsenyu!", kreynele
swell (v), geshvoln/ongedroln vern;
  "Swell with pride", "vern breyter vi
  lenger"
swim (n), der shvum
swim (v), shvimen
swimming pool (n), der shvimbaseyn
swindle (v), bashvindlen, opnarn
swine, der khazer (H)
swing (children's) (n), di hoyde
swing (movement) (n), der makh, der
  shvung
swing (v), vign
Swiss (adj), shveytser
Swiss (person) (n), der shveytser
switch (n), di iberbayt
switch (electrical) (n), der oysshliser
switch (v), aribergeyn, iberbaytn zikh
swollen, geshvoln, ongekvoln
sword, di shverd
sycophant, der khoynef (H); (to be a
  s.), unterlekn, untertantsn

synagogue, dos beys-medresh (H)
  (Jewish orthodox), di shul
synagogue procession (carrying the
  Torah scrolls), hakofes (H)
syrup, der sok

T

table, der tish
tablecloth, der tishtekh
tack (n), der shtift
tack (v), tsuknopkeven
tag (n), der tsetl; (game), yogerlekh
tail, der ek
tail coat, der frak
tailor, der shnayder
take (v), nemen; (take medicine),
  aynnemen
tale, di dertseylung, di geshikhte, di
  mayse (H)
talk (n), reyd; (speech), di rede
talk (v), redn; "Stop talking" (v),
  shvaygn
tall, hoykh, shtoydriyohu (R) (coll); "A
  tall man", "der drong" (hum.) (lit.,
  pole)
tally, shtimen
Talmud, di gemore (H), der talmud (H)
tame (adj), getsamt
tame (v), ayntsamen
tamper with, tshepen
tap (faucet), der shpunt
tape (n), di lente
tape (adhesive) (n), der klepband
tape (music) (v), rekordirn
tape recorder, der magnetofon, di
  rekordirke
tar (n), di dyegekhts, di smole
tardy (to be) (adj), farshpetikt
target, der tsil, di tsilbret
Tarter, der toter
task, di arbet; "This is no mean task",
  "folg mikh a gang"

taste (n)   **this**

taste (n), der geshmak, der gust, der tam (H)

taste (v), farzukhn, filn dem tam, zukhn

tasteful, mit geshmak

tasteless, on tam (H)

tasty, batamt (H), geshmak

taunt (v), yekn

tavern, di kretshme (R), di shenk

tax (n), der shtayer

tax (v), bashtayern; (strain), onshtrengen

tea, di tey, di tshay (R)

teabag, dos sentserl

teach, lernen (Jewish studies); "teach a lesson", onlernen

teacher, der lerer, der rebe (H)

teacher of Hebrew, der melamed (H) (Jewish)

teacher's wife, di melamedke (H)

tear (rip) (n), der ris

tear (rip) (v), raysn, tseraysn

tear (weeping) (n), di trer(n)

tearfully, mit geveyn

teaspoon, dos (tey-)lefele

tedious, nudne

teenager, der tsenerling

telephone (n), telefon; (long distance telephone call), der vaytklung

telephone (v), onklingen

tell, dertseyln (relate)

tell, heysn (request)

temple, dos beysamikdesh (H) (Jewish) (The Temple)

temple (forehead) (n), di shleyf, der shtern

temptation (n), der nisoyen (H), der yeytser-hore (H); "Yield to temptation", nikhshl vern (H-Y)

tempting (be t.) (v), zayn a nisoyen (H)

ten, tsen

tense (adj), ongetsoygn

tent, dos getselt

tenterhooks (to sit on), zitsn (vi) oyf shpilkes

terrible, geferlekh, paskudne (R)

terrific, gvaldik; "Terrific!", gvaldovne! (Y-R)

terrifying (adj), shreklekh

terror, di eyme (H), der shrek

testicle(s), di beytse (di beytsim) (H)

thank (v), danken; "Thank G-d!", "borkhashem" (H), danken got, got tsu danken; "Thank you", a dank dir, ikh dank aykh

thanks (n), der dank

that (adj), der, dem, di, dos, yene; "That man there", otayener (R-Y)

that (conj), az

the, der (m), di (f), dos (neuter), dem (dative), di (pl.)

theatre, der teater

theft, di geneyve (H)

them, zey

then (at that time), demolst; (in that case), imkeyn (H); (therefore), bekheyn (H), derfar, deriber

there, dort, dortn

There! (there you are), ot hostu dir

therefore, bekheyn (H), derfar, deriber; (and therefore), uvkheyn (H))

they, zey

thick, grob

thickness, di greb

thief, der ganef (H)

thigh, der dikh, di polke (hum.)

thimble, der fingerhut

thin, dar; "thin person", di darinke (f), der darinker (m)

thing, di zakh

think, denken, klern, trakhtn

thinker (speculative), der denker

think it over, batrakhtn zikh

third (adj), drit

third (n), dos dritl

thirst, der dorsht

thirsty, dorshtik; (to be t.), darshtn

thirteen, draytsn

thirty, draysik

this, der (m), di (f), dos (neuter), di (pl.); (emphatic), ot der/di/dos, der doziker, di dozike, der/di/dos/di o

thistle, di shtekhlke
thorough, fulshtendik
though, afile (H), khotsh; (as though),
  punkt vi
thought (n), der gedank
thoughtful, fartrakht
thoughtless, umbaklert
thousand, der toyznt
thread (n), der fodem
thread (v), aynfedemen
threaten, strashen (R)
three, di dray; (cards), dos draytl
three-story (house), der draygornik,
  di trokhetazhne (R)
threshold, di shvel
thrifty, shporevdik
throat, der gorgl, der haldz
throb (v), tyokhken
throne, der tron
through (prep), durkh
thumbtack, di knopke
thunder (n), der duner
thunder (v), dunern
thunderbolt, der blits un duner
Thursday, der donershtik
thyme, der timyan
ticket, der bilet
tickle (v), kitslen
tid-bits, dos nasheray
tide (n), der yam-fleyts (H-Y); "The tide
  turned", "dos redl hot zikh
  ibergedreyt" (the fortune changed)
tidy up, tsuklaybn
tie (bond) (n), der (far)bund
tie (necktie) (n), der shnips
tie (a knot) (v), farbindn
tiger, der tiger
tight, eng, ongetsoygn
tighten, ontsien; (t. a screw), farshroyfn
time (instance) (n), dos mol; "Once",
  "eyn mol"
time (span) (n), di tsayt, der zman
  (H); "Any time", "abi ven"; "Every
  time", "yeder mol"; "What time is it?",
  "vifl iz der zeyger?", "vos iz der tsayt?"
timid, moyrevdik (H)

timid man/woman, der/di lemishke
  (lit. porridge) (R)
tin (adj), tsinen
tin (the metal), dos blekh; (a tin), dos
  tsin
tinsmith, der blekher; (wife), di
  blekherke
tiny, kleyntshik, montshink, pitsimonike
  (R) (coll. pitsik), pitsink; "Tiny bit",
  dos kapetshke, dos pitsl
tip (end) (n), der shpits; (hint), der
  onvunk; (money), dos birgelt, dos
  trinkgelt
tip (money) (v), gebn birgelt/trinkgelt;
  (tip off), oyszogn
tip over (v), iberkern
tipsy, farshnoshket
tip-toe, "oyf di tsipkes"
tire (n), der (gume)reyf
tired, farmatert, mid; "be tired of", zayn
  zat fun
tissue paper, dos vishpapir, dos
  zaydpapir
to, tsu; (destination), in; (names of cities
  and countries), keyn; (to limit of), biz
to and fro, ahin un aher
toad, di broske, di luhashke, di ropukhe
toad-stool, dos sam-shveml (H-Y)
toady, der teler-leker (plate licker), der
  unterleker, der untertentser (to dance
  attendance)
toadying (n), di khnife (H)
toast (bread) (n), der tost; (drink), der
  tost
toast (bread) (v), tsubroynen
toast (drink) (v), oystrinken lekoved
  (Y-H)
toaster, der tsubroyner
tobacco, der tabik, di tabike (R)
today, haynt
to-day's, hayntik
to-do, der hu-ha, der tareram
together, in eynem, tsuzamen; "Bring
  together", tsuzamenfirn; "two
  together", zalbe tsveyt; "three
  together", zalbe drit, etc.

toil (n), di horevanye, di mi, di pratse (R)

toil (v), horeven, matern zikh

toilet (n), der klozet

toilet paper, dos asher-yotser-papir (H)

toilet seat, di klozetbret

tomato, der pomidor (I)

tombstone, di matseyve (H)

tomorrow (adv), morgn

tomorrow (n), der morgn

tongue, di tsung; (language), dos loshn (H); (pl.), di leshoynes

tonsil(s), der mandl(en)

too, tsu; (also), oykh; "Too bad!", nebekh!

tool (n), der makhsher (H); (pl.), di makhshirim

tooth, der tson; (pl.), di tseyn

tooth-ache, der tseynveytik

top (high point) (n), der shpits

top (lid) (n), dos eyberl

top (spinning), dos dreydl

top (prep), oybn; "On top of (in addition)", dertsu; "to top it off", tsu di ale zakhn

topcoat, der ibertsier, der mantl

topic, di teme; (rabbinical), di sugye (H)

torch, der shturkats

torment (n), dos maternish

torment (v), (oys)matern, (oys)mutshen (R)

tormented, gematert, gemutshet (R)

tortoise, di tsherepakhe (R)

touch (n), der onrir, der rir

touch (v), onrirn, tshepen, tsurirn

touched (mentally), gerirt

touchy, shpirevdik; (topic), delikat

tour (v), arumforn

towards, tsu

towel, der hantekh; (dish towel), di stsirke (R)

town, dos shtetl

town hall, dos rot'hoyz

toy (n), dos shpilkhl, di tsatske (R); toys, shpilvarg

tractate, der maymer (H)

tractate (of the Talmud), di mesekhte (H)

train (railway), di ban

train (v), (oys)shuln; (animals), (oys)trenirn

traitor, der farreter, der izmenik (R)

translate, fartaytshn, iberzetsn

translation (n), di fartaytshung, der iberzets, di iberzetsung

trap (n), di pastke (R); "To set a trap", "khapn in a pastke"

travel (n), dos arumforn

travel (v), forn

tray, di tats

treasure (treasury) (n), der oytser (H)

treasure (v), tayer haltn

treat (n), di laketke (R), der maykhl (H)

treat (pay for) (v), mekhabed zayn (H-Y)

tree, der boym; (pl.), di beymer

trial (legal) (n), der mishpet (H), der protses

trial (test) (n), der (oys)pruv; "Trial and error", "tref un toes" (Y-H)

triangle, der drayek

tribute (n), der koved (H); "pay tribute to", opgebn koved

trick (n), di kunts; (deceit), der drey

trick (v), opnarn

trickle (n), dos ritshkele

trickle (v), kapen (R), rinen

tricky, farfirerish, kuntsik

trifle (n), di kleynikeyt, di shmokhte

trifles (n), shmontses

trigger-happy, "bald khapt er zikh shisn", shiserish

trim (v), arumshnaydn, opniglen

tripod, der drayfus

triumph (n), der nitsokhn (H)

triumph (v), menatseyekh zayn (H-Y)

troop (n), dos khayel (H), di trupe, zelners (pl. only)

trot (v), tlisen

trouble(s) (n), di tsore(s) (H); "What's the trouble?", "vos iz?"

trouble (v)   **uncomfortable**

---

trouble (v), mien zikh (H-Y)

troublemaker, der shterer, der trumbanik (R)

trough (drinking trough), di korete (R); (feeding), der zholeb

trouser leg, der hoyz

trousers, hoyzn

trout, di stronge (R)

trowel, di kelnye (R)

true, emes (H); "come true", mekuyem vern (H-Y)

truism, der farshteyt-zikh

truly, emesdik

trumpet, der trumeyt; der shoyfer (H) (ram's horn) (Jewish)

trunk (snout), der shnuk; (torso), der tul; (tree), der shtam

trust (n), der tsutroy; (confidence), dos nemones (H)

trust (v), getroyen

trusted, bagleybt

trustee, der nemen (H)

trustee (in synagogue), der gabe (H)

truth, der emes (H); "in truth", in emesn

try (n), der pruv

try (v), prubirn, pruvn

t-shirt, dos (arbldike) laybl

tube, dos traybl; (squeezable), di tube; "inner tube", der petiv

Tu-Bishvat, der khamishoser (H)

Tuesday, der dinstik

tulip, der tulpan (R)

tumbler (glass), der kelishik (R)

tuna fish, der tunfish

tune, di melodye, der nign (H) (Jewish)

tuning fork, der kamerton

turkey, der indik (R)

Turkey (country), di terkay

turn (bend) (n), der (oys)drey

turn (sequence) (n), der nekst, di rey; "at every turn", keseyder (H)

turn (v), dreyen; "turn back" (v), umdreyen; "turn in" (drive), farforn; "turn off" (v), farleshn, oysleshn; "turn on" (v), ontsindn; "turn out" (result), oyslozn zikh; "turn over", iberkern; "turn up" (in a strange place) (v), farvalgern zikh

turnip, di brukve (R)

turnover (meat-filled), der knish, dos krepl (R)

twelve, tsvelf

twenty, tsvantsik (tsvontsik)

twin, der tsviling

twirl, dreydlen

twist (n), der drey, der krim; (dance), der tvist

twist (change meaning), tsedreyen

twist (make crooked) (v), fardreyen

twist (turn over) (v), iberkern

twisted (distorted), tsedreyt

two, tsvey

type (n), der tip

type (v), (op)tipirn

typewriter, di shraybmashin

U

ubiquitous, iberal, umetumik

ugliness, di mieskeyt (H-Y)

ugly, mies (H); (ugly person), der/di mieskeyt

ulcer, dos geshvir, der parkh

umbrella, der shirem

unaware, nit visndik

unbuttoned (shirt), tsekhrastet

uncalled-for, umneytik

uncanny, tshudne (R)

uncertain, "hengen oyf a hor" (to hang on a hair), umzikher

uncle, der feter

unclean (ritually, Jewish), treyf (H)

uncomfortable, umbakvem

unconcerned, umbazorgt; "Be unconcerned about", "arn vi der farayoriker shney" (bothered like last year's snow), nit arn

uncover, opdekn, oysbleyzn

under, unter; (to go under), untergeyn

underclothes, dos untervesh

underhand, dreydldik

underpaid, nit dertsoln

understand, farshteyn

understandable, farshteyik, gring tsu farshteyn

understanding (n), der durkhkum, dos farshtendenish; "Reach an understanding", "kumen tsu a tolk"

understood, farshtanen

undertaking (n), di unternemung

underwear (long), gatkes (R), dos (unter)vesh

undo (open), oyfmakhn; (nullify), makhn tsu gornit

undress, oyston zikh

uneasy (anxious), umruik

unexpected, umgerikht

unfair, umyoysherdik (H)

unfit (adj), umpasik

unfit (to declare u.) (v), farbrakirn

unfold (develop), antviklen

unfortunate, . . . nebekh, umgliklekh

unfortunately, "nebekh!", tsum badoyern

unhappy, umgliklekh; (be u.), zayn fintster

unharmed, besholem (H); (come out u.) "opshnaydn trukn"

unintentional, nit-vilndik

union, der farband, der fareyn

unique, eyntsik

unite, fareynikn

United States, di fareynikte shtatn

unity, dos akhdes (H), di eynikeyt

unknowingly, beloy-yoydim (H)

unknown, umbakant

unless, saydn

unlucky, shlimazldik (Y-H)

unlucky person, der shlimazl (G-H); (very unlucky person), der shlim-shlimazl

unmanageable, "vi a beyn in haldz" (like a bone in the throat)

unnatural, umnatirlekh

unnecessarily, umzist

unnecessary, umneytik

unobtrusively, shtilerheyt

unpleasant, prikre, umayngenem

unpleasant person, der paskudnyak (R) (der paskudnik)

unplug (v), opshtekn

unprofitable, nit loynen zikh

unravel, funanderplontern

unruly, tseyushet

unseen (adj), umbamerkt

unseen (adv), umbamerkterheyt

unsuccessful (venture), "nit-gerotn"; (person), on hatslokhe (H), on mazl (H)

unsuitable, "toygn oyf kapores" (H), umpasik

until, azh, biskl, biz, biz vanet; "until now", adayem (H), biz aher

untrue, nit emes (H); "Entirely untrue", "nit-geshtoygn nit-gefloygn" (see intr) (Y-E)

unusual, umgeveyntlekh

unusually, bazundersh

unveil, oyfdekn

unwell, "nit mit alemen" (not with everyone)

unwilling, onkheyshekdik (H)

unzip, oyfshleslen

up (adv), aroyf

upheaval, dos iberkerenish

uphold, shtitsn, unterhaltn, zayn getray

upkeep, der oys'halt

upright, shteyendik; (righteous), rekhtfartik

upset (adj), tsetrogn

upset (v), oyfregn, tserudern

upset (knock over), kapoyer varfn

upset (worry), oyfregn, tserudern

upside down, kapoyer, "mitn kop arop un mit di fis aroyf"

upstairs, der oybn (up there)
upstairs (direction), aroyf
up-to-date, azhur(ik)(F), derfirt biz
  haynt
urinate, mashtn zayn (H-Y), pishn
urine, di hashtone (H), dos pishekhts
usable, toygevdik; (be u.), toygn
usage, der banits, der hergl (H)
use (n), der banits; "Be of use", nitsn,
  toygn; "Have no use for", "darfn oyf
  kapores" (H); "It's no use", "farfaln!"
use (v), (ba)nitsn, (ba)nutsn
used (adj), genitst
used (accustomed) (adj), tsugevoynt
used (to) (aux), flegn
useless, "helfn vi a kozak an eynore"
  (H) (to help like giving a Cossack an
  Evil Eye), "helfn vi a toytn bankes" (to
  help like cupping a corpse), umzist
usual, geveyntlekh
uterus, di heybmuter
U-turn, "der khof-oysbeyg" (H-Y)

V

vacancy, der frayer ort
vacant, leydik, pust
vaccinate, vaktsinirn; (against
  smallpox), shteln pokn
vacuum (v), opshtoybn
vacuum cleaner, di shtoybmashin
vagabond, der shleper
vagina, di mutersheyd
vagrant, der shleper
vague, nepldik, tseshvumen
vain (conceited), gadlesdik (H); "In
  vain", "in der velt arayn", umzist
vain person, der gadlen (H); (pl.), di
  gadlonim
valley, di dolene, der tol
valuable, tayer, vertful
value (n), der batref, der shats, der/di
  vert
value (v), haltn tayer, (op)shatsn

valve, der ventil
Vandyke beard, dos komets-berdl (H-Y)
vanish, farshvundn vern, nelm vern (H-Y)
vapour, di pare
varicose veins, gedrolene odern
variety (n), di farsheydnkeyt
variety (a v. of), alerley, kol miney (H)
various, alerley, farsheydn
veal, dos kelberns
vegetable, dos grins; (vegetables), dos
  gortnvarg (pl. only)
veil (n), der shleyer; (bridal), dos
  dektikhl
veiling (of the bride), dos badekns
  (Jewish)
vein, di oder
velvet (adj), sametn
velvet, der samet
velveteen, der plis
vendor, der farkoyfer
vengeance (n), di nekome (H), di
  oprekhenung
vengeance (to take), kiln zikh dos
  harts, oprekhenen zikh
ventilate, oysluftern
ventriloquist, der boykhreder
verdict, der psak-din (H)
verdigris, der grinshpon
verge, der grenets; "be on the verge of",
  haltn bay (baym)
vernacular, di vokhedike shprakh (the
  week-day tongue)
verse (biblical), der posek (H)
versus, kegn, keneged (H)
very, zeyer
vessel (container), di keyle (H)
vest, der zhilet
vex, "trenen di odern"
vibrate, vibrirn
vicious, beyz, rotskhish (H)
victim, der korbn (H) (see Y-E); "War
  victims", di milkhome korbones (H)
view (sight) (n), der oysblik;
  (opinion), di meynung
village, dos dorf, der yishev (H)

vim, dos heybekhts, der koyekh (H)
vine, kleterbleter, der vaynshtok
vinegar, der esik
vineyard, der vayngortn
violence, di hits
violent, hitsik
violet (adj), lila, violet
violet (flower), di fyalke (R)
violin, der fidl
V.I.P., der godl (H)
virgin, di psule (H)
virility, der koyekh-gavre (H)
vise, di klem; (fig.), der urvant
visible, kentik
visit (v), "kumen tsu gast"; "Visit the
    sick", mevaker-khoyle zayn (H-Y)
visitor (welcomed), der oyrekh (H)
vital, "neytik in lebn" (necessary in life)
vivacious, zhvave
vocal, shtim; "Be vocal", makhn koyles
    (Y-H)
voice (n), dos kol (koyles, koylim) (H),
    di shtim
void, botl (H), posl (H); "Void in sixty",
    "botl beshishim" (H) (If the contents
    of a meat dish exceeds by sixty times
    the quantity of dairy food that
    contaminated it, the contamination is
    ignored); "make void", paslen
volume (book), der band
volume (capacity), der farnem
volume (loudness), di hoykhkeyt
volume (turnover), der oysker
voluntary, frayvilik
volunteer (n), der frayviliker
voluptuous, tayvedik (H)
vomit (n), dos brekhekhts, di keye (H)
vomit (v), brekhn
vote (n), di shtim
vote (v), shtimen
vow (n), der neyder (H)
vow (v), menader zayn (H-Y)
voyage (n), di nesie (H)
vulgar, prost
vulture, der grif

W

wade, topshen zikh
wade through snow or mud,
    shlyopen
wage, dos getsolt, di peyde
wage-earner, der fardiner
wager (n), der vet
wagon, di droskhe (R), di fur, der vogn
wailing (n), di yelole (H)
wailing wall, der koysl-ma'arovi (H)
waist, di talye; (of a garment), der ston
wait (v), vartn; "Wait till you hear this!",
    "nu . . . nu!"
wait (on tables) (v), sarvern
wake (someone) (v), (oyf)vekn
wake up (v), oyfkhapn zikh
walk, der shpatsir; (gait), der gang, der
    hilekh (H)
walk (v), shpatsirn
walk (go for a w.) (v), geyn shpatsirn
wall (n), di vant
wallet, dos baytl, der polyares, der
    portmone (F)
wallpaper, tapetn
wall-to-wall, gantsdilik (whole floor)
walnut, der veltshener nus
walrus, der morzh, dos yam-ferd (H-Y)
wander, navenad zayn (H-Y), voglen
    zikh
Wandering Jew, der eybiker yid (the
    eternal Jew)
want (n), der bager, dos velenish
want (v), veln
war (n), der/di krig, di milkhome (H);
    "make war", krign, milkhome haltn (H-
    Y)
warm (adj), varem; (person), hartsik
warm (n), der/dos tsholnt (a dish kept
    warm for the Sabbath) (Jewish) (F)
warm up (v), onvaremen; (oneself),
    varemen zikh
warning (n), di hasroe (H), di
    vorenung
wart, der vortsl

war victims, di milkhome korbones (H)

was, flegn, geven

wash (v), vashn

washed up, kaput (vernacular) (G), poter (H)

washer (n), dos bletl, dos shaybl

wash hair, tsvogn

washing (before burials), di tehare (H) (Jewish)

washing machine (n), di vashmashin

washtub, di balye

wasp, di vesp

waste (n), der opfal

waste (v), tsepatern

waste away (like a dying animal), peygern

wastebasket, dos keyberl

waste time, tseraybn

watch (guard) (n), di shmire (H)

watch (timepiece) (n), dos zeygerl

watch (v), "haltn an oyg"; "Watch (someone) carefully", "kukn oyf di finger"; "Watch your step", "pamelekh vu du geyst" (watch the fingers)

water (n), dos vaser

water (animals) (v), onpoyen (R)

watermelon, der arbuz, di kavene

wave (hair) (n), di ondulirung

wave (motion) (n), der makh

wave (water), di khvalye (R)

waver (hesitate), kvenklen zikh

wavy, gekhvalyet

wax (n), der vaks

wax (v), (on)veksn

way (manner), der oyfn (H); "way of life", der shteyger lebn

way (road), der derekh (H), der gang, der veg

ways (habits), postemkes

we, mir

weak, shvakh

weakling, der shvakhinker

weakness, di shvakhkeyt

wealth, dos ashires (H), dos negides (H), di raykhkeyt

weapon (n), der vofn

weapons, dos kley-zayen (H) (same in pl.)

wear (v), trogn

wear (put on), onton

weasel, dos vizele

weather, der veter

weather (v), baykumen, iberhaltn

weave (v), oysvebn

web, dos geshpins, dos geveb

wedding, di khasene (H)

wedding ring, dos kdushn-fingerl (H-Y)

wedding supper, di khupe-vetshere (H-R) (Jewish)

wedge (n), der klin

wedge in (v), araynshparn

Wednesday, der mitvokh

weed, dos vildgroz

week, di vokh; "A week ago", farakhttogn (eight days ago)

week-end, der shabes-zuntik, der sof-vokh (H-Y)

weigh (v), (op)vegn

weight, di vog; "gain weight", ontsern zikh; "lose weight", optsern zikh

welcome (n), di bagrisung, dos kaboles-ponem (H)

welcome (v), bagrisn, mekabl-ponem zayn (H-Y)

welcome (by shaking hands), sholem gebn; "You are welcome", aderabe (H), zol dir voyl bakumen

well (adj), gezunt

well (adv), gut; Well?, "nu?" (R), "tu?" (R); "Well!" (so what?), meyle (H); "Well done", "a yasher koyekh" (a sh-koyekh) (H); "Well, well!", "ze nor ze"

well (n), der brunem

west, der mayrev (H)

wet (adj), nas

wet (v), bagisn, banetsn, farnetsn

whack (n), der frask, der khmal

whacked out, oysgemutshet

whale, der valfish

what, vos; "what else?" (sure),
"vodẹn?"; "What for?", lemạy (H), tsu
vos?; "What kind?", vọsara?; "What
then?", vozhe?

wheat (adj), veytsn

wheat (n), der veyts; (whole wheat),
der klạyenveyts

wheel, di rod; (small wheel), dos redl

when, az, ven

when (question), ven

where?, fun vanet (from where), vu,
vuhin

whether, az, tsi; "Whether . . . or", "tsi
. . . tsi" (R)

whey, di srọvetke

which, velkhe, vos

which (interrogative), velkhe, voser

while (conj.), beshạs (H), beys (H);
(suffix with adj), . . . erheyt (eg. while
young, yungerheyt); (suffix with n.),
. . . vayz (eg. while a child, kindvayz);
"A little while", a vạylinke

whimper (v), pkhiken (R), vimpern
(R)

whine (n), der pishtsh, der pkhik, der
yomer

whine (v), pishtshen

whip (cat-o'-nine-tails), der kantshik

whip (whack) (v), shmaysn

whiskey, der bronfn, der shnaps

whisper (n), di sheptsh

whisper (v), sheptshen

whistle (n), der fayf; (instrument), dos
fayfl

whistle (v), fayfn, svishtshen
(piercingly)

white, vays; "white meat", der beylik;
(egg white, eye white), dos vaysl

who, velkher, vos

who (interrogative), ver

whole (adj), gants, gor

wholesale (adj), hurt; (adv) oyf hurt;
(n), der hurt

whore, di nafke, di zoyne (H)

whortleberry, di shvartse yagde (P)

whose (interrogative), vemens

why, far vos, varum, vozhe; "Why of all
things", "vos epes?"; "Why then",
almay (H)

wicked (adj), beyz, shlekht

wicked man, der roshe (H)

wicked woman, di marshạs (H)

wide, breyt

wide awake, ọysgetshukhet

wide open, breyt ofn

widespread, farshpreyt

widow, di almone (H)

widower, der almen (H)

wife, di froy, di vayb; Old wives', babske

wig, der parụk, dos sheytl (Jewish)

wild (adj), vild

wildcat strike (n), dos shtrayk(l) far
zikh

will (bequest), di tsavoe (H)

will (desire), der rotsn (H), der viln

will (v), veln

"God willing", mịrtseshem (H)

willow tree, di vayde, di verbe (R)

win (v), gevinen

win (in competition) (v),
oyskonkurirn

wind (n), der vint

wind (v), ondreyen, viklen zikh

window, der fentster; (display), di
vitrine (F)

windy, vintik

wine, der vayn

wing, der fligl

winged, bafliglt

wink (n), der vunk

wink (v), pintlen

winter, der vinter

wipe (v), (op)/(oys)vishn

wire (adj), drotn

wire (n), der drot

wire (fasten) (v), tsụdroteven;
(provide wires), durkhfirn drotn in

wireless (n), der rạdyo

wisdom, di khokhme (H), der seykhl
(H)

wisdom tooth, der khokhme-tson
(H-Y)

wise, klug

wise crack, di khokhme (H)

wise guy, der khokhm (H); (pl.), di khakhomim (pl. is used only for sages of old)

wish (n), der farlang

wish (v), glustn zikh, veln, vintshn, volt veln (n); "I wish that . . . ", halevay volt

wishful thinking, "der halevay gedank"

witch (f), di makhsheyfe (H)

with, mit; (at the house of), bay

without, on; "do without", bageyn zikh on

witness (n), der eydes (H) (sing and pl)

witness (v), zayn an eydes fun

wizard, der mekhashef (H)

woe, di tsore (H), der vey; "Oh woe is me", a brokh iz mir!, oy vey iz (tsu) mir!

wolf (n), der volf

wolf (food) (v), fresn, opfresn

woman, di froy, di vayb; "Beautiful woman", di krasavitse (R)

womb, di trakht

wonder (n), der vunder

wonder (v), klern

wonder at (v), vundern zikh

won ton(s), dos krepl(akh) (R)

wood, dos holts

wood chip(s), dos shpendl(ekh)

woodpecker, der pik'holts

woods, der vald

wool (adj), voln

wool (n), di vol; "To pull the wool over the eyes of", "farredn di tseyner"

word, dos vort; "Man of his word", "der vorts-man"; "To send word to", "lozn visn"

words, diburim (H), reyd

work (n), di arbet; (hard labour), di pratse (R)

work (v), arbetn

workable, oysfirlekh

work hard, horeven

work out (solve), oysarbetn

workshop, der varshtat

world (of people), der oylem (H), di velt; "This world", der oylem-haze (H); "World to come", der oylem-habe (H)

worldly, erdish, oylem-hazedik (H); "Worldly possessions", farmegns

worm, der vorem; (pl.), verem

worn, opgenitst

worried, bazorgt, fardayget (Y-H)

worry (n), di dayge (H)

worry (v), daygen (H), zorgn; "I should worry!", "bin ikh bedales" (H) (am I in poverty?)

worse, erger; "if worse comes to worse", in ergstn fal; "None the worse for it", "es hot im gornit geshat"; "No worse than anyone else", "mit laytn glaykh"

worth (n), der shats, der/di vert

worth it, keday (H); "It's not worth (doing, going etc.) . . . ", "siz nit keday"

worthless, hefker (H), hefker petrishke (H-Y) (worthless parsley), "hefker tsibeles" (H-Y) (worthless onions), khay kak (H), on a vert

worthy, vert

would-be, kloymershtik, oykh mir a . . .

would that, halevay (H)

wound (n), di vund

wound (v), farvundikn

WOW!, "eyn kleynikeyt!", "gvaltik!", "hu-ha!"

wrap (v), (ayn)viklen

wrapper, der aynhil

wreath, der krants

wren, der rob

wrench (n), der mutershlisl

wretched, klogedik, nebekhdik

wriggle (v), tsaplen

wriggle out, dreyen zikh

wring (hands) (v), farbrekhn; (neck), aropdreyen

wring out, oysdreyen

wrinkle (n), der kneytsh

wrinkle (material) (v), tsekneytshn

wrinkled, tsekneytsht

wrist, dos (hant-)gelenk; "wrist-watch", dos hant-zeygerl
write, shraybn; "write up", bashraybn
writing(s), der ksav (di ksovim) (H); "in writing", biksav (H)
wrong (adj), farkert, krum, umgerekht (unjust)
wrong (n), di avle (H)

X

x-ray (camera), der rentgen-aparat
x-ray(s) (pictures), der rentgen-shtral(n)
x-ray (v), durkh'iksn

Y

yard (court), der hoyf; (36 inches), der yard
year, dos yor; "Declining years", oyf der elter; "Last year", far a yorn; "Last year's", farayorike; "Next year", iber a yor
yeast, heyvn; "by leaps and bounds", vi oyf heyvn (as if on yeast)
yellow, gel
yes-man, der omeyn-zoger
yesterday, nekhtn; "Day before yesterday", eyernekhtn
yet (after all), dokh, fort, fundestvegn; "Not yet", nokh nit
Yiddish (adj), yidish
Yiddish (language), dos mame-loshn, dos yidish; (archaic), dos ivre-taytsh
yield (n), dos getrog
yield (give way) (v), nokhgebn, optretn
yield (produce) (v), trogn
yoke, der yokh
yokel, der zhlob
yolk, dos gelkhl

Yom Kippur, der yinkiper (H)
you (sing. and familiar), du
you (pl. and formal), ir
you (acc. of you pl.), aykh
you (obj.), dir
you (polite) (Jewish), a yid; "where do you come from ", fun vanet kumt a yid?
young (adj), yung
young man, der yunger-man
your (sing.), dayn; (pl.) dayne
your (pl.), ayer; (pl.) ayere(ire)
yours, dayner; (pl.) ayere
youth (n), der bokher, der boytshik (anglicism), der yung
youth (collectively), di yugnt

Z

zebra, di zebre
zero, der nul
zero in (on) (v), derpintlen zikh (tsu)
Zion, dos tsien
Zionism, dos tsienizm
zip-up, farshleslen
zipper, dos (blits)shlesl
zone (n), di zone
zone (v), (ayn)zonirn
zoo (n), der zo'o-gortn
zoological, zo'ologish

Interesting Yiddish Translations

brothel, dos shandhoyz (shame house)
busybody, der kokhlefl (cook spoon)
call girl, dos lebmeydl (alive girl)
cannibal, der mentshnfreser (man eater)
chorus girl, dos blishtshmeydl (sparkle girl)
c.o.d., nokhtsol (later pay); shikn oyf nokhtsol (send c.o.d.)
constipation, di farhaltung (holding back)
contraceptive, der trog-farhiter (pregnancy preventor)
corn (toe), dos hineroyg (hen's eye)
corrode, tsefresn (devour)
corset, dos shnirlaybl (string vest)
crocodile tears, tsibele-trern (onion tears)
diabetes, di tsukerkrenk (sugar sickness)
dropsy, di vaserkrenk (water sickness)
echo, dos viderkol (repeat voice)
elevator, di heybmashin (lift machine)
escalator, di vikltrep (wrap steps)
fairyland, dos ergetsland (somewhere land)
fender (car), der blote-fligl (mud wing)
first aid, di gikhe hilf (quick help)
flying saucer, dos fli-telerl (flying saucer)
fondling, kutsenyu-mutsenyu
freckle, dos zumer-shprenkl (summer spot)
frigid woman, di kalte kuznie (cold forge) (hum.)
gaudy, shrayik (screaming)
genitals, di geshlekht-organen (sexual organs)
giggle, khikhikn
gimmick, der dzhimdzhik
glamour girl, dos blishtshmeydl (sparkle girl)
glutton, der geshmater haldz (converted throat)
gums, dos tseynfleysh (teeth flesh)

halitosis, der moyl-reyekh (mouth odour)
handkerchief, dos noztikhl (nose cloth)
harlot, di gasnfroy (street woman)
heckler, der tsvishnrufer (between caller)
hernia, der vinklbrokh (groin fracture)
honeymoon, der honik-khoydesh (honey month), di kushvokh (kiss week)
hook-and-eye, mendl un vaybl (Mendl and wife)
hydrophobia, di vasershrek (water fright)
impotence, di mener-shvakhkeyt (man's weakness)
intangible, nit ontsutapn (not to be felt)
involvement, di arayngeflokhtnkeyt (to be intertwined)
know-it-all, der altsveyser (all knower)
long distance call, der vaytklung (distant ring)
mainspring, di traybfeder (drive feather)
messenger, der/dos shikyingl (send boy)
miss (non-hit), der farbayshos (passed shot)
one-way street, di ahingas (that way street)
pentagon, der finfek (five corner)
philander, shpiln a libe (play a love)
pivot, der dreypunkt (turn point)
promiscuous, seksuel nit iberklayberish (sexually not choosy)
protractor, der vinkl-mester (angle measure)
pun, di vertershpil (words games), der kalambur (F)
puzzle, di geduldshpil (patience game), di trefshpil (guess game)
quiz programme, der her-un-tref (hear and guess)
ravine, der (barg) shpalt (hill split)
rayon, di kunstzayd (synthetic silk)

rectangle, der grodek (even corner)
refund, der kriktsol (return payment)
ridge, der bargrukn (hill spine)
sherbert, dos frukhtayz (fruit ice)
skirt, dos (halbe) kleydl (half a dress)
skyscraper, der volkn-kratser (cloud
    scraper)
sleet, der graypl-regn (pellet rain)
slope, der bargarop (down-hill), der
    bargaroyf (up-hill)
slow-motion, di krikhgikhkeyt (crawl
    speed)
smart aleck, der beser-veyser (better
    knower)
sole (fish), di yam-tsung (sea tongue)
sparkler, der kalter fayer (cold fire)
spick-and-span, finkldik un fekhldik
    (sparkling and glittering)
spiral staircase, di shvindltrep (dizzy
    steps)
triangle, der drayek (three corner)
tripod, der drayfus (three foot)
U-turn, der khof-oysbeyg (khof
    (Hebrew C-shaped letter) -turn)
Vandyke beard, dos komets-berdl
    (kamats (Hebrew T-shaped vowel)
    beard)
ventriloquist, der boykhreder (belly
    talker)
vernacular, di folkshprakh (people's
    language), di landshprakh (country
    language), di vokhedike shprakh
    (week-day language)
wall-to-wall, gantsdilik (whole floor)
yes-man, der omeyn-zoger (amen-
    sayer)

Idioms
Di Idyomes

afraid, dershrokn; 'he is afraid", "di hoyt tsitert oyf im" (his skin is shivering)

ail, krenken; "What ails you?, "vos felt dir?", "vos tut dir vey?"

annoy, "tshepen zikh tsu"

any, "Any day now", "az nit haynt, iz morgn" (if not today, then tomorrow)

appear, vayzn zikh; "To all appearances", "vi es zet oys"

argue, taynen (H); "He argues the point speciously", "er dreyt mitn grobn finger" (he turns with his thumb (large finger)), "to argue endlessly", "hakn a tshaynik" (bang a teapot)

attaboy, "ot azoy!", "a lebn oyf dayn kop" (a life on your head)

bait (v), "tsapn dos blut" (drain or tap the blood)

bargain (n), di metsie (H); extraordinary bargain", "a metsie fun a ganef" (a bargain from a thief)

be, zayn; "To be or not to be . . . ", "zayn oder nit zayn, do ligt der hunt bagrobn" (to be or not to be, there lies buried the dog)

before, eyder; "Before you know it", "eyder vos ven"

birds of a feather, "fun eyn teyg geknotn" (kneaded from one batch of dough)

bite (v), bisn; "Have a bite to eat", "khapn epes" (grab something)

bitter, galik; "The bitter end", "der same sof"

blanket, di koldre (R); "Wet blanket!", "zoyere-ugerke!" (sour pickle), "bitere tsibele" (bitter onion)

bone(s), der beyn(er); "More bones than meat", "kay un shpay" (chew and spit)

bother, arn; "Bother with", "patshken zikh"; "Not bothered in the least", "arn vi der farayoriker shney" (bothered like last year's snow); "Too much bother", "es loynt nit" (it doesn't pay); "What bothers you?", "vos kotert dikh?"; "You needn't have bothered" (sarcastic), "a dank dir in noz arayn" (thank-you in your nose)

bribe (v), untershmirn; "az me shmirt fort men" (if you grease you ride)

bully (v), balebateven; "Stand for no bullying", "nit lozn zikh shpayen in der kashe" (not allow spitting in the porridge)

burden (n), di mase (H), der yokh; "be a burden", "zitsn oyfn haldz" (sit on the throat)

business, dos gesheft; "Mind your own business", "shtek zikh nit" (don't stick your nose in)

can, kenen; "How can this be carried out?", "vi kumt di kats ibern vaser?" (how does the cat cross the water?)

cart, der vogn; "Put the cart before the horse", "khapn di fish far der nets" (catch the fish before the net)

cheap, bilik; "Cheap as dirt", "bilik vi matse-vaser", "bilik vi borsht"

coal, koyln; "Carry coal to Newcastle", "firn shtroy keyn mitsrayim"(carry straw to Egypt)

commemorate, "batseykhenen dem ondenk fun . . . "

commend, "nokhzogn a shabes" (repeat a Sabbath)

congratulate oneself, "patshn zikh in baykhl" (pat one's belly)

corner (v), "farshtupn in a vinkl" (relegate to a corner)

coy, kloymersht shemevdik (H-Y) (feigned shame), "lozn zikh betn" (allow oneself to beg)

crack of dawn, "ven got aleyn shloft nokh" (when G-d is still asleep)

crocodile tears, "tsibele-trern" (onion tears)

crowded (densely crowded), "kop oyf kop" (head to head)

damn him!, "A ruekh in zayn tatn arayn" (a devil in his father); "I'll be damned!", "take?"

dare (v) (challenge), aroysfodern; "How dare you?", "vi kumstu?"; "I dare you", "anu pruv nor"

day, der tog; "We haven't all day!", "der tog shteyt nit" (the day doesn't stand still)

deal, "A good deal" (a lot), "a hibsh bisl"; "big deal!", "a tayere metsie" (H) (a dear bargain)

dead, geshtorbn; "He's dead", "er ligt mitn pupik aroyf" (he's lying stomach up)

design, di kavone (H); "Have designs upon", "sharfn zikh di tseyner" (sharpen one's teeth)

desperate, fartsveyflt; "be desperate", "krikhn oyf glaykhe vent" (climb on straight walls)

destitute, orem; "Become destitute", "blaybn in eyn hemd" (remain with one shirt)

detail (n), di pitshevke (R); "In great detail", "mit ale pitshevkes"

difficulty, di shverikeyt; "With great difficulty", "mit grine verem" (with green worms)

dime, dos tsenele; "A dime a dozen", "valgern zikh in di gasn" (be scattered in the streets)

dirt-cheap, "bilik vi borsht" (cheap as borsht)

discourage, opredn; "leygn shteyner oyfn hartsn" (put stones on one's heart)

distance, di vaytkeyt; "This is some distance", "It's a far cry", "folg mikh a gang" (hum.) (obey my course)

distant relative, "ferds fus podkeves an eynikl" (grandchild of the horseshoes of a horse's foot)

distraught, tsekhusht, tsetreyslt, tsetraytlt; "zayn vi nit keyn higer" (be as if not belonging here); "arumgeyn on a kop" (go around headless)

domineering woman, "a yidene a kozak" (a Jewess like a Cossack) (Jewish)

downhearted, dershlogn; "zayn vi unter der vant" (be as if under a wall)

"draw the words out", "shlepn far der tsung" (drag ahead of the tongue)

dressed up to the nines, "in esik un in honik" (in vinegar and in honey)

drop (n), der tropn, dos kapetshke (R); "At the drop of a hat", "abi vos" (only what)

dupe (n), dos nebekhl, der yold; (to dupe), "onhengen a lung-un-leber oyf der noz" (hang a lung and liver on a nose)

earshot (within); "vi vayt der oyer greykht", (as far as the ear reaches)

earth, di erd; "To the ends of the earth", "vu di velt hot an ek" (where the world has an end)

easy, gring; "Take it easy!", "khap nit!" (don't grab); " hob tsayt!" (have time), "I didn't have an easy time with him", "bay im hob ikh nit keyn honik gelekt" (with him I didn't lick any honey)

edible, "khotsh nem un es es" (at least take and eat it)

effort, di mi; "Make every effort", "leygn zikh in der leng un in der breyt" (lie down in the length and width), to extend oneself

"eke out a living", "oysshlogn zikh dos bisl parnose" (knock out a bit of earnings)

end, der sof (H); "Stand on end", "shteyn kapoyer"; "Where the world has and end", "vu der shvartser fefer vakst" (where black pepper grows) (hum.)

enough, genug; "to be hardly enough", "klekn oyf a tson" (to last on a tooth)

equivocate, "plontern mit der tsung" (stammer with the tongue)

everything, alts, altsding; "everything goes!", "hefker tsibeles" (abandoned onions); "hefker petrishke" (abandoned parsley)

excellent house, "a hoyz fun hayzerland"

excess (carry things to excess), "ibertsien dos shtrikl" (over pull the leash)

excuse (H), der terets; "your answer doesn't hold water", a foyler terets, (a lazy excuse)

exhausted, "faln fun di fis" (fall off your feet)

expectation(s), di vartung(en); "Great expectations", "leyg zikh nit keyn feygelekh in buzem" (Don't count your chickens before they're hatched) (lit; don't put birds on your bosom)

explain things in detail, "araynleygn a finger in moyl" (put a finger in one's mouth)

fall, faln; "To barge into a conversation like a bull in a china shop", "araynfaln vi a yovn in suke" (To fall like a Russian soldier into a Sukkah)

falter, "plontern mit der tsung" (confuse with the tongue)

fits and stars, "ven nit ven", (when and if)

flatter (v), "krikhn in di oygn" (crawl into the eyes)

fold (v), farleygn; "Sit with legs folded", "zitsn oyf terkish" (sitting Turkish style)

fondling, "dos kutsenyu-mutsenyu" (hum.)

forget, fargesn; "aroysgeyn fun zinen" (leave the memory)

frequently, ale vayle; "ale montik un donershtik" (every Monday and Thursday)

frigid woman, "di kalte kuznie" (cold forge)

"full blast"; "mitn fuln bren", (with full burn); "oyf tish un oyf benk", (on tables and benches), "oyf vos di velt shteyt", (that on which the world rests)

"full to the brim", "ful vi an oyg" (full as an eye)

futile, umzist; "Make futile attempts", "krikhn oyf glate vent", (climb on smooth walls); "Talk futilely", "redn tsu der vant", (to talk to the wall)

galore, lerov (H); "vifl s'harts glust" (as much as the heart desires)

genitals, "di geshlekht-organen" (sexual organs)

glare, "raysn di oygn" (tear out the eyes); "oys'shteln a por oygn (oyf)" (display a pair of eyes)

glutton, "der geshmater haldz" (H-G), (converted throat)

go, geyn; "Not know how to go about it", "nit visn mit vos men est es" (to not know with what to eat it); "Go on!", "gey shoyn gey!"

good (successful), gerotn; "As good as the next person", "a glaykher yakhsn mit andere" (be an equal nobleman with others); "Be good at", "zayn a berye oyf" (H); "Be very good at", "zayn a maydem" (H); "Good for nothing", "toyg oyf kapores" (H); "It's a good thing that he came", "a marokhe vos er iz gekumen" (a good fortune that he came); "Not too good", Nit foygldik" (not like a bird), "Pretty good", "nishkoshe" (H); "What good is it?", "vos toyg es?"

gossip, di pliotke (R), dos rekhiles (H); "Become the object of gossip", "araynfaln in laytishe mayler" (fall into respectable mouths)

grandeur (glory), di gdule (H); "a gdule oyf zayn bobe" (Much glory to his grandmother)

grin (v), shmokhn; "lakhn mit tseyner" (toothy laugh)

guarded speech, "halbmoylik" (with half a mouth)

guinea-pig, dos yam-khazerl (sea-pig) (H) ; "use as a guinea-pig", "lernen zikh shern oyf bord" (learn by cutting off one's beard)

half, halb, khotsi (H); "Be half dead", "fokhn mit der neshome" (fan with the soul)

hand, hant; "Hand-and-glove", "knipl-beknipl" (knot in knot); "Live from hand to mouth", "esn fun arbl" (eat from one's sleeve); "Lend a hand", "untershteln a pleytse" (put under a shoulder)

HAPPY BIRTHDAY!, !!mit mazl geyert zikh" (may you add years with luck), "mazl tov tsu dayn geburtstog"

"harmless person", "nit tshepen keyn flig oyf der vant" (to not touch a fly on the wall)

"harem-scarem", "khap-lap"; "vi a farsamte moyz" (like a poisoned mouse)

hastily, "oyf gikh", "oyf eyn fus" (on one foot)

hat, dos hitl, der hut; "Talk through one's hat", "zoygn fun finger" (suck one's finger)

head, der kop; "Head over heels", "strom-halavoy"

heaven, der himl; "For heaven's sake!", "gvald geshrign!" (shout woe)

heel (foot), di pyate (R); "Take to one's heels", "nemen di fis oyf di pleytses" (hum.) (to take one's feet to one's shoulders), "makhn vayivrekh (H) (hum.)

hell, dos gehenem (H); "Go to hell", "gey in dr'erd (go into the ground); "Hell has broken loose", "es tut zikh khoyshekh" (H) (it is dark); "To hell", "tsu al di shvartse yor" (to all the black years) (devil)

"hem and haw", "dreyen mit der tsung" (to turn one's tongue)

hoard, der oytser (H); "He has a hoard (of savings)", "er hot a knipl" (he has a bundle)

home, di heym; "Feel completely at home", "zayn vi a fish in vaser" (be as a fish in water)

honeymoon, der honik-khoydesh (Y-H) (honey month); di khasene-nesiye (H) (marriage voyage), 'di kushvokh" (kiss-week)

honour profusely, "arumtrogn oyf di hent" (carry around on one's hand)

hope (n), di hofenung; "Carry on without hope", "geyn mitn kop durkh der vant" (to put one's head through a wall)

hook-and-eye, "mendl un vaybl" (Mendl and wife)

horse, dos ferd; "Beat a dead horse", "raysn zikh in an ofener tir" (to quarrel in an open door); "from the horse's mouth", "fun rekhtn tsapn" (from the proper tap)

hot cakes, latkes (R); "Sell like hot cakes", "farkoyfn zikh vi matse-vaser" (H-Y)

"How about that?", "vi gefelt dir di mayse?" (how do you like the story?)

humiliate oneself, "shvartsn zikh dos ponem" (blacken one's face)

hurry, dos aylenish; "What's the hurry?, "vu brent?" (where is something burning?)

hurt (adj), tsemazikt (Y-H); (battered), vey ton (v); "Hurt in a fight", "krign klep" (receive blows); "My feet hurt", "di fis tuen mir vey"

idea, der gedank; "I don't have the slightest idea", "freg mikh bekheyrem" (H)

idle (unoccupied), "shling-un-shlang", "pust-un-pas"

ignore, "makhn zikh nit visndik fun" (pretend not to know); "es ligt im in der linke peye" (it's lying in his left earlock); "he doesn't care about it", "hern vi dem koter" (to listen like a tomcat)

ill, krank; slightly ill, nit mit alemen (not with everyone)

illiterate, "nit kenen keyn tseylem fun keyn alef" (not knowing a cross from an aleph)

impatient, umgeduldik; "Be impatient", "shpringen fun der hoyt" (jump from one's skin)

impossible, ummeglekh; "Attempt the impossible", "krikhn oyf glate vent" (climb on smooth walls); "geyn mitn kop durkh der vant" (put one's head through the wall); "shlogn zikh kop in vant" (bang one's head against the wall)

impotent, "on koyekh" (H); impotence, "di menershvakhkeyt" (male weakness)

improbable, "nit leygn zikh oyfn seykhl" (not to rely on one's intellect)

incoherent (he is), "es klept zikh bay im nit a vort tsu a vort" (one word doesn't adhere to another)

incompatible, "vi a lulev (H) (Succoth palm) mit an esreg" (H) (citron)

intangible, "nit ontsutapn"

intercourse (sex), der tashmesh(-hamite) (H); "seksuele-batsi'ungen"

involvement, "di arayngeflokhtnkeyt" (be wrapped up in)

irrelevant (be), "klepn zikh vi arbes in vant" (stick like peas to a wall)

ivory, "der helfandbeyn" (elephant bone)

jaw, "der bordbeyn"; (chin bone), "der kayer" (chewer), "der pisk" (R) (animal)

jump (n), der shprung; "Be one jump ahead", "haltn mit eyn trot vayter"

know, visn; "What do you know!", "herst a mayse!"; "Know-it-all", "der altsveyser"

laugh, lakhn; "Laugh on the wrong side of the mouth", "lakhn mit yashtsherkes" (lizards); "Split one's side laughing", "tsezetst vern lakhendik"

leap (n), der shprung; "Grow by leaps and bounds", "vaksn vi oyf heyvn" (grow as if with yeast)

least, klenst; "Not in the least", "oyf a hor nit" (not on a hair); "to say the least", "to put it mildly", "eydl geret" (courteously said)

leer, shiklen; "esn mit di oygn" (eat with the eyes)

length, di leng; "Go to great lengths", "shpringen fun der hoyt" (jump from one's skin)

life, dos lebn; "Live the life of Riley", "lebn vi got in ades" (live like G-d in Odessa)

like (v), glaykhn (anglicism), holt hobn; "If you like", "gezunterheyt"; "A likely story!", "punkt!"

"listen attentively", "onshteln moyl un oyern" (fix mouth and ears upon)

live (v), lebn; "Live it up", "lebn a khazershn tog" (live a piggish day); "I should live so", "khlebn" (honestly) ((contraction of) "ikh zol azoy lebn")

matter, "No matter", "alts eyns"; "No matter how good", "vi gut es zol nit zayn"; "No matter what", "ove-tove"

meaningless, on a zinen; "By all means", "avade" (H), aderabe (H); "By no means", "far keyn fal . . . nit"; "By what means?", "vi azoy?"

meddler, "der kokhlefl" (dipper) (cooking, stirring spoon)

mediate, "araynleygn zikh in sholem" (H) (put one's effort into peace)

mess (n), der balagan (H), di blote (R), dos patshkeray; "Make a mess of things", "farkokhn a kashe" (cook up a porridge)

mincemeat, dos kreplfleysh; "Make mincemeat of", "makhn ash (un blote) fun" (make ash and dirt of)

mind, der moyekh (H); "Make up your mind", "nu shoyn!"; "ahin oder aher!" (there or here); "Never mind", "meyle!"; "I don't mind", "fun maynet vegn"

miserable, klogedik, nebekhdik; "Make life miserable for", "farshvartsn di yorn" (blacken the years)

moan (v), yenken; "okhtsn un krekhtsn" (moan and groan)

"monkey-business", "der kunkl-munkl

"more and more beautiful", "vos vayter alts shener" (the further the more beautiful)

mountain, der barg; "Make a mountain out of a mole-hill" "makhn fun a flig a helfand" (make an elephant from a fly); "makhn fun a vort a kvort" (make a quart from a word)

move, rirn zikh; "Move heaven and earth", "aynleygn veltn" (tear down worlds), "rirn a vant" (move a wall)

much, a sakh; "Make much of", "makhn a tsimes fun" (make a stew)

mum, sha!; "Keep mum", "shvaygn vi yorkes hunt"

mumble, beben; "redn unter der noz" (talk under the nose)

naive, tmimesdik (H-Y); "Be naive", "keyn tsvey nit kenen tseyln" (to not be able to count to two), naive person, der tam (H), der/di tomem (H)

need, darfn; "Not need to", "farshporn"; "Not needed at all", "darfn oyf kapores" (to need like a scapegoat fowl); "That's all I need", "mer felt mir nit" (I'm not missing anything else)

new, nay; "What's new?", "vos hert zikh?"

New Year's Eve, "der silvester-ovnt"

next door, "mit a tir vayter" (A door further); "a tir lebn a tir" (a door near a door)

non-committal, "mitn halbn moyl" (with half a mouth)

non-existent, "nit-geshtoygn nit-gefloygn" (re: resurrection of Christ) (hum.)

nonsense, "blote!"; "Talk nonsense", "redn fun hits" (heated talk); "hakn a tshaynik" (bang a teapot); "Stuff and nonsense!", "a nekhtiker tog" (yesterday's day)

not, nit (nisht); "Is that not so?", "ayo?"; "Not at all!", "gor!"

nothing, gornit, keyn zakh nit; "Be nothing compared to", "zayn a hunt antkegn" (be a dog against)

now, itst, yetst; "Every now and then", "ale vayle"; "Just now", "nor vos"

nuisance, der tsutshepenish, der nudnik (person) (R); "Make a nuisance of oneself", "krikhn in di oygn" (climb in one's eye)

object, der kheyfets (H); "Money is no object", "a rendl aroyf a rendl arop" (up a gold coin, down a gold coin)

obvious, klor; "klor vi der tog" (clear as the day); "belabour the obvious", "brekhn zikh in an ofener tir" (to break into an open door)

off, avek; "We're off!", "HAYDA !"

outdo, aribershtaygn; "farshtekn in gartl" (relegate to a belt) (hum.)

overdo, "ibertsien dos shtrikl" (overstretch a string), iberkhapn di mos (overtake a measurement)

passion, di laydnshaft; "Be passionate", "hobn heys blut" (have hot blood)

patronize, "Look down upon", "kukn fun oybn arop oyf" (to look down upon from above)

philander (v), "shpiln a libe" (play a romance)

plot against (v), "grobn a grub oyf" (dig a mine against)

popular, folkish; "To become (unduly) popular", "arayngeyn in shustergas" (go into the street of shoemakers)

premonition, dos forgefil; "I have a premonition", "dos harts zogt mir" (my heart tells me)

presentable (to be p.), "nit hobn mit vos zikh tsu shemen" (not to have anything to be ashamed of)

press (v), kvetshn; "I'm badly pressed for time", "di hoyt brent oyf mir" (my skin is burning)

price (n), der mekekh(H); "At a fair price", "in glaykhn gelt" (in equal money)

probable (be), "kenen gring gemolt zayn"; "Most probably", "gikher far alts"

progress (n), der gang; "Make progress", "rukn zikh fun ort" (proceed from a place)

promiscuous, mufkerdik (H); "seksuel nit iberklayberish" (not sexually choosy)

pronounce, aroysredn; "Have trouble pronouncing", "brekhn zikh di tsung (tseyn)" (break one's tongue (teeth))

provoke, tsebeyzern; "aroysbrengen fun geduld" (bring out of patience)

pry into, "araynshmekn zikh", "araynshtekn di noz" (stick in one's nose)

pucker up, "makhn a vaynshl fun di lipn" (make a sour cherry of the lips)

pushover (be a), "zayn gring vi a hor fun milkh" (be easy as a hair from milk)

puzzled (be), "oysshteln a por oygn" (display a pair of eyes); "Look puzzled", "brekhn zikh dem kop" (break one's head)

quick, shnel, gikh; "Touch to the quick", "nemen di leber" (take the liver)

rags, di shmate (R); "In rags and tatters", krue-blue, "opgerisn un opgeshlisn"

rave (v), bredyen; "redn fun hits" (heated talk); "rave about", "loybn in himl arayn" (to praise to the heavens)

reason (n), der farvos, der tam (H); "For no good reason", "glat in der velt arayn" (straight into the world); "It stands to reason", "der seykhl trogt oys" (common sense bears out); "There is a reason for everything", "yeder vorem hot zayn dorem" (every worm has its intestines)

respectable, orntlekh; "Look respectable", "hobn a ponem" (H) (have a face)

"Respectfully yours", "mit (groys) derekh-erets" (H)

restless, umruik; "To be restless", "nit kenen aynzitsn" (be unable to sit still)

returns, "Many happy returns", "biz hundert un tsvantsik" (may you live to 120)

revile, "zidlen un shnidlen" (curse and swear), "shlogn kapores mit"

rhyme (n), der gram; "Without rhyme or reason", "on a tam un on a ram" (on a shtram un on a gram)

rich, raykh; "Strike it rich", "araynfaln in a shmaltsgrub"; "rich as Croesus", "raykh vi koyrekh"

rid, poter (H); "Good riddance", "a sheyne reyne kapore"

righteousness (ironic), betsedek; "With righteousness", "biz tsu der keshene" (As far as the pocket)

robust, "gezunt vi a poyer" (healthy as a peasant)

ropes, der shnur(n), der shtrik; "Know the ropes", "visn vu a tir efnt zikh" (to know where a door opens)

round, "All the year round", "a kaylekhik yor"

rub, "There's the rub", "do ligt der hunt bagrobn" (there lies buried the dog)

rub (v), raybn; "Rub it in", "shitn zalts oyf di vundn" (pour salt into the wounds)

ruin, der khurbm (H); "He ruined me", "er hot mikh gekoylet on a meser" (he slaughtered me without a knife)

run; "Have a run in one's stocking", "farlirn an eygl in zok" (lose a stitch in a sock)

sake; "For the sake of", "tsulib"; "For my sake", "fun maynet vegn"

say, zogn; "You don't say!", "azoy gor!"; "I say!", "her nor!"; "That's what you say!", "es ret zikh ayn"

scare (v), ibershrekn; "He is scared", "di hoyt tsitert oyf im" (his skin is shivering)

scatter, tseshitn; "Widely scattered", "tsezeyt un tseshpreyt"

scorn (v), farakhtn; "makhn ash (un blote) fun" (make ash and dirt of)

scratch (n), der krats; "Start from scratch", "onheybn fun (der) alef" (start from the letter a)

scrawl (n), "kotsheres mit lopetes" (R) (pokers and spades), patshken mit der pen

self-satisfied, "patshn zikh in baykhl" (hum.) (pat oneself in the belly)

sensitive, shpirevdik; (touchy), honerove (hum.); "Be sensitive", "nemen zikh tsum hartsn"

shaky, vakldik; "oyfn hinershe fis" (on chickens feet); "be shaky", "haltn zikh oyf mishkoyles" (H), (stand on a balance)

shame, di shand; "Shame on you!", "du zoltst zikh shemen in dayn vaytn haldz" (Blush deep down in your throat)

"It's a pity and a shame", "a kharpe un a bushe" (H), "a kharpe un a shande" (H-G)

short, kurtz; "In short order", "eyns-tsvey" (one two)

show (v), vayzn; "Show off", "krikhn in di oygn" (crawl in one's eye); show-off (n), der oysfayner

"Shrug one's shoulders", "kvetshn mit di pleytses"; "shrug off", "avekmakhn mit der hant" (push aside with the hands)

shudder, groyln; "es geyt mir iber a groyl (kelt)" (a terror overtakes me)

shut, farmakhn; "Keep one's mouth shut", "haltn s'moyl"

"Shut one's eyes to", "kukn durkh di finger oyf" (look between the fingers at)

side, di zayt; "Be on the side of", "haltn mit"

silence, di shtilkeyt; "Be silent", "onnemen a moyl mit vaser" (fill a mouth with water), farshtopn dos moyl (clog up the mouth)

skin, di hoyt; "Get under your skin", "farkrikhn unter di negl" (crawl under the nails)

skinny, dar; "hoyt un beyner" (flesh and bones)

sky, der himl; "Out of a clear sky", "fun heler hoyt" (from fair-coloured skin), "in mitn derinen", "plutsem in a mitvokh" (suddenly on a Wednesday (midweek))

smattering (have a), "kenen oyfn shpits meser" (know as much as on the tip of the knife)

snicker, "lakhn in arbl" (laugh up one's sleeve)

snivel (v), "tsien mit der noz" (pull with one's nose); "rinen fun noz" (run from one's nose)

so, azoy; "So as to . . . ", "kedey tsu . . . " (H-Y); "So be it", "zol zayn azoy"; "So do (am) I", "ikh oykh"; "So what?", "iz vos?"; "So there!", "zest?"; "So and so", "aza un aza" (azoyner un azelkher); "Is that so?", "azoy?"

society, di khevre (H), "High society", "di hoykhe fenster" (high window)

"Sometimes one way, sometimes another", "vi a mol"

speed (n), di gikh(keyt); "At full speed", "hendem-pendem", "mit der fuler gikhkeyt"

"Spick-and-span", "finkldik un fekhldik"

splendid, "hakndik un tshakndik", mitn gantsn tshak (with total splendor)

squat (v), "zitsn oyf di pyates" (sit on the heels)

squeamish, migldik, mlosne (R); "Feel squeamish", "gendzlen in boykh", "mloyen baym hartsn"

squint (v), kukn kose (look aslant); "farzhmuren di oygn"

stagger, pritshmelyen (R); "unterhakn di fis" (chop the feet from below)

stand (v), shteyn; "Stand out", "varfn zikh in di oygn" (throw oneself in other's eyes)

step (n), der trot; "A step away", "a katsnshprung" (a cat jump)

sticks (coll.), di hek; "Out in the sticks", "(ergets) in a hek", "in drerd oyfn dek" (at the bottom of the earth)

stone, der shteyn; "Leave no stone unturned", ""zukhn mit likht" (search with light)

stone-deaf, "toyb vi di vant" (deaf as the wall)

straddle, tsegoplen; "ayngoplen mit di fis"

straw, di shtroy; "The last straw", "dos reshtl tsu di tsores" (the remnants of the troubles)

strength, der koyekh (H); "With all one's strength" "mit ale koykhes"

stress, der druk; "Stress and strain", "drik-un-shtik"

stride (n), der shpan; "In one's stride", "mir-nit dir-nit"

suicide, der aleynmord, der zelbstmord; "Commit suicide", "zikh onton a mayse" (do a story on oneself)

surmise (n), der onshtoys; "Hog-wash!", "boykh svores" (Y-H)(belly surmises)

swarm (v), royen zikh; "shviblen un griblen"

swell, ongedroln vern; "Swell with pride", "vern breyter vi lenger" (become wider than longer)

talk, redn; "He does all the talking", "a breyte deye hot er" (he has a wide idea)

task, di arbet; "This is no mean task", "folg mikh a gang"

tide, der shtrom; "The tide turned", "dos redl hot zikh ibergedreyt" (the fortune reversed)

time, di tsayt; "What time is it?", "vifl iz der zeyger?"; "Any time", "abi ven"; "Every time", "yeder mol"

tipsy, farshikert (Y-H), "farshnoshket"

tip toe, oyf di shpits finger, "oyf di tsipkes"

toady, "der teler-leker" (plate-licker)

to-do, hu-ha!; "To make a big to-do", "makhn a tsimes" (make a stew), makhn a tareram

"trial and error", "tref un toes" (Y-H)

trick, di kunts; "Play a dirty trick", "opton a mayse", opton a shpitsl

trigger-happy, "bald khapt er zikh shisn" (he quickly takes to shooting), "bay im iz bald geshosn" (with him one is soon shot)

trouble, di tsore (H); "Brew up trouble", "farkokhn a kashe" (cook up a porridge)

unbelievable, "nit geshtoygn nit gefloygn" (Neither arose nor flew) (re: Christ)

uncertain, nit tsu gloybn, umzikher; be uncertain (outcome), "hengen oyf a hor" (hang on a hair)

unconcerned, umbazorgt, "be unconcerned about"; "arn vi der farayoriker shney" (to bother like last years snow), "arn vi di vant", (to bother like the wall) nit arn

understand, farshteyn; "Reach an understanding", "kumen tsu a tolk"

unharmed, besholem (H); "come out unharmed", "opshnaydn trukn" (get off dry)

unknown, umbakant; "This is the unknown factor"; "do ligt der hunt bagrobn" (here lies buried the dog)

unmanageable, "vi a beyn in haldz" (like a bone in the throat)

unsuitalbe, umpasik; "toygn oyf kapores"

untrue, nit emes (H); "nit" etc. (see unbelievable)

unwell, umpas; "nit mit alemen" (not with everyone), loy-aleykhemdik (H) (hum.), (not unto you)

upside down, "mitn kop arop (un mit di fis aroyf)", (with the head down and with the feet up)

useless, umzist; "helfn vi a toytn bankes" (help like cupping a corpse), "helfn vi a kozak an eynore" (help like giving an Evil Eye to a Cossack)

U-turn, "der khof-oysbeyg" (a curve like the Hebrew C-shaped letter khof)

Vandyke beard, "dos komets-berdl" (beard like the Hebrew T-shaped vowel komets)

ventriloquist, der boykhreder; (belly talker)

vernacular, di vokhedike shprakh (week-day speech)

vex (v), "trenen di odern"

"Watch someone carefully", "kukn oyf di finger" (watch the fingers); "haltn an oyg", (Keep an eye on)

wool, di vol; "Pull the wool over the eyes", "farredn di tseyner" (distract the teeth)

worry (v), daygen (H), zorgn zikh; "Buck up! Don't worry", nit gedayget"; "I should worry", "bin ikh bedales" (H) (I am in poverty), "mayn bobes dayge" (My grandmother's worry) (sarcastic)

Yiddish-English Dictionary

A

a (ind. art.), a

abi (R), any, as long as, if only; "abi gezunt" (R-G), if only healthy, nothing else matters

"adayem haze" (H), "to this very day"

adenoy, (G-D), the Almighty (H) (my Lord)

aderabe (H), on the contrary, please, with pleasure, you are welcome

adir (H), mighty, (used only in "gvir adir", "mighty rich man")

adurkhgeyn (G) (durkhgeyn), to go through

afile (adv) (H), even, though; "afile nit", "not even"

agev (H), by the way

dos agmes-nefesh (ages-nefesh) (H), aggravation, heartache

di agode (H), legend, tale

der agres (R), gooseberries (sing and pl)

aheym (G), home(ward)

aheymkumen (v) (G), to come home

akegn (G), against, opposite

der aker (n), acre, plough

akern (v) (G), to plough

akher (H), after

akhpern (v) (G), to revere

dos akhrayes (H), responsibility

akhrayesdik (H), responsible

di akhsanye (H), hotel, inn

akht (G), eight

akhtsik (G), eighty

akhtsn (G), eighteen

akhuts (H), besides, except

der akshn (sing) (H); akshonim, obstinate person(s)

dos akshones (H), obstinacy

ale (G), all, everyone

der alef (H), a or o, first letter of the Hebrew Alphabet

der alef-beys (H), a, b, c's, alphabet

aleksander mukden (G), Alexander the Great (of Macedon)

alerley (G), all kinds, variety

aleyn (G), alone, self

di aliye (H), a calling up to a Torah reading; (der oyfruf (G)), ascent

al-kol-ponim (H), at any rate, by all means

der almekhtiker (G), almighty, (G-D)

der almen (H), widower

di almone (H), widow

alt (G), old

amatoreven (v) (F), to dabble

amer, on the other hand (followed by a question), then, thus

dos amkho (H), Jews, the common people (Jewish)

amol (Y-G), at one time, once, once upon a time

der amorets (H), ignoramus, illiterate person, rude person

dos ampernish, argument, bickering

ampern zikh, to argue, to quarrel

ander (an ander) (G), next, second, the other

andersh (G), different, otherwise, something else

an erekh (H), approximately

anider (G), down

"der ani-maymen" (H), credo (lit. I believe)

der antik, antique, rarity; "an antik", something exquisite

antloyfn (G), to run away

antshuldikn (v) (G), excuse, pardon

antshuldikn zikh, apologize

antshuldik (t) (mir), excuse me, pardon me

der apifyur (H), the pope

der apikoyres (H), heretic, non-believer in Judaism

der aptsas (n), heel (shoe)

der araber (G), Arab(s)

arayn (G), in

araynfaln (G), be deceived into, interrupt, to fall in; "araynfaln vi a yovn in suke", (lit. to fall like a Russian into a Sukkah) "To barge into a conversation"; "falt mir nit arayn in di reyd", "do not interrupt me"

der arayngang, entrance; "arayngang farvert", no admittance

araynganvenen (zikh) (G-H), to sneak in

arayngeyn (G), to enter

araynleygn (G), bury, invest, lay oneself out, to put in; "shtarbn iz nokh vi es iz, ober dos araynleygn in drerd, dos bagrobt a mentshn", "dying isn't too bad in itself, it's laying the man in the earth that buries him"

araynshparn (G), to wedge in

araynshparn zikh, push one's way in

der arbe-
   kanfes (four wings) (H) (di tsitses) , four tassels of a Jewish religious under-garment, signifying the omni-presence of G-D

der arbes, pea(s) (sing and pl)

di arbet (n) (G), work

der arbeter (G), workman

arbetn (G), to work

der arbl, sleeve (sing and pl)

der arbuz (R), watermelon

ariber (R), across, over

ariberbrengen (v) (G), to bring over

ariberklaybn zikh (G), to move into a new house

ariberpeklen zikh (G), to die (lit. to bring over bag and baggage)

aribertrogn (G), to bear, to move (by carrying), to relay, to transfer

dos arikhes-yomim (H), longevity, long life

der arikhes-yomim-shats (H-Y), life expectancy

arn, to concern oneself, to mind

arop (G), down

aropglitshn (Y-G), to slide down

der aroploz (G), a chute, descent, landing

aroplozn (Y-G), lower, to let down

der aroppluntsh (Y-G), splashdown (spacecraft)

aroyf (G), up

der aroysgang (n) (G), exit

aroysgeyn (G), to exit, to go out

der aroysloz, graduating class, (stock) issue, release

aroyslozn (G), to issue

aroystraybn (G), banish, drive out, expel

arum (G), around

arumgeyn (G), go around, to wander

der arumkuk, inspection, survey

arumkukn (G), to look around

arunter (G), down

di arure (H), shrew

a sakh (H), many, much

asern (v) (H), to forbid, (ritual) (Jewish)

dos ash (G), ash, ashes

di asife (H), meeting

dos ashires (H), wealth

der askn (H), one active in public life

der atomkoyp (Y-G), atomic pile

atsind, at present, now

avade (H), certainly, of course

avek (G), away

avekfaln (G), to collapse

avekleygn (Y-G), to lay, to lie down, to set down

"aveksharn zikh" (G), to die, "to shuffle away"

di aveyre (H), a sin

di avle (n) (H), wrong

di avyomuter (F), aircraft carrier

der avyon (F), airplane

ayer (G), your

aykh (G), you

ayln, to hurry; "ayl zikh", "get a move on", "hurry up"; "ayl zikh nit", "take your time" (don't hurry)

di ayl-sho (G-H), rush hour

aynbeygn, to bend; "aynbeygn zikh", to bend (crouch)

der aynbinder (G), bookbinder

aynbindn (v), to bind (a book)

der aynfal (Y-G), idea, notion
aynfaln (Y-G), to collapse, to occur
"vos falt aykh ayn?", "how dare you?", "what's the idea?"
der aynflus (n) (G), influence
ayngeboygn (Y-G), bent, curved
ayngeleygt, pickled
dos ayngemakhts (n) (Y-G), preserves
ayngeshpart (G), stubborn
aynkhazern (H), memorize, to study
aynleygn (G), to destroy, to place on deposit, to raze
"Lig ayngeleygt", "Lay still!", "Shut up!"
aynnemen (G), appease, capture, over-run, subdue, to take (medicine); "aynnemen a mise meshune" (G-H), "To suffer an unnatural death"
aynpakn (G), to pack, to package, to pack up
aynpakn zikh, to pack one's things
dos aynredenish, misconception, self delusion
aynredn (Y-G), coax, persuade; "er vil mir aynredn . . . ", "He wants to talk me into . . . "; "aynredn zikh", to delude oneself
aynrikhtn (Y-G), to soil
aynshlofn (G), to fall asleep
der ayntsol (Y-G), deposit, installment payment
ayntsoln (v), to make payments, to pay in
aynzinken (G), to dunk, to sink
dos ayzn (G), iron; (der ayzn), flatiron
az (G), as, if, that, when, whether
aza (Y-G), "such a"
dos azes (H), impudence
azh (R), even
di az'hore (H), warning
azoy (Y), "is that so", like that, so
di azye (Y), Asia; "di kleyn-azye", "Asia Minor"

B

babske refues (R-H), old wives' remedies
der badarf (n), need
badarfn (G), happen to, have to, need, require
badarft zayn (G), happened to be
badekn (G), to cover
dos badekns (G-Y), veiling (of the bride) (Jewish)
der badkhn (H), buffoon, jester (Jewish)
der bafal (Y-G), a mugging, an attack
bafaln (v), to attack, invade
baganvenen (Y-H), embezzle, to rob
bagaystern (v), to inspire, to rouse
bagaystert (G), enthusiastic
di bagaysterung, enthusiasm
bagegenen (G), to meet
dos bagegenish, date, encounter, meeting
bageyn (G), to commit; "bageyn zikh on", "to do without"
der bagrob (n), rebuff, scolding
bagrobn (adj), buried
bagrobn (v) (G), to bury, to put the kibosh on someone, to rebuff; "do ligt der hunt bagrobn", "this is the unknown factor"; 'zayn oder nit zayn, do ligt der hunt bagrobn", "To be or not to be, etc"
der bahalter, shelter
bahaltn (G), to hide
bahavnt (G), expert, well versed
di bak(n) (G), cheek(s)
bakant (adj), acquainted, famous
der bakanter (G), acquaintance, friend
bakenen (mit) (v), introduce (to); "bakenen zikh", be introduced to, meet
baklogn (G), to complain
bakn (G), to bake
di bakoshe (H), plea, request
der bal-akhsanye (H), innkeeper

der bal-aveyre (H), sinner
bald (G), soon
der bal-deye (H), a man whose opinions are respected, person in authority
balebateven (Y-H), to keep house, to manage
balebateven iber/mit (Y-H), bully, throw one's weight around
dos balebatishkeyt (H-G), economy, household
balebetshen (Y-H), to babble, to mumble, to talk nonsense
der balebos (H), householder, master, owner; (pl.) balebatim
di baleboste, efficient female, mistress
balegern (v), to besiege
di balegerung (G), a siege
der balegole (H), coachman, drayman; illiterate, ignorant person
der bal-gayve (H), an arrogant man
der bal-kaas (H), an angry man, choleric
der bal-khay (H), animal, any living thing, possessor of life; "der tsar baley-khayim", "sorrow for living things (animals)"
der bal-khov (H), debtor
der bal-koyre (H), the reader of the Torah in a synagogue (Jewish)
der bal-makhloykes (H), hair-splitter, quarrelsome man
der bal-melokhe (H), artisan, craftsman
der bal-moyfes (H), miracle worker
der bal-mum (H), a cripple, a man with a physical defect
der bal-nes (hanes) (H), miracle worker
dos balones (H), eagerness, interest
der bal-shem (H), miracle worker
bal shem tov (H), Israel Ben Eliezer, (1700-1760); (lit. master of the name (G-D))
der bal-tayve (H), a lustful man
di bal-tayvenitse (H), a lustful woman

der bal-tfile (H), reader of the prayers (Jewish)
der bal-tkie (H), blower of a shofar (Jewish)
der bal-tsdoke (H), a charitable man, philanthropist
der bal-tshuve (H), a penitent (returner to the fold), "There, where the bal-tshuve stands even the saints cannot stand": The godless reply; "Because of the smell"
bamant (adj) (G), a married woman
di ban (G), a train
di banke(s) (R), cupping glass(es) (used to draw blood); "es vet helfn vi a toytn bankes", it's helpless, it's useless
der banket, banquet (secular); "gebn a banket", "give a banquet"
der bar (n), bar
di bar(ne), pear
barabaneven (R), to drum
der barabanshtshik (R), drummer
der baran (R), a ram
barekhenen (G), calculate, consider
der barg (G), heap, hill, mountain
der barmenen (H), a corpse
di bar-mitsve, Jewish boy's thirteenth birthday when he assumes religious responsibilities
di barsht (G), a brush
bashaymperlekh, evident, obvious
der bashefer (G), creator (G-D)
der basheftiker, employee
basheftikn (G), to employ
di basheftikung, employment, pursuit
bashert, fated, predestined
di (der) basherte(r), bride (or groom) to be
bashtayern, to tax; "bashtayern zikh", to contribute
di bashtayerung, taxation
bashteln, (Y-G), cover, to order
di bashtelung (n), appointment, order (merchandise); "makhn oyf bashtelung", to make to order
bashteyn (G), allow, consent

der bashteyteyl, component, ingredient

bashuldikn, to accuse

der bashuldikter, accused

di bashuldikung, accusation, charge

bashvindlen (Y), to swindle

di basmalke (H), princess

di bas-mitsve, Jewish girl's thirteenth birthday (see bar-mitsve)

di bas-yekhide (H), only daughter

der batlen (n) (H), a man with no occupation, a non-person

batlen (v) (H), fiddle away the days

dos batlones (H), impracticality, inefficiency

der batrakht, consideration; "nemen in batrakht", take into consideration; "nit kumen in batrakht", be out of the question

batrakhtn (G), consider, to deliberate

di batrakhtung, (medical) check-up, deliberation, examination

batsoln (G), to pay, to pay for

der bavaybter (Y-G), married man (bewived)

bavornen (G), safeguard, to insure

bay (G), at, with; "bay undz", "at our place"

dos baydl, cottage, covered wagon, tent

baym (G), in the process of, when, while

der bayshpil (G), example; "tsum bayshpil", "for example"

der bayt, (ex)change; "makhn a bayt", to trade

der baytl (G), purse, wallet

baytn (G), to change, to exchange; "baytn dos rendl" (G-Y), change one's gold coin, ducat" (for less)

baytn zikh (v), change, take turns, trade

der bazetser, settler

bazetsn (Y-G), to seat, to settle (a country), to take possession

dos bazetsns (Y-G), seating (of the bride) (used in this sense only) (Jewish)

bazetst, manned, occupied

bedeye hobn (H-G), have a mind to

bedieved (H), afterwards, in retrospect, subsequently

befeyresh (H), clear, decided, explicit

der beged (H), garment, (pl. begodim)

begimatrie (H), according to the numerical value of the letters in the alphabet (Jewish)

di beheyme (H), beast, fool, head of cattle

bekhayim (H), alive

bekheyn (adv) (H), so, therefore

der bekheyn (n) (H), implication

dos bekies (H), proficiency, skill

bekoved (H), honourably

belaz, "if you'll pardon my French", "in the language of the strange people"

benemones (H), honestly, my word of honour

beney-bris (H), sons of the convenant (B'nai Brith)

benken (G), to long for

dos benkenish (n) (Y-G), homesickness, longing

der ben-melekh (H), prince

der ben-toyre (H), scholar

der bentsh, thud

bentshn (G), bless, to grant, to say grace; "Got zol im bentshn (used ironically) mit dray mentshn: eyner zol im haltn; der tsveyter zol im shpaltn; der driter zol im bahaltn", "may G-D graciously send three persons upon him: one to hold him; the second to split him; the third to bury (conceal) him"

der ben-yokhid(l) (H), only son

der ber (G), a bear; "der groyser ber", the Big Dipper

di bereze (G), birch (tree)

der/di berye (H), clever efficient person; "zayn a berye oyf", be good at

beser (G), better

der beser-veyser (Y-G), smart Alec, (better-knower)

beshas (H), during; "beshas mayse" (H), at the same time, (the hour of the deed)

besholem (H), at peace, intact, safely

"beshum oyfn veyinyen" (H), "under no circumstances"

der bes-medresh (H), prayer and study house, small orthodox synagogue (Jewish)

der bes-oylem (H), cemetery ("house eternal") (see "ort")

besprovolotshne (R), wireless

di bet (G), a bed

beteve (H), customarily, naturally (by nature)

dos betgevant (G), bedding

betlen, to beg

der betler (G), beggar; (di betlerke) female beggar

betn (G), to ask for, to beg, to plead; "ikh bet aykh", please

betsedek (H), with righteousness (ironically) - (B,TS,D,K, - "Biz TSu Der Keshene" - "as far as the pocket".)

beyde (G), both

der beygl (G), bagel (doughnut-shaped bread roll) (Jewish)

dos beygl, small sheet

der beyn (G), bone; "mit di beyner", just like

der beysamigdesh (H), The Temple (in Jerusalem) (Jewish)

der beys-hakvores (H), cemetery (lit. house of burials) (see "ort")

der beys-khayim (H), cemetery ("house of life"), (See "ort")

der beys-tfile (H), house of prayer

beyz (G), bad, evil; "dos beyz-oyg", "the evil eye"

beyzern zikh (G), be angry with, scold

di beyzkeyt, malice

bifrat (H), especially

bifresye (H), in public, openly

der bik (R), a bull

der biker-khoylim (H), mitsvah of visiting the sick

di bikhershank, bookcase; (pl.) bikhershenk

bikhlal (H), altogether, in general

di biks, gun, rifle

dos bild (G), a picture

bilik (G), cheap

bilkher (G-Y), more deserving, preferable

di bime (H), pulpit (Jewish)

bimzumonim (H), in cash

bin (G), am

bisl (G), few, little

bislekh (G), small amounts

bislekhvayz (G), a little at a time, little by little

bite (G), "please"

di bite (G), request

biz (G) (bizkl), until

bizkhus (H), because of the merit of

der bizoyen (H), disgrace, shame

der blat (n) (G), leaf, newspaper, page, (pl. bleter)

blaybn (G), to remain, to stay

dos blekh (G), tin (the metal)

der blekher (G), tinsmith

di blekherke, the tinsmith's wife

bleyz (adj), dull

der bleyz (G), blank, gap

der bleyztants (Y-G), striptease

di blezl-gume, bubble gum

bli kets (H), endlessly

di blintse (R), cheese-filled pancake

der blishtsh (R), a sparkle, glamour

blishtshen (R), to shine, to sparkle

dos blishtshmeydl (R-Y), glamour girl

der blits (G), flash, stroke of lightning; "a blits im in kop", "a lightning stroke in his head"; "blits shnel", instantly

blitsn, to lighten

blondzhen (R), to get lost, to go astray

di blote (R), marsh, mess, mud, puddle

blotik, (R), messy, muddy

bloyz, only

der bloz, blow, gust

blozn (G), to blow

di blum (bliml) (G), a flower
der blumentop (G), flowerpot
di blumen-tsibele, flower bulb
dos blut (G), blood
blutik (G), bloody
blutikn, to bleed
der bob (bebl), bean (beans)
di bobe (R), grandmother
"di bobe mayse" (R-H), "baloney!", "cock and bull story", fairy tale, old wive's tale, "rubbish!"
di bobke (R), bean; "bobkes", nothing, "Nuts!"
di bod (G), a bath; (pl. beder)
dos bod, resort; (pl. beder)
bodn, to bathe; "bodn zikh", to take a bath
der bodner (G), cooper (barrel maker)
der bodyung (G), (name of derision, worse than "balegole"), good for-nothing, loafer, rowdy
der boke (H), master, skilled person; (pl. bekiim)
der bokher (H), bachelor, young man
di boksn, phylacteries (old usage)
bombardirn (v), to bomb, to shell
di bombardirung, bombing, shelling
di bombe, a bomb
di bord (pl. berd), beard, chin; "a mayse mit a bord", an old story
der bordbeyn, jaw
borekh shepotrani (H) (hum), Good Riddance!
borkhashem (H), "thank G-D"
der borsht (borshtsh) (R), beet soup
borves, barefoot
der boser vedom (H), "flesh and blood", mortal, ordinary man
botl (H), of no effect, void; "botl beshishim" (H), void in sixty" (If the contents of a meat dish exceeds by sixty times the quantity of dairy food that contaminated it, the contamination is ignored)
boyberik (Y), back of the beyond (Sholem Aleichem's mythical village)

der boydem, attic; "oyslozn zikh a boydem", to come to naught, to fizzle
boyen (G), to build; "boyen oyf", depend upon, rely on
der boykh (G) (dos baykhl), belly, stomach; (pl.), di baykher
der boykhreder, ventriloquist
boykh svores (G-H), hogwash (belly surmises), scuttlebut
der boykhveytik, indigestion, stomach ache
der boym, tree; (pl.), beymer
der boyml, edible oil
boymldik, bland, oily
der boyre (H), the Creator
der boytshik (E-R) (anglicism), lad, young fellow
brayen (G), to brew, to talk at length; "vos zol ikh aykh lang brayen", "to make a long story short" (why should I talk to you at length?)
der breg (R), bank, edge, shore; "der breg yam", beach, coast; "oyfn breg", ashore
brekhevdik, breakable, fragile
brekhn (G), to break; "brekhn teler", "to break plates" (betrothal)
brekhn (G), to vomit
der bren, burn, fervor, verve; "mitn fuln bren", full blast
brenen (G), to burn
brenevdik, flammable
brengen (G), to bring
dos brenholts, firewood
breyt (G), broad, wide
breytgaystik, broadminded
breytlhartsik, generous
di breyre (H), a choice
breyredik (H), optional
di briln, eyeglasses
brilyant (adj), brilliant
der brilyant(n) (n) (G), diamond(s)
brilyantn (adj), darling, diamond, precious
der bris (H), covenant (re: circumcision ceremony, as in B'nai B'rith) (Jewish)

der briv (G), letter (correspondence)

dos brivele (brivl) (G), a message, a note (little letter)

di brokhe (H), benediction, blessing

der bronfn, brandy, whiskey; "traybn bronfn", to distill liquor

broygez (H), angry

dos broyt, bread

der bruder (G), brother (pl. di brider)

dos brum-ayzn, Jew's harp (lit. hum-iron)

der brunem (n) (G), well

di brust (G), breast, chest; (pl.), brist

dos bukh (G), book, (pl. bikher)

di bulbe(s) (R), potatoe(s)

der bund, Jewish Labour Bund (Socialist Party)

der bund (n), league, tie

der bundist, follower of the Bund

der bunt (R), bundle, rebellion

der buntar, rebel

bunteven, to incite rebellion

bunteven zikh, to rebel

bur (H), ignorant

der burshtin, amber; (adj), burshtinen

burtshen (R), to grumble, to mutter

di bushe (n) (H), disgrace, shame, (stronger than "shande")

der bushl (n), bushel, stork

der buyan (R), hoodlum, hooligan

der buzem, bosom

di buzem-keshene (G-R), breastpocket

D

dafke (H), absolutely, for spite, just

der dakh (G), roof

di dakh-dire (G-H), penthouse

dakhtn zikh, to seem to

der dales (H), poverty

dos dales-hoyz (H-G), slum

der dalfn (H), pauper

danen (danet), here, this place; "biz danen", up to here; "durkh danen", this way

der dank (n) (G), thanks; "a dank dir", "thank you"; "a dank dir in noz arayn (sarcastic thanks)", "you needn't have bothered" (thank-you up your nose); "iber dank", against one's will

danken (G), to thank

dar, lean, thin

darfn (G), be supposed to, ought to, to need

di darinke (m., der darinker), lean, thin person

darshenen (H), interpret (Jewish), lecture, to preach

der das (H), religion

davnen (H-Y), to say one's prayers (Jewish); "davnen betsiber" (H), "to pray as a congregation (minyan)"

"daven farn omed" (H-Y), "davn before the pulpit" (lead the congretation in prayer) (Jewish)

der dayen (H), a judge, rabbi's associate

di dayge (H), care, worry; "a dayge hob ikh", "I don't care"; "dayges parnose", "worry for one's livelihood"; "mayn bobes dayge", "I should worry" (my grandmother's worry)

daygen (H), to care, to worry

"nit gedayget", "buck up!"

dayn (G), your (singular)

dehayne (H), for example, namely, such as

dos dekl (G), cover, lid

dekn (G), to cover

der demb (domb) (G), oak tree

demolst, at that time

denken (G), to reason

der (G), he, the

derbay, at that, hereby, nearby; "zayn derbay", be present; "nit zayn derbay", be absent

derbayik, adjacent, nearby, neighbouring

der derekh (H), manner, way; (pl. drokhim)

der derekh-hateve (H), course of nature

der derekh-hayoysher (H), the righteous way, the way of justice

derfar (G), therefore

der derfolg (G), success

derfun (G), of it, thereof

derhaltn (G), maintain

deriber (G), consequently, for that reason, therefore

der derkherets (H), good manners, respect

derlebn (G), experience, to live to see, to survive; "ir zolt derlebn iber a yor", many happy returns (may you live to see another year)

derleyzn (G), to redeem

di derleyzung, redemption, salvation

derlozn (G), to admit, to permit

dermonen (dermanen) (G), to exhort, to mention, to remind

dermonen zikh, to recollect, to reminisce

di dermonung, mention, remembrance, reminder

dertseyln (G), to relate, to tell

dertseyln biz, to count as far as

di dertseylung, account, narrative, story

dertsien (G), to bring up, to raise, to stretch

di dertsiung, education, upbringing

dertsu (G), in addition to, on top of, to boot

dervargn (dervergn) (G), to choke

dervayl (dervayle) (G), for the time being, meanwhile

dervaylik, temporary

dervayzn (G), to prove, to show

dervegn zikh (G), to dare, to venture

dervisn zikh, to find out, to get wind of

dervorgn (G), choked, swallowed up

derzen (G), to discern, to glimpse, to spot

derzen zikh, to appear in view

der detsember (G), December

di deye (H), authority, influence; "a breyte deye hobn", "to do all the talking" (to have a wide idea); "mit der deye tsu", with the intention of

der deyfek (H), pulse

der dibek (H), wandering evil spirit of which a person may be possessed; (pl.), dibukim

diburim (H), words; "redn klore diburim", to not mince words, to speak explicitly

der dil (n), floor

der din (H), the law (Jewish); "alpi din", according to Jewish law, lawfully

dingen, to hire, to lease, to rent

dingen zikh, to bargain

der dinger, lessee

der dingopmakh, lease agreement

di dingung, charter, lease

di dinst (G), servant

der dinstik (G), Tuesday

di dinstmeydl (G), maid, servant girl

der din-toyre (H), a lawsuit before a rabbinical court

dir (G), you, (objective case, sing.)

di dire (H), apartment, housing

dos dire-gelt (H-Y), rent

do (G), here

dokh (G), still, yet

der dokter (G), doctor

der dolar (doler) (G), dollar

der donershtik (G), Thursday

der dor (H), generation; "oyf dor-doyres", for generations; (pl.), doyres

dort (dortn) (G), there

dos (G), that, the

der dover-akher (H), scoundrel; (f), di dover-akherte

doziker (G), the said, this; "der doziker", this; "di dozike", the said, these

dray (G), three

draygorndik (G), three stories high

drayik, triple

draysik (G), thirty

draytsn (G), thirteen

der dreml (R), a nap; "khapn a dreml",
  "catch forty winks"
dremlen, to doze, to nap
dos dreydl (G), spinning top, toy
dreyen (G), to turn; "dreyen mitn
  grobn finger" (to turn with a fat finger
  (thumb)), "to argue a point
  speciously"
dreyst, bold
di dreystkeyt, boldness
di dreytir, revolving door
drikn (G), to have heaviness, to
  oppress, to press, (M.S.); "zol im drikn
  in hartsn", "may he have heaviness of
  the heart"
di drikung, pressure
der drik-un-shtik, stress and strain
drit(n/er) (G), the third; "der driter
  min", the neuter (third) gender
dos dritl (G), a third
dritns, thirdly
di droshe (H), a sermon (Jewish)
di droshke (R), carriage (horse-
  drawn), wagon
der droysn (G), out of doors
du (G), you, (sing.)
duln (v), to annoy, to bother; "duln a
  kop", to pester
der duner (G), thunderbolt; "a duner
  zol im trefn", "may a thunderbolt
  strike him"
dunern (v), to thunder
durkh (G), through, (prep.)
durkhvertlen zikh (G), exchange
  angry words, to have an argument
dushenyu (R), sweetheart

E

efsher (H), perhaps
efnen (G), to open
der ek (G), corner, end, extremity, tail
ekht, authentic, genuine, pure, real
dos eksl, steer

ele (H), but, but if; "ele nit", but if not,
  or else
di elektrie, electricity
der elektriker, electrician
elektrish (Y), electric (adj) (I.O.)
elf (G), eleven
elter (G), older; "oyf der elter", "in old
  age"
di eltern (G), parents
di eltern (G), declining years
der emes (H), true, truth; "di emese
  velt", "the beyond" (the true world);
  "in der emesn", "really, truly"
emetser (G), someone
di end(n) (n) (G), end(s)
endikn (G), end, graduate
dos England, England
dos English (adj and language),
  English
der entfer (n) (G), answer
entfern (v) (G), to answer
epes (G), somehow, something,
  somewhat
der epl, apple
er (G), he
di erd (G), earth; "gey in dr'erd", "go to
  hell"
di ere (G), era
di ere (G), honour, (obsolete)
erev (H), on the eve of
erger (G), worse
ergets (G), somewhere
ergste (G), worst
erlekh (G), honest, noble
dos ernvort (G), parole, word of
  honour; "oyf ernvort", on parole
ersht (adj), first, former, initial; "der
  ershter", the first; "tsum ershtn", at
  first
ersht (adv), only
ershtns, firstly, in the first place
dos erts-isroel (H), Palestine, (Land of
  Israel) (Israel after 1948)
es (G), it
dos esn, food
esn (G), to eat

der esreg (H), citron, (for Sukes)
(Jewish)
etlekhe (G), every, few, several
der evyen (H), a poor man; (pl.),
evyoynim
dos ey(er) (G), egg(s)
eyberflekhlekh, superficial
der eybershter (G), G-D, the Lord; (lit.
the all-highest)
eybik (G), ever, forever
der eydem (H), son-in-law
eyder, before, rather than
der eydes (n) (H), witness (same in
pl.); "zayn an eydes", to attest to
eydl (G), gentle, noble, refined
eyernekhtn (G), day before yesterday
dos eyfele(kh) (H-Y), baby(ies) (pet
name for children), birdy(ies), infant
di eyflshaft, infancy
eyflvayz, in (one's) infancy
eygn (G), own. (n); "mayn eygn hoyz",
"my own home"
eygntlekh (adj), actual, virtual
eygntlekh (adv), actually, as a matter
of fact
der eykher yisroel (H), apostate,
heretic
der eyl (H), G-D; "eyl rakhum
vekhanun" (H), merciful and gracious
G-D"
der eyl, ale, oil
di eyl (G), ell, (measurement of length)
eyli, eyli (H), "MY G-D! MY G-D!"
eyn (adj) (G), one; "eynmol", "one
time"; "in eynem", "together"
eynfakh(e) (adj) (G), plain
der eyns (G), one, (number); "alts-
eyns", no matter, regardless; "eyns-
tsvey", in no time, in short order
eynse, one o'clock
di eynskeyt, oneness
der eysek (H), affair, business,
concern; (pl.), asokim; "shmuesn
eysek", to talk shop
di eytse (H), advice
eytsen (H), to advise, to counsel

der eyver (H), limb; (pl.), eyvrim; "der
(menlekher) eyver", penis

F

der fakt(n) (G), fact(s), reality;
"gegebene faktn", data
der fal (n), fall
faln (G), to fall
far (G), for
far a (G-Y), what kind of; "ze nor vos far
a gevaldn er makht", "look at the row
he's kicking up"
faran, existing
farayorik (Y-G), last year's
farbay (G), gone by, passed away
farbetn (Y-G), to invite
di farbetung (n), invitation
farblaybik, permanent
farblaybn (G), to be left, to remain
farblondzhen (R), to lose one's way;
"vern farblondzhet", "to be lost", "to
go astray"; "ver farblondzhet", "get
lost!"
farbrakirn (Y-G), to declair unfit, to
reject
di farbrakirung, condemnation,
disapproval
fardayen, to digest
fardayget (Y-H), worried; "a yid is
fardayget", "a Jew is a worrier"
di fardayung, digestion
fardinen (G), to earn
der fardiner (G), wage earner
dos fardinst, earning
dos fardinstl, odd job
fardrisn (Y-G), to be sorry, to irk
der fardros, chagrin, resentment
fareybikn (G), to immortalize
farfaln (Y-G), alas, doomed, "it's no
use", lost, over and done with, too
bad, "what's done is done"
farfaln vern (Y-G), to disappear
farfirn (Y-G), to mislead, to seduce

di farfirung, seduction

farforn (Y-G), head off, overshoot, put up at, smash, to turn (drive) in; "er iz undz farforn di veg", "he headed us off"

farfoylt (G), gone bad, rotted

farfoylt vern, to decay, to rot

fargenigik, pleasurable

der fargenign (G), delight, joy, pleasure

fargesn (G), forget

di fargesung, oblivion

fargeyik, momentary, passing, transient

fargeyn (G), pass (away), penetrate, (sun) set

farginen (G), to not begrudge, to not envy; "nit farginen", begrudge, envy

der farhalt, tie-up

farhaltn, arrest, constipate, delay, detain, to hide; "farhaltn zikh", be delayed

di farhaltung, constipation, detention

der farher, audition, hearing, interrogation

farhern (Y-G), to examine, to mishear

farheyrat (G), married

dos farhit-mitl, precaution

farhitn (G), to prevent

farhitndik, preventive

di farhitung, prevention

farkatshen (Y-G), to roll up sleeves, to tuck

der farker, intercourse, traffic

farkert (G), contrary, conversely, inversely, the opposite, vice versa

farkirtsn (G), abbreviate, abridge, curtail, to shorten

di farkirtsung, abbreviation, abridgement

der farkler, design, scheme

farklern, contrive; "farklern zikh", reflect, sink into thought

farklert (Y-G), absorbed, pensive, preoccupied

farklingen, (Y-G), to fill with a ringing sound; "dos gelekhter fun di kinder farklingt dos hoyz", "the children's laughter sets the house ringing"

farknasn (Y), to betroth

farknast, engaged

di farknasung, betrothal, engagement

farkokhn (Y-G), concoct, to cook up; "farkokhn zikh (in)", to become an enthusiast (of)

der farkoyf, sale, sales

farkoyflekh, negotiable

farkoyfn, to sell

der farkrim (di farkrimung), distortion

farkrimen, deform, distort; "farkrimen zikh" (Y-G), grimace, to look sour, "to make a face"

farkrimt, deformed, distorted, slanted

der farlang, request, wish

farlangen (G), to ask for, to request

farlaten (Y-G), to patch

farleygn (Y-G), to fold (arms), to mislay, set (trap); "farleygn zikh oyf", plunge into, set one's heart on

farleykenen (Y-G), denounce, deny, disclaim, disown; "nit tsu farleykenen", undeniable

farlirn (G), to lose; "farlirn zikh", to become lost

di farlobung (G), betrothal, (obsolete)

farlorn (G), lost

farlozn (adj), deserted, forlorn

farlozn (v) (Y-G), to leave (behind)

farlozn zikh, rely on

farmakhn (G), to close

dos farmegn (n) (G), estate, fortune

farmegns (G), a vast sum, possessions, worldly goods; "a farmegns vifl", it is surprising how much

farmestn zikh, to compete, to vie

farmishpetn (Y-H), to sentence

di farmishpetung, conviction

der farmog, holdings, property

farmogn (G), to own

farn (far dem) (G), be for, before

der farnakht (Y-G), dusk, evening

farnakhtlekh, toward evening
farnemen, occupy, take up; "farnemen zikh", turn, veer
di farnemung, occupation (of territory)
farredn (Y-G), to becloud with talk, to digress in speech
di farrekhn-konte, charge account
der farreter (n), traitor
farrikhtn (Y-G), to correct, to repair
farsamen (Y-H), to poison
farsarkhenen (Y-H), to stink up
farshemen (Y-G), to shame; "farshemen zikh", become ashamed/embarassed
farshikern (Y-H), to booze away, to get drunk
farshikert, drunk
farshleslen, to zip up
farshlisn (G), to lock in, to lock up; "farshlisn zikh", to lock oneself in
farshmayet (Y), bustling, busy
farshmekn (Y-G), to be aromatic; "di royzn hobn farshmekt dem tsimer", "the roses filled the room with the their perfume"
farshraybn (Y-G), record, to take down
farshraybn zikh, to register
di farshraybung, entry, registration
farshteln (Y-G), to block, to conceal, to disguise
farshteln zikh, disguise oneself, impersonate
farshtelt, disguised, in disguise
farshteyn (Y-G), to understand
farshteyt-zikh, agreed, naturally, of course
der farshteyt-zikh (Y-G), truism
farshtinken (Y-G), to stink up, (the place)
farshvartsn (Y-G), blacken; "farshvartsn di yorn", to make life miserable for
farshvern zikh, to conspire, to plot; "farshvern zikh nit tsu", to swear off . . .

di farshverung (Y-G), conspiracy
farstrakhirn (Y-G), to insure
fartaytshn (Y-G), to interpret, to translate
di fartaytshung, interpretation, translation (esp. from Hebrew to Yiddish)
der fartekh, apron
fartik (G), finished
fartrogn (adj), absent-minded
fartrogn (G), carry away, to endure; "nit tsu fartrogn", intolerable
di fartrogung, tolerance
farvoglt, homeless
farvoglt vern, roam far from home, turn up somewhere
der farvos (G), reason
far vos, why
farzamen, to miss (by being late)
farzamen zikh, to be delayed
di farzorg, welfare
farzorgn, to bestow, to equip, to provide, to supply, to take care of
farzorgt, apprehensive, worried
di farzorgung, supply
farzukhn, (Y-G), to taste
farzukhn fun, to sample
di fatsheyle, cloth, kerchief, scarf, shawl
der fayer (n) (G), fire
fayern, to celebrate
di fayerung, celebration
der fayf, catcall, whistle
dos fayfl, whistle (instrument)
fayfn (G), to whistle
fayn (adj) (G), fine
faynt hobn, to dislike, to hate
der fefer (n) (G), pepper
dos fefermints, peppermint
dos feld (G), cemetery (Jewish), domain, field
feldmestn (Y), the measuring of graves with a string which is later used as a candlewick in the synagogue service
der feler (G), a defect, an error; (Y), beau (jargon), fellow (jargon)

feln (G), to lack, to miss; "es felt emetser", "someone is missing"

felndik, absent, missing

dos fendl (G), pan, pennant

der fentster (G), window; "di hoykhe fentster", high society

dos ferd (G), fool, horse (sing. and pl.); "zay nit keyn ferd", "don't be an ass"

di fershke (R), peach

fertsik (G), forty

fertsn (G), fourteen

di festung (G), fortress

der feter, uncle

der fidl (G), fiddle, violin

filn (Y), to feel (touch), to fill, to perceive

filn zikh, to feel (emotion)

finf (finef) (G), five

der finger (G), finger, toe; (pl. the same)

fintster (G), dark, sinister

fir (G), four

firn (G), to lead, to live; "er firt a khazershn lebn", "he leads (lives) a pig's life" (well off)

der fish (G), fish

dos fisl (G), leg (of furniture), little foot

der flam (n) (G), flame

flegn (G), used to, (was)

dos fleshl, bottle

dos fleysh (G), flesh, meat

der fleysher (G), butcher (purveyor of meat)

fleyshik (adj) (Y-G), meat, (re: dietary laws) (Jewish)

flien (G), to fly

di flig (G), a fly

der fligl, wing

flikn (Y) to pluck feathers, (e.g. from a chicken)

dos flivarg (Y-G), aircraft

der flokn, a club, a stick

der flot (G), fleet, navy

der floy (pl. fley), flea; "hobn fley in der noz", "have a bee in one's bonnet" (lit. have flees in one's nose)

der fodem (n), thread; "mit koshere fodem" (coll), " with knobs on" (with kosher thread)

folgevdik (adj), docile

di folgevdikeyt, obedience

folgn (G), obey, take advise of

fonfen, to mumble incoherently, to talk sonorously

fonfevate (fonfate), talking through the nose

der fonye (foni) (R), a Russian, a soldier

der for, lead (in a game), short trip

forn (G), to ride, to travel

forshteln, to introduce, to present, to represent

forshteln zikh (G), to imagine, to introduce oneself, to speculate; "shtel zikh for", "just imagine!"

di forshtelung, concept, performance, play, show

fort (G), for all that, nevertheless, still

der foter (G), father

der foygl (feygele), bird, homosexual (slang); (pl.), feygl, foyglen; "feygele", dear child (lit. little birdy)

foyl, lazy, putrid

der foyler (foylyak) (G), lazy person, sluggard; "der foyler terets" (H), "doesn't hold water" (lazy excuse)

di foylung, decay

di foyst, fist; "lakhn in di foystn", "laugh in one's sleeve" (laugh in one's fists)

di frage (n) (G), issue, question

der frak, frock coat, tails

dos frankraykh (G), France

dos frantseyz(ish), French (language)

frantseyzish (G), French

der frantsoyz, Frenchman

der frask (R), a box on the cheek, a slap on the face

fray (adj) (G), free

der fraydenker (G), freethinker

der fraynd (G), friend, relative

fraynd (title), Miss, Mr, Mrs

di frayndshaft (G), friendship

der fraytik (G), Friday

fregn (G), to ask, to enquire
fremd (G), foreign, strange
der fremder (G), stranger
der fremdtseykhn, quotation mark
der freser (G), gourmand
fresn (G), to eat like an animal, to wolf
di freyd (G), joy
der freyd-farshterer, killjoy
freylekh (G), cheerful, happy; "dos
  freylekhs", "a cheerful tune"
di freylekhkeyt, cheer, happiness
fri (G), early
der friling (G), spring, (season)
frirn (G), to freeze
di froy (G), wife, woman
frum (G), orthodox, pious
der frumak (G-R), bigoted, fanatical
fuftsik (G), fifty
fuftsn (G), fifteen
ful (mit) (G), full of, lots, much, plenty
fun (G), from, of
fundestvegn (Y-G), however,
  nevertheless
der funt (n) (G), pound
der furgon-oyto, station wagon
der fus (pl. fis) (G), foot, leg
der futer, fur, fur coat
di fyalke (G), violet (flower)

G

der gabe (G), synagogue trustee, (pl.
  gaboyim)
di gabete (G), wife of "gabe"
dos gadles (H), arrogance, conceit,
  pride
der galekh (H), priest
der ganef (H), rascal, thief, (see
  "khoyshed zayn")
der gan-eydn (H), garden of Eden,
  paradise
der gang (n) (G), conduct, course, way
gants (G), all, whole; "in gantsn",
  altogether, fully, quite

gants (G), quite
gantsdilik (Y-G), wall-to-wall, (whole
  floor)
ganvenen (H), to steal
di ganz (G), (pl. genz) goose, ("silly
  woman", as "goose" in Eng.)
di gas (G), street; "oyf der yidisher gas",
  in Jewish society
der gast (G), guest
gatkes (R), long underwear
dos gavres (H), virility
di gayve (H), haughtiness, pride
der gazlen (H), robber
di gdule (H), glory, grandeur, (a word
  of mockery, sarcasm); "a gdule oyf
  zayn bobe", "much joy to his
  grandmother" (sarcastic); "a groyse
  gdule", a big deal (sarcastic)
gebildt (G), well educated
gebn (G), to give
der gedank (n) (G), idea, thought
di gedanken-keyt, train of thought
gedenken (G), to remember
gedenkevdik, memorable
der geder, limitation, restraint
gederem (H), intestines
der gedoyer, duration
gedoyerdik, long-lasting
gedoyern, to continue, to last
dos gedrang, congestion, implication,
  inference, throng
gedroln (G), afflicted with varicose
  veins
gedrungen (zayn g.), be implied,
  follow
di geduld (G), fortitude, patience
geduldik, patient
di geduldshpil, puzzle
di gefar (G), danger
gefeln (G), to please; "epes gefelstu mir
  nit haynt", "somehow you don't please
  me to-day" (in reference to health)
geferlekh (G), frightening, terrible
dos gefilekhts (n) (G), filling, stuffing

gefilte (G), stuffed; "gefilte fish", "boiled chopped fish balls" (technically should be called gehakte fish (chopped fish))

gefinen, to find

geflokhtn (G), braided

gegangen (G), gone

dos gehalt (G), salary

dos gehenem (H), hell

gel (G), yellow

dos gelekhter (G), laughter

dos gelenk (hant-gelenk), wrist

der gelernter (G), a learned man

dos gelt (G), funds, money

gemasert (H), denounced

gematert (G), far-fetched, forced, laboured; "siz a gematert, gemutshet lebn", "it's a dog's life" (see "gemutshet")

gemeynt (G), alleged

gemolt, imagined, painted; "es ken gemolt zayn", "it is possible"; "es ken nit gemolt zayn", "it is impossible"

di gemore (H), Talmud

gemutshet (R), tormented, tortured

der general (Y), general, overhead (expenses)

di geneyve (ganeyve) (H), larceny, theft

genitsevet (R), altered, turned (as a coat)

genoy (G), exactly

genug (G), enough

ge'oynish (adj) (H), brilliant, extremely intelligent

der ger (H), proselyte to Judaism

dos geretenish (Y-G), crop, plentiful harvest, plenty

dos gesheft (G), business

der gesheftsman (G), businessman

di geshikhte (G), history, story

geshmadt (H), converted from Judaism to another religion

dos geshrey (G), a scream, a shriek

dos geshtank (n), stench

geshtoygn (G), "nit geshtoygn nit gefloygn", entirely untrue (lit. neither arose nor flew) (in reference to Christ)

geshvister (G), brothers and sisters, siblings

geshvoln (G), swollen; "geshvoln vern", to swell

der get (n) (H), divorce

getn (H), to divorce

di geule (H), the coming of the messiah, the redemption of the Jews

gevald (gevalt, gvald, gvalt) (G), a clamour, "HELP!"

di gevald (gvald), force, violence; "er hot es genumen mit gevald", "he took it by force"

gevaldeven (gvaldeven) (G), rant, rave, scream, shriek

"gevald geshrign" (geshrien) (G), "for G-D's sake!", "how can it be?", "utterly impossible!"

geveltikn (n) (G), to dominate, to rule

di geveltikung, domination

geven (G), (has) been, was

dos geveyn (G), lament; "mit geveyn", "tearfully"

geveynen zikh, to get used to

geveynt, accustomed to, used to

geveyntlekh, common, commonly, usual, usually

gevinen (G), to win, to win over

dos gevins, gain, prize, winnings

gevorn (G), became

gevor vern (gevoyr vern) (G), to discover, to find out, to learn

geyik, acceptable, current

geyn (G), to go

dos gezeml (G), a clump, a cluster, a collection, a crowd, a gathering

gezen (G), seen

dos gezikht (G), countenance, face, (n)

gezolt zayn (G), should have happened

gezunt (adj) (G), healthy, strong

dos gezunt (n) (G), health, strength; "a gezunt dir in kepele", "bless your dear little head"; "tsu gezunt", G-d bless you (in response to a sneeze), may this help you (upon administering medicine)

"gezunterheyt", in good health, with the best of luck

der giber (H), hero; "shimshn agiber", Samson

gikh (G), quickly, rapid

gildn (G), golden

der gildn, zloty

dos gile-aroyes (H), incest (Jewish)

der gilgl (H), reincarnation

glat (G), flat, smooth, smoothly; "glat azoy", "just so", "without a special purpose"

glaykh (G), even, good, just, straight

di glaykhheyt, equallity

dos glaykhvort (glaykhvertl) (G), anecdote, joke

di glezele (G), small glass

dos glezl (G), lens, small drinking glass

gliklekh (G), happy, lucky

der glok (G), bell

der gloybn (n), belief, conviction, faith

gloybn (gleybn) (v), to believe

dos gloz (n) (G), glass (drinking and material); (pl. glezer)

dos gmiles-khesed (H), interest-free loan

gneyvish (H), rascally, (sometimes used to describe ingenuity, trickery)

di gnod, favour, grace, mercy

gnoteven, to oppress

der godl (H), great man, V.I.P

der goen (H), scholar of unusual brilliance; "a goen oylem", "a world genius"

der goles (H), diaspora, exile

gomur (H), complete

der gopl, electric plug, (table) fork

gor (G), altogether, quite

der goresh (H), divorcé, divorced man

der gorgl (gergele) (G), Adam's apple, larynx, throat

gornit (gornisht) (G), nothing

der gornit, a good-for-nothing, a nobody

der got (G), G-D

gotenyu (G), G-D (affectionate diminutive) "dear G-D", "holy smoke!"

der goy, gentile man

di goye, gentile woman

Goyml (H), prayer said by Jews after escaping great danger

der goyrl (H), fate, lot (I.O.)

der goyses (H), person dying

goysesn, be dying, be in mortal agony

goyver zayn (H-Y), to conquer, to overcome; "er iz goyver geven", "he mastered himself"; "nit goyver tsu zayn", invincible

goyzer zayn (H-Y), to decree (something unfavourable); "er iz goyzer", "he decrees"

graylekh, most certainly, with pleasure

grestn (G), greatest

greyt (G), prepared, ready

greytn, to prepare; "greytn tsum tish", set the table

gribenes (grivn), rendered fat

griblen zikh, to bore into, to brood, to rack one's brains

grin (G), green; "ikh bin gel un grin gevorn", "I was flabbergasted"

gring (G), easy, light (in weight)

der grus (n) (G), regards; "mit grus, ayer/dayn", sincerely yours

gro (groy), grey

grob (G), fat, thick; "der grober yung", "boor"

der groshn (R), penny, (pennyworth), small coin

groys, large

dos groz (G), grass

di grushe (H), divorced woman, divorcée

der gubernator (G), governor

der guf (H), body

der guf-geboy, physique

di gumiḷazye (R) (coll.), high school

gut (G), good, well; "gants gut", "quite well", "very good"

der guter-bruder (G), friend

di guzme (H), exaggeration

der gvaldglok, burgler alarm

gvaldik, mighty, terrific

gvaldovne! (G-R), TERRIFIC! (comically)

der gvar (H), a strong, manly person

der gvir (H), rich man

der gvir adir (H), "mighty rich man"

di gvirishaft (H-G), riches, wealth

der gvul (H), boundary, domain, limit

di gzeyre (H), evil decree (aways stern)

H

hafle-vofele (H), amazing, "miracle upon miracle", remarkable

di hakkhoshe (H), denial, retraction

"haklal", "aklal", (like "nu") (H), "be that as it may", "to make a long story short", etc

hakn (G), to chop; "hakn a tshaynik", bother (bang a teapot), "to chatter, argue endlessly"; "hakn in", to beat violently

hakodesh-borkhu (H), , "the Holy One, blessed be He", the Lord

hakofes (H), synagogue procession carrying the Torah scrolls

der haldz (G), neck, throat; "du zoltst zikh shemn in dayn vaytn haldz", "shame on you" (blush deep down in your throat); "ibern haldz", more than enough; "krikhn fun haldz", be coming out of one's ears

halevay (H), would that; "der halevay-gedank" (H-G), "wishful thinking"

di halokhe (H), religious law of Judaism (lit. "Going the way one should go")

haltn (G), to believe, to engage in, to hold; "haltn baym", to be about to; "haltn in eyn ... ", to continually do something; "Haltn milkhome", "Be at war"; "Ikh halt punkt farkert", "I believe the exact opposite"

di halvoe (n) (H), loan

di hamtsoe (H), device, idea

der handl, commerce, dealings, trade

handlen, to act (behaviour), to proceed; "handlen in", to deal in, to trade

di handlung (G), action, deed

di hanoe (hanoye) (H), enjoyment, fun, pleasure; "hanoe hobn" (H-Y), enjoy oneself

di hant (G), hand, (pl. hent)

der/dos hantekh (G), towel

dos hantgelenk (gelenk), wrist

der har, lord, master, owner

der harbst (G), autumn

hargenen (H), to kill, to murder; "ver gerharget!", "Drop dead!"

di harmonye, accordion, harmony

dos harts (G), heart, shirt front; "es iz mir arop a shteyn fun hartsn", "I got a load off my chest" (a stone off my heart); "fun tifn hartsn", "from the bottom of my heart"

der has, hatred

hashem-yisborekh (H), the Lord; (lit. blessed name)

di hashgokhe (H), care, custody, providence (G-D), supervision

di hashpoe (n) (H), influence

hashpoedik, influential

di hashtone (H), urine

di haskole (H), the Jewish Enlightenment movement in the 19th century

di haskome (H), agreement, approval, consent

hasn (G), to despise, to hate

di hatslokhe (H), success

di havdole (H), division, separation (Jewish) (ceremony separating the Sabbath from the week)

di havtokhe (H), a pledge, a promise
haynt (G), to-day
hayntik (G-Y), modern
haynt-morgn, any day now
hayntveltik (G-Y), modern
hayoytse midvoreynu (H), it follows from what we said
hebreyish (adj), Hebrew
dos hebreyish, Hebrew (language)
hefker (H), ownerless, worthless; "hefker petrishke" ("worthless parsley"); "hefker tsibeles" (H-R), "everything goes" ("worthless onions")
dos hekdesh (H), filthy place, (flophouse)
hekher (G), higher, louder
hekhern (G), to promote, to raise (prices or wages)
di hekherung, promotion, raise
der held (G), hero; "der groyser held", "big-shot" (big hero)
helfn (G), to help
dos hemd (G), shirt; "dos letste hemd", the shirt off one's back
dos hemdl, book jacket; "blaybn in eyn hemd", become destitute
hengen (G), to hang
der henglaykhter (G), chandelier
di hentshke(s) (Y), glove(s)
herevdik, audible
hern (G), to hear, to obey
der her-un-tref (Y-G), quiz, quiz program, (hear and guess)
di hesofe (n) (H), raise (in pay)
der hesped (H), eulogy, (funeral oration)
di hetsoe(s) (H), cost(s), expenditure(s), expense(s)
dos heybekhts, pep, vim
di heybmashin, elevator
heybn (G), to be indignant, to lift; "es heybt im", he is indignant; "heybn in himl arayn", exhalt, "to praise to the skies"
heylik (G), holy

di heym (H), home; "di alte heym", the Old Country; "in der heym", at home
heymish (G), cosy, domestic; "dos heymishe shtetl", "cosy village"; "der heymisher mentsh" (G), "just folks", "one of our kind"
der heymplats, homestead
der heypekh (H), contrary, opposite; "leheypekh", "on the contrary"
der heyrat (G), marriage (in disuse, di khasene (H), is better)
heys (G), hot
heysn (v) (G), call, tell; "vi heystu?", "what are you called?", "what's your name?"
heyzerik (G), hoarse, sore throat
der hezek (H), a loss
der higer (G), local (man)
der hikevatn (G), one who stammers
der himl (G), heaven, sky
di himl-linye, sky-line
di hindl (hun) (G), chicken, hen
der hinkediker, lame person, limping person
hinken (G), to limp
hintish (adj), canine, mean, rotten
dos hintl, pup
hintn (G), behind, in back
der hintn (n) (G), back, behind (body part-seat), rear
hipsh (adj), considerable, sizable; "a hipshe bisl", "quite a few"
historishe (G), historic
di historye, history, tale
der hiter, custodian, guard, guardian
dos hitl (G), cap, hat
hitn, to guard, to observe, to protect, to take care of; "hit zikh", "beware of', "watch out"
di hits (n) (G), fervour, fever, heat, hot spell, violence
hobn (G), to give birth, to have
di hodevanye, upbringing
hodeven (R), to breed, to bring up, to cultivate, to feed, to raise, to rear; "hodeven di genz", "to breed geese"
der hodever, breeder, grower

di họfenung, hope

họferdik (adj) (G), chipper, self-confident

hofn (G), to hope

họleptses (khọleptses), cabbage rolls, stuffed cabbage

holt-họbn, to be fond of, to care for, to like; "ikh hob ir holt", "I like her"

dos holts (G), wood

homen (H), Haman (anti-Jewish, Persian minister of old)

der hon (hendl) (G), rooster, (pl. hener)

der họnik (G), honey; "honik lekn", "to have it good" (always in the negative); "bay im hob ikh keyn honik nit gelekt", "I didn't have an easy time with him"; "ir hot in belsen keyn honik nit gelekt?", "you had a hard time in Belsen?", "mentsh! men hot unz sogar keyn sakharin gegebn!", "man, they hardly gave us any saccharin"

di hor (G), bit, hair, iota; "a hor greser", a bit larger; "hengen oyf a hor", to hang on a thread (hair)

der horb (R), hump, hunchback

hot (G), has

dos họtseplots, a remote place; "fun họtseplots", from heaven knows where

der hoyker, a hump, a hunchback

hoykerdik (adj), hunchbacked

der hoykerdiker (n), a hunchbacked person

hoykh (G), high, tall

di hoyt, flesh, skin; "hoyt un beyner", skin and bones; "fun heler hoyt", out of thin air

der hoyz (G), pant leg

dos hoyz (n) (G), house

hoyzn, pants, trousers

der hoz, hare; "shisn tsvey hozn mit eyn shos", "kill two birds with one stone" (shoot two hares with one shot)

der hu-ha!, bustle, hullaballoo, to-do, Wow!

der hụltay, debauchee, person of loose morals

hulyen (R), to carouse; "a hulye ton", "to have a fling"

di hun (hindl) (G), chicken, hen; (pl. hiner); "der alter hiner freser", "oldtimer", "tough old rooster" (old chicken eater)

der hundert (G), hundred

der hunger (G), famine, hunger, starvation

hungerik, hungry

hungern (G), to be hungry

der hụngertoyt, starvation

der hunt (G), dog, (pl. hint)

der hust, cough

hustn (G), to cough

I

"i . . . i" (Y), "both . . . and"

"i dos", even then

iber (G), over

iberbetn (G), to beg pardon; "iberbetn zikh", "to make up"

ịberblaybn (G), leave over, remain

der ịberfal (G-Y), an ambush

iberfaln (G-Y), to ambush, to assail, to attack

iberfirn (G-Y), to ruin (transitive), to spoil

iberfirn zikh (intransitive), be spoiled, to spoil

iberforn (G-Y), overtake (by vehicle), to run over

ibergeblibn (G), left over

iberhipern (iberhipn), to omit, to pass over, to skip

iberik (Y), left over, overly, particularly, superfluous

di ịberikeyt, redundancy

iberkern (G), to switch, to turn over, to twist around; "iberkern dem pelts", "switch loyalties"

der iberkler, hesitation

iberklerik, hesitant

iberklern (G), to reconsider, to think over; "nit iberklerndik", indiscriminately

iberton (G-Y), to change clothes of; "iberton zikh", change one's clothes

ibertraybn (G), to exaggerate, to overdo

dos iber-yor (H-Y), leap year

der iker (H), principle; "der iker", above all, especially

ikh (G), I, me

der ikh, ego

di ikhed shtible (H-G), private room for bride and groom

der ile (H), genius, scholar-prodigy, (pl. iluim)

im (G), him

der impet (Y), impetus, momentum; "flien/forn mitn impet aleyn", to coast (fly/drive with momentum alone)

der impetveg (Y-G), runway

der imshtand (shtand) (Y), standing, station, walk of life

di imyenye (R), estate

"im yirtse hashem" (H), G-D willing, "if it pleases G-D" (often pronounced mirtseshem or mirtshem)

der indik (R), a turkey

der ingber (G), ginger

dos ingber-vaser, ginger-ale

inteligent (adj), intelligent

der(/di) inteligent(ke) (G), intelligent (wo)man

di inteligents, intelligence, intelligentsia

der inteligents-vifler, I.Q.

der inyen (H), matter, subject, (pl. inyonim); "kolishe inyonim", "communal affairs" (public life)

der ipesh (H), a bad odour, a stench, a stink

ipeshn (v), to stink

ir (G), you (2nd person pl.)

ir (G), her

ire (G), your

di ir habiro (H), capital city

di italye, Italy

der italyener (G), Italian (person)

italyenish (adj), Italian

dos italyenish (italeynish), Italian (language)

itst, now (yetst)

itster (G), now

iz (G), is

der izmenik (R), traitor

K

der kaas (H), anger; "in kaas", "angry, annoyed"

kaasn zikh oyf (H-Y), be angry at

der kaboles-kinyen (H), acceptance of the purchase (in a shidekh (betrothal)) (Jewish)

der kadish (H), prayer for the dead (Jewish)

dos kadokhes (H), fever; "a naynyorik kadokhes", "a nine year fever" (a curse); "es toyg oyf kadokhes", "it's worthless"

der kaftn, a gabardine, a topcoat (worn by observant Jews)

kakhabe (H), actually, exactly

kakn, to defecate

di kale (H), bride

di kale-moyd (H-G), girl, (eligible spinster)

kalemutne (R), dejected, gloomy

der kalendar (G), calendar (non-Jewish dates)

kalt (adj) (G), cold

der kam (keml), comb, crest (of a mountain), ridge

kamo shonim (H), how many years

der kamtsn (H), miser, stingy person

di kane, enema

der/di kant, edge, rim
der kant, county, region
der kantshik, "cat-o'-nine-tails" (whip)
der kap, cape (land), drop, little bit
der kapelyush (R), derby hat
der kapelyush-makher (R-G), big shot, (lit. hat-maker, "brass hat")
kapen (v) (R), drip, drop, hang, trickle
dos kapetshke (R), a drop, a little, a tiny bit
der kapital (G), capital, funds
der/dos kapitl (G), chapter (of a book); "onheybn a nay kapitl", to turn over a new leaf
di kapore (H), Yom-Kippur scapegoat fowl (Jewish); "a sheyne reyne kapore" (G-H), (always this order of words) "good riddance", serves him right!
kapores (H), atonement (Jewish), religious ceremony; "es toyg oyf kapores", "it's good for nothing"; "oyf kapores!", "like a hole in the head"; "shlogn kapores", "beating the animal (or fowl) of atonement" (Jewish ritual)
di kapote (R), top coat (gabardine) (Jewish)
kapoyer, reverse, topsy-turvy, upside down
der kaptsn (H), pauper, poor man, (connotation more subtle than "oreman"); "kaptsn! vu krikhstu?", "kaptsn!, know your place!"
karbn (v), to notch, to score
di karete (R), carriage, chariot, coach
karg, almost, not enough, stingy; "a karger vokh", "almost a week" (a stingy week)
der karger, stingy person
karik (adv), back
di karsh (G), cherry; "makhn a karsh", to pucker up/purse one's lips
di kashe (R), porridge; "farkokhn a kashe", "brew up trouble" (to cook up a stew)
di kashe (n) (H), question

der kasril (H), cheerful pauper, "orem ober freylekh" (poor but happy)
kasrilevke (H-Y), any mythical far-off place, Sholem Aleichem's mythical town
der kater (Y), catarrh, cold, (cloth) cutter (jargon), (ship) cutter
der katoves, fun, jest; "on katoves", "no joke", "seriously"; "oyf katoves", "for fun", "in jest"
di kats (ketsl) (G), cat
der katsef (H), butcher
di katshke (R), a duck, ("gabby woman")
der katukh (R), chicken coop
di kave (R), coffee
di kavone (H), intent, motive
kavyokhl (H), as if it could be possible (re: G-D)
kayen (G), to chew
der kayer, jaw
kayklen (G), to roll. ("rock with laughter")
kaylekhdik (kaylekhik), globular, round
kayln (v) (R), to slaughter (in a non-kosher way); "er hot mikh gekoylet on a meser", "he ruined me" (he slaughtered me without a knife)
der kaysn (H), short-tempered man, (one who flies off the handle easily)
di kdushe (H), holiness, sanctity
keday (H), advisable, worthwhile; "siz nit keday", "it's not worth (doing or going etc.)"
kedey (H), in order that
kegn (G), against, opposite
di kehile (H), community, congregation, organized Jewish community
der keler (G), cellar
der kelev (H), a mean person, a vicious dog
der kelner, waiter
dos keml (G), camel, comb
kenen (G), able to, to know (language, skill), to recognize

kenen oysnveynik (G), to know by heart

der kener (G), connoisseur, expert, one who knows

kentik (G), apparent, marked, noticeable, visible

dos kerbl, ruble, Russian coin

der kern (n), kernel, nucleus

kern (v) (G), to sweep

kern (v) (G), turn around, turn over, turn up

kern (v), may, might; "zey kern veln epes", they may want something

di keshene (R), pocket, pocketbook (coll)

der keshene-ganef (R-H), pickpocket

di kest, chestnut, room and board (Jewish)

di keyle (H), instrument, vessel; "di puste keyle", "empty headed (windbag)"; "di tayere keyle", "subtle brain"

keyn (G), no, not, to, towards (travel to plus country); "ikh for keyn Miami", "I'm travelling to Miami"; "ikh hob nit keyn . . . ", "I don't have any . . . "; "keyn ayen-hore" ("keyn eyn hore"), "knock on wood" (no evil eye)

keyner (G), no one

keynmol (G), never

di keyt, chain, mountain range

der keyver (n) (H), grave, tomb; "der keyver oves" (H), "grave of the fathers"; "der keyver-yisroel" (H), "Jewish grave"

der kez (G), cheese

der khabar (R), a bribe

khakhatuln, to laugh out loud

der khakren (H), speculative thinker

di khale (H), braided white loaf of bread, Sabbath bread

khaleshn (H), to faint

der khalfn (H), money changer

dos khaloshes (H), faint, nausea, weakness

di khaluke (H), charity fund, partition

der kham, boor, cad, extremely rude person

der khamer (H), ass, blockhead

"dos khaneles eygele" (H-G), pansy (little Hannah's eye)

khanfenen (H), to flatter, "ir khanfet mir" is highly offensive; "khanfenen zikh", engage in flattery

der khanike (H), Chanukah, feast of the Maccabees, festival of lights

der khap (R), a clasp, a grip, a snatch; "mit a khap", "with a start"

khap-lap (khap-lap-tsap) (R), haphazardly, helter-skelter

khapn (R), to catch, to snatch; "khap nit" (R-G), don't grab, "take it easy"; "khapn zikh", "remember suddenly"; "khapn zikh tsu", to throw oneself at

der kharakter (G), character

der kharif (H), brilliant, sharp-minded one (in Talmud)

dos kharifes (H), acumen, sagacity

di kharote (H), changing one's mind, regret, remorse

kharote hobn (v) (H-Y), to regret, to repent

di kharpe (H), disgrace

di khasene (H), wedding; "khasene hobn", "get married"

di khasene gehate (H-G), married woman

der khasene gehater (H-G), married man

khas-vekholile (H), G-D forbid

khas-vesholem (H), G-D forbid

di khate (R), cabin, hut, peasant cottage

der khaver (H), fellow, friend (pl. khaveyrim)

di khaverte (H), comrade, girl friend

di khaye (H), animal, beast, living thing; "di vilde khaye" (Y-H), wild animal

dos khayil (H), army, troops; "eyshes khayil" (H), "woman of valor" (housewife)

dos khayim (H), life; "lekhayim", "to life"; "makhn a lekhayim", to toast (make a to life)

khay kak (R), worthless

der khazer (H), greedy person, pig, (pl. khazeyrim); "az men est khazer, zol rinen iber dem moyl", "go the whole hog", "in for a penny, in for a pound" (when one eats pig, it should run over his mouth); "lebn a khazershn tog", "living it up"; "vil men zayn a gvir, darf men zikh farshraybn oyf tsvantsik yor a khazer", "if one wants to become a rich man, one must sign up for twenty years as a swine"

der/di khazer-shtal (H-G), filthy house, pigsty

der khazn (H), cantor

di khaznte (H), cantor's wife

der khesed (H), loving-kindness; "der gmiles khesed" (H), "interest-free loan"; "khesed shel emes" (H), "true grace"

di khevre (H), association, group; "di khevre-kedishe" (H), "burial society" (voluntary) (Jewish)

der kheyder (H), room; (pl. khadorim), after-hours Hebrew classes

dos kheylev (n) (H), fat, tallow

der kheylik (H), part, portion, (pl. khalokim)

der kheyn (H), charisma, charm

dos kheyn-gribele(kh) (H-G), dimple(s)

der kheyrem (H), ban, excommunication (Jewish)

der kheyshik (H), eagerness, patience; "hobn kheyshik tsu", have a mind to

di kheyune (H), livelihood, living, means of support; "tsien kheyune fun", "make a living from"

khezhbenen (H), to calculate

der khezhbm (H), an accounting, bill, estimate; "der khezhbn-hanefesh" (H), "accounting of the soul", introspection, meditation

der khiber (H), addition, composition

di khiber-mashin (H), adding machine

der khilel (H), desecration, violation; "der khilel-hames" (H), "desecration of the dead"; "der khilel-hashem" (H), blasphemy (desecration of the name); "der khilel-haziveg", adultery (desecration of marriage)

di khine, China

der khinezer, Chinese person

khinezish (adj), Chinese

dos khinezish (language), Chinese

der khisorn (H), a defect (in character); (pl. khesroynes)

der khitrak, sly person

khitre (R), crafty, sly

di khitrekeyt, craft, cunning

khlebn (Y-G), honestly, (contraction of "ikh zol azoy lebn", "I should live so")

khlipen (R), to sob

di khmare (R), a cloud

di khnife (H), flattery, toadying

der khnyok (R), bigot, oaf, unreasonable conservative

der khokhm (H), sage, wise guy (pl. khakhomim) (pl. used only for sages of old)

di khokhme (H), wisdom, wise crack

der kholem (H), a dream (pl. khaloymes); "poyser kholem zayn", "to interpret a dream"

kholemen (H), to dream

di kholere (kholerye), cholera; "a kholere (kholerye) oyf im", "to hell with him"

kholile (H), G-D forbid

der khomets (H), non-kosher bread during Passover (Jewish)

der khor (G), choir

khorev (adj) (H), destroyed, waste; "khorev makhn" (H-Y), to annihilate, to destroy, to ruin

khoser-deye (H), insane

khoshev (H), esteemed, important

der khoshev (H), dignitary

der khosid (H), Chasid, pious man

der khosn (H), bridegroom, (pl. khasanim); "der khosn-bokher (H), eligible (marriageable) man; "khosn doyme lemelekh", "a bridegroom is like a king"

der khotsef (H), an arrogant man

khotsh (R), although, at least, if only, one might as well

khotshbe (R), at least

khotshe (R), see khotsh

khotsi (H), half

der khoydesh (H), month; (pl. khadoshim)

der khoyle (H), a patient, a sick person; "der khoyle-mesuken" (H), dangerously ill person; "der royfe-khoylim", "healer of the sick"

der khoynef (H), flatterer, sycophant

khoyshed zayn (H-G), suspect of

der khoyshekh (H), darkness, gloom; "es tut zikh khoyshekh", "all hell has broken loose"

der khoyv (H), a debt

der khoyzek (H), derision, mockery, ridicule; "es hot a ponim fun khoyzek", "it looks ludicrous"; "makhn khoyzek", "to mock"

khoyzekdik (H), ludicrous

der khreyn (R), horse radish

khropen (R), to snore

der khruz (kruz) (H), proclamation (rabbinical)

der khshad (H), suspicion; "hobn a khshad" (Y-H), to suspect

dos khshives (H), importance (things as well as persons), prestige

der khtsos (H), midnight prayers and study (Jewish); "oprikhtn khtsos", "rise at midnight for study and prayers (Jewish)"

der khumesh (H), five books of Moses, the Pentateuch

di khupe (H), (wedding) canopy (Jewish)

di khupe-vetshere (H-R), wedding supper

der khurbm (H), catastrophe, damage, destruction, "the Holocaust"

di khutspe (H), arrogance, gall, nerve

di khvalye (R), a wave

der khvat (R), a brave and clever young man

der kibed (H), refreshments to visitors, tribute; (pl. kibudim); "tsuteyln di kibudim", "to do the honours"

"der kibed-av, kibed-eym" (kibed-av-voeym), "honour due one's father, honour due one's mother"

der kidesh (H), benediction over wine (Jewish); "der kidesh-hashem" (H), martyrdom for being a Jew (Jewish)

dos kikhl(ekh) (G), cookie(s)

kil (adj) (G), aloof, cool

di kile (n) (R), hernia, rupture

kimat (H), almost; "kimat hot a mol dem taytsh fun gornit", "a miss is as good as a mile" ('almost' can sometimes be translated as 'nothing')

der kiml, caraway seeds (no pl.)

di kimpet, childbirth, labour

dos kind (G), child; "geyn tsu kind", "to be in labour"; "kind-un-keyt" (G), kit and caboodle, kith and kin, "young and old"

kinderlekh (G), little children

der kindl-kontrol, birth control

di kine (n) (H), envy

der kinig (n), king

der kintsler (G), artist (painter)

der kise-hakoved (H), G-d's throne

der kishef (H), magic, witchcraft

der kishef-makher (H-G), magician

di kishke (R), hose, intestine, stuffed derma; "di blinde kishke", appendix; "di grobe kishke", colon; "di grode kishke", rectum

der kit (R), putty

der kitayets (R), Chinese

der kitser (n) (H), abstract, summary; "a kitser", "in a word", "in short"

der kitsl, tickle

kitsldik, ticklish

kitslen, to tickle
di kitsve (H), dole, public charity
di kladke (klatke) (R), foot bridge
di klafte (H), bitch, (female dog)
der klal (H), community at large, the
public; "der klal-tuer", community
leader, one active in community work;
"der klal-yisroel", "community of
Israel", Jewry, "Jews as a whole"
der klap, blow, hit
klapn (G), to bang, to clap, to make a
noise
klaybn (G), to collect, to gather, to
pick
klekn, suffice, to be sufficient
klekoydesh, clergy (Jewish)
klener (G), smaller
klenst (G), smallest
klepn (G), to glue, to paste, to stick;
"klepn zikh", to adhere, to cling to, to
stick to
klern (G), to contemplate, to purify, to
think
kleterbleter (G), climber leaves, ivy
di kletke (R), a cage
dos kleyd (G), a dress, a gown
di kleyderbarsht, whisk broom
di kleydung (G), apparel, clothing
kleyn (G), small
di kleynikeyt (G), small thing, trifle;
"eyn kleynikeyt!", "no small thing!",
"what a bother!", "wow!"
di kleyt (R), a shop
dos klezayin (H), arm, arms, weapon
der klezmer (H), musician (pl.
klezmorim)
der klin (G), a wedge
klingen (G), to phone, to ring, to
sound
klingers (G), coins (that which rings),
dough (money)
di klipe (H), demon, evil spirit, shrew
der klistir, enema
di klole (H), a curse
klor (G), clear (adj)
der klots (G), wooden beam; (coll.),
clumsy person (klats), dolt

di klots-kashe (G-H), perplexing
question, stupid question
kloymersht (H), allegedly, as it were,
ostensibly, so to speak
der kloyster (G), church
di kloyz (G), chapel, small synagogue
klug (G), clever
der klump (n) (G), clump
di klyamke (R), door handle, knob
di klyatshe (R), mare
der knaker (hum.), bigshot, braggart,
smart aleck
dos knasmol (G), betrothal dinner
kneln (hum.), to teach
dos kneydl, dumpling, pudding ball
(pl. kneydlekh)
dos kneytl, synagogue candle; "leygn
kneytlekh", "to make things worse for
someone being punished"
dos knipl (G), hoard of savings or
some money (tied in a corner of a
handkerchief or in a sock), knot
knipl-beknipl (G), palsy-walsy
der knish (R), meat bun
der knobl (G), garlic
der kodesh (H), holy man, martyr
(Jewish), saint; "shpringen kodesh",
toadying (to rise on toes and fall back
on heels) (in the synagogue)
der kodshe-kodoshim (H), holy of
holies, inner sanctum
dos koel (H), community (Jewish)
dos kokhn (n), cooking
kokhn (v) (G), to cook
dos kol (H), voice
der kolboynik (H-R), a rascally know-
it-all, jack of all trades
di kolboynitse (H-R), female know-it-
all
kolishe (H), communal
kol miney (H), all kinds
der kolner (R), a collar
der kol nidre (H), prayer on the eve of
Yom Kippur (Jewish)
kolzman (H), as long as
der komets (H), symbol for
pronunciation "O" under "alef'

der kompliment (G), compliment
di konferents (G), conference
der kop (G), head; "geyn mitn kop durkh der vant", "knock yourself out", "to do the impossible"; "zikh shlogn kop in vant", "beat your brains out", "to carry on without hope"
dos kop-dreyenish (G), bother, mental confusion, worry
der korbm (n) (H), sacrifice, victim; "er iz a korbn fun zayn eygener akshones", "he is the victim of his own obstinacy" (pl. korbones)
der korev (H), a relative; (pl. kroyvim)
di kort (n), playing card; "makhn a kertl", to have a game of cards; "shpiln in kortn" (v), to play cards
di kose (n) (R), scythe
kosher (H), honest, ritually clean (Jewish); "der khazer shtelt aroys dos koshere fisl", "put over a fraud" (the pig thrusts out its kosher little leg)
der koshik (R), basket
koshn (R), to mow
di kotinke (R), kitten, pussycat (term of endearment)
der koved (n) (H), honour, respect
koydem kol (H), first of all
der koyekh (H), strength; (pl. koykhes)
der koyen (H), priest (Jewish)
der koyfer-beiker (H), agnostic, atheist, one who denies the existence of G-D
koyfn, to buy
di koyl, ball, bullet, coal, sphere
der koyletsh (R), braided white loaf of bread
koym, barely, scarcely; "koym-koym", by the skin of one's teeth"; "koym mit tsores", "at long last", "with great difficulty"
der koymen, chimney, smokestack
der koymen-kerer, chimneysweep
der koyne (H), customer
der koyp (n), hill, pile

koyrim faln (H-Y), to kneel (in religious service)
der kozak (R), Cossak
der kramp (n) (G), cramp
di krankn-shvester (n) (G), nurse
dos krankn-shvesteray (n) (G), nursing
di krasavitse (R), beautiful woman
der krats (G), a scratch
kratsn (G), to stratch
dos kraytekhts(er) (G), herb(s)
der krekhts, moan
krekhtsn (Y), to complain, to groan
di krenk (G), disease, sickness
krenken (G), to be sick, to mortify, to sicken; "oyskrenken" (coll.), "to regret", "to suffer for"
krepirn (G) (coll.), to croak, to suffer (not of animals)
dos krepl(ekh) (R), meat-filled turnover(s)
di kretshme (R), inn, tavern
der kretshmer, innkeeper
kreynele (Y-G), sweetheart! (my little crown) (title)
di krig (n) (G), fight, quarrel, war
krign (v), to get, to obtain, to war
krign zikh (v), to quarrel
krikhn (G), to crawl
der krizh (R), small of the back
di krom (R), a store
di kropeve (R), stinging nettle
krum (G), crooked, lame
der ksav (n) (H), writing; (pl. ksovim)
di ksube (H), marriage contract (Jewish); (pl. ksubes)
di ku (G), a cow; (pl. ki)
kuflshmoynedik (H), eightfold
der kugl (G), pudding
kukn (G), to look
di kulye (R), bundle (straw), crutch
kumen (G), to come
kumendik (G), coming, due, next
der kuneleml (H), an awkward, clumsy, naive person
der kupe, railroad compartment
di kupe (R), a heap
kurts (G), short

der kush, kiss; "a kush gebn/ton", to kiss
kushn (G), to kiss
di kushvokh (Y-G), honeymoon (kiss week)
kveln (Y), to gloat, to take pride
der kvetsh (n) (G), squeeze; (coll.), a crank
kvetshn (G), to squeeze
der kvitsh, scream
kvitshen (v), to scream, to shriek
di kvure (H), burial; "brengen tsu kvure", "to bring to burial"

L

der lakey, lackey
lakhn (G), to laugh
der laks, lox, salmon, smoked salmon
der lamdn (H), scholar
der landsman (G), countryman, old-country man
der landsmanshaft (G), association of old-country men
lang (G), long
di lape (R), claw, paw; (coll. for "large hand")
di laske (R), kindness (condescendingly)
di late (R), a patch; "leygn lates", to patch, to sew on patches
di latke (R), pancake
dos layb (G), body, flesh
der laybserdak (G-R), Jewish religious undergarment (see arbe kanfes)
der laybserdrek (G-R), contemptuous expression for "laybserdak"
dos layb-tsudekl (G), body coverlet to which "tsitses" are attached
laydn (G), to bear, to suffer
di laydnshaft (G), passion
layehudim (zayn l.) (Y-H) (hum.) (Jewish), there is gaiety, there is joy, there is rejoicing

layen (v), to lend to
layen bay, to borrow from
laykht (G), easy
laykhter (G), easier
der laykhter, candlestick
der laylekh, bed sheet
der layt, adult, (respectable) people
di layvnt, canvas, felt (material), linen
lebedik (G), alive, lively
di leber (G), liver
lebn, alongside, next to
dos lebn (n) (G), life
lebn (v), to live (be alive)
dos lefele (lefl) (G-Y), pit of the stomach, teaspoon
der lefl (G), spoon, (tablespoon), spoonful
der lehakhesnik (H), a defiant, spiteful person
lehavdl (v) (H), to make a distinction (between sacred and profane); "lehavdl beyn hakhayim vehameysim", "to distinguish between the living and the dead" (also "if you'll forgive me")
leheypekh (H), on the contrary, the opposite (in ideas)
lekhatkhile (H), at first, initially, originally
lekhayim (H), to life (a toast)
lekhayim toyvim ul'sholem (H), to good life and to peace
lekholapokhes (H), at least
lekhoyre (H), apparently, it seems
lekn (G), to lick
lekoved (H), in honour of, on the occasion of
lemanashem (H), be sure to, don't fail to, for G-D's sake
der/di lemishke (R), Caspar Milquetoast, milksop, naive person
lemoshl (H), for example
der lempert (G), leopard
der lerer (G), teacher (secular)
lernen (G), to study, to teach
lernen zikh (v), to learn, to study
der lets (H), jester, mocker
dos letsones (H), derision, mockery

letst (G), last, latest

di levaye (H), funeral (cortege)

di levone (H), moon; "halbe levones", parentheses

der levyosn (H), leviathan

der leyb (G), lion

leydik (G), empty

der leydik-geyer (G-Y), loafer, (one who goes empty handed)

leyenen, to read

leygn (G), to lay, to lie; "leyg zikh nit keyn feygelekh in buzem", "don't count your chickens before they're hatched" (don't put little birds in your bosom)

leygn zikh, to lie down, to turn in

di leym (G), clay

leykenen, to deny; "leykenen shteyn un beyn", to deny everything (to deny stone and bone)

di leytse(s) (R), rein(s)

der leyvi (H), Levite

leyzn (G), to get money for selling, to take in receipts; "gebn tsu leyzn", to patronize; "git mir tsu leyzn", "buy something from me", patronize me

di libe (v) (G), love, love affair, romance; "shpiln a libe", to court, to have a love affair

libersht (G), rather; "libersht hobn/ veln", prefer

libn, to love; "libn zikh", to love each other, to make love

der lign (n) (G), a lie; "zogn a lign", to lie

lign (v) (G), be situated, to lie

lignay (H), adversely

lignen (G), to tell a lie

der ligner (G), liar

di likht (G), candle(s), light, (same in pl.)

lila (adj), purple, violet

di lilye, lily

link (adj) (G), left

der linker (n) (G), left handed person, politically "left"

link'hantik, left-handed

links, to the left

di lite, Lithuania

der litvak, Lithuanian Jew

der lodn (n), shutter

lodn (v), to charge (electrically), to sue

loet (H), greedy

der loker (n), ambush

lokern, to lurk, to watch

der loksh(n) (R), noodle(s); (slang) Italian person

lomir (G-Y), let's (contr. of "lozn mir")

der lomp (G), lamp

di lonke (R), lawn, meadow

der loshik (R), colt

dos loshn (H), language; "dos mame-loshn", "mother tongue", Yiddish

dos loshn-hore (H), vilification, wicked tongue

dos loshn-koydesh (H), holy tongue (Hebrew)

di loyb, praise

loybn (v), to praise; "loybn in himl arayn", to praise highly, to rave about

loyfn (v), to run

loyt, according to

lozn (G), to allow, to leave, to let

der lozung, slogan

der luekh (H), calendar (Jewish dates only), tablets (on which Mosaic laws were first engraved)

di luft (G), air

der luftmentsh (G), a man without a means of support

der lulev (H), palm branch (for Succoth) (Jewish)

di lung(en) (G), lung(s)

M

der mabl (H), a flood

ma dokh (G), if even, since even, when

di mageyfe (H), epidemic, pestilence, plague

der magid (H), itinerant preacher, orator

di make (H), affliction, plague, pox; "er hot makes", "he has nothing at all"

di makhateniste (H), in-law (female)

der makher (G), commission agent, lobbyist

di makherayke, contraption

dos makhloykes (n) (H), feud, quarrel

makhmes (H), because of

makhn (G), to make; "makhn shabes", "to celebrate the Sabbath"

der makhnes-oyrekh (makhnes orkhim) (H), hospitable person, one who invites in poor on the Sabbath (Jewish)

makhnes-oyrekh zayn (H), to extend hospitality

der makhsher (n) (H), appliance, tool, (pl. makhshirim)

di makhsheyfe (H), witch (female); "di alte makhsheyfe", "a mean old woman"

makkhesh zayn (H), to deny

makrev zayn (H), to sacrifice

der malbesh (H), garment (pl. malbushim)

der malekh (H), angel

di malene (R), raspberry

di malke (H), queen

der malkhamoves (H), angel of death (not used literally)

maln (mal zayn, male zayn) (H), to circumcize

di mame (G), mother

dos mame-loshn (G-H), mother tongue, Yiddish

mamesh (H), literally (to intensify an exaggeration); "er hot im mamesh tserisn vi a hering", "he literally tore him apart like a herring"

der mamzer (H), bastard

der man (G), husband, man, (pl. mener)

der mandl(en), almond(s), tonsil(s)

di mapole (n) (H), defeat, setback

der marants (pomerants) (R), orange

"maresh-oylem zayn" (h), cause a sensation, "storming of worlds" (intellectual rather than a physical feat)

der mark (G), market-place

di marke(s) (R), postage stamp(s)

di marshas (H), wicked woman (der roshe, wicked man)

di mase (n) (H), bulk, mass, pulp

masern (H), to betray, to inform against

di mashke (H), beverage, liquor

mashmoes (H), probably, supposedly

dos mashmoes (H), probability

mashpie zayn (H-G), to influence; "er iz mashpie geven", "he was influenced"

maskem (H), agreed

maskem zayn (H-Y), to agree, to consent to

di masline(s) (H), olive(s)

di maslinke, buttermilk

der masmid (H), dedicated Talmud student

di matbeye (H), a coin, sum of money (hum.)

matern (G), to torment

dos maternish, hardship, torment

matern zikh, to slave, to toil

der materyal (Y-G), material

di matone (H), donation, gift

matriekh zayn (H-G), to burden, to impose upon, to trouble; "matriekh zayn zikh dafke tsu", "go out of one's way to"; "matriekh zayn zikh un", "be so kind as to", "to take the trouble to"

di matse (H), unleavened bread (biscuit) for Passover (Jewish)

matse-vaser (H-G), matso water; "bilik vi matse-vaser", "cheap as dirt"; "me hot es tsekhapt vi matse-vaser", "it was snapped up like hot cakes"

di matseyve (H), tombstone

matsliekh zayn (H-G), to be lucky, to be successful, to prosper

mavdl zayn (H-G), distinguish, separate

der maydem (H), adept person, expert

der maykhl (H), delicacy, pleasure (pl. maykholim) (food)

der maymer (H), article, tractate

mayn (G), my

mayrekh zayn (H-G), to expatiate, to talk/write at excessive length

der mayrev (H), evening prayer (Jewish)

di mayse (H), story; "di emese mayse", cancer (the real thing); "gekhapt be'eys mayse", "caught in the act"; "gekhapt in der mayse", "caught in it"; "gor a mayse", "what kind of a story is that?"

di mayse-bereyshis (H), the story of the beginning, (creation)

di mayse-gvir (H), as becomes a man of wealth

di mayse-nes (H), miraculous event

di mayse-noyre (H), a tale of dread; "arbetn maysim", "make a great to-do"; "herst a mayse!", "what a story!"; "heybt zikh on a mayse!", "once you begin, there'll be no end"; "mayse on a sof" (H-G), "a dragged out affair"; "opton a mayse", "play a dirty trick"; "vos iz di mayse?", "what's wrong?"; "zikh onton a mayse", "commit suicide"

di mayse-shehoye (H), actual occurrence

mayse-sotn (H), "the devil take it"

mayse-soykher (H), business like, "the way of a business man"

maysim-tatuim (H), wickedness

maysim-toyvim (H), good deeds (pl. only); Parent's prayer; "toyre, khupe un maysim toyvim", "Torah, wedding canopy and good pious deeds"

dos mazl (H), luck

mazldik (H), lucky

mazltov (H), congratulations (good luck!)

der mazltov (H), congratulations

me (men) (Y), one; "me tor nit", "one must not"

medie zayn (H-Y), to announce, to declare, to inform, to notify

di medine (H), country, state (of Israel)

di medoe (H), advertisement, announcement, notice

mefarnes zayn (H-G), to support (a family)

megadl zayn (H-G), to raise children

megazem zayn (H), to exaggerate; "er iz megazem", "he exaggerates"

megn (G), may, to have permission

megulgl vern (H-G), to be reincarnated, turn up (in a surprising place)

der mehalekh (H), distance, gap, interval

di mehume (H), riot, stampede, turmoil

mekaber zayn (H-G), to bury (Jewish)

mekabl-ponem zayn (H-G), to congratulate, to honour, to welcome

mekalel zayn (H-G), to curse

mekane zayn (H-G), to envy; "ikh bin im mekane", "I envy him"

mekayem zayn (H-G), to fulfil, to materialize

der mekekh (n) (H), price

mekhabed zayn (H-G), to honour

der mekhaber (H), author

mekhadesh zayn (H-G), to bless (the new moon) (Jewish), to innovate, to renew

mekhalel zayn (H-G), to desecrate; "er iz mekhalel shabes", "he desecrates the Sabbath"

der mekhashef (H), magician, wizard

di mekhaye (H), joy, relief, refreshment; "zikh mekhaye zayn", to be delighted, to enjoy oneself greatly, "to be refreshed"; "zikh mekhaye zayn vos", "to be happy that"

mekhaye-meysim zayn (H-Y), resurrect the dead

di mekhile (H), forgiveness; "betn mekhile", to apologize

der mekhutn (H), male in-law (pl. makhatonim)

di mel (G), flour

der melamed (H), teacher (of Hebrew), (pl. melamdim)

di melamedke (H), wife of a melamed

di melodye (G), melody (other than Jewish music)

di melokhe (H), craft, occupation; "a melokhe iz a melukhe", "an occupation is like a kingdom"

di melukhe (H), kingdom, state

der melumed (H), learned man (Jewish)

der memune (H), caretaker, custodian, supervisor

men (G), one (person), they

der menadev (H), donor

menadev zayn (H-G), contribute (money)

menakhem-ovl zayn (H-Y), comfort a mourner, "pay a condolence call"

menatseyekh zayn (H-G), to be the winner, to defeat, to triumph

dos mendl, hook

dos mendl un vaybl (Y-G), hook and eye

di menie (H), obstacle

di menoyre (H), Menorah, (seven branched candelabrum) (Jewish)

der mentsh (G), good fellow, man, (pl. mentshn-people)

mer (G), more; "mer nit", "no longer", "no more"

der/di mer (n), carrot; (pl. mern)

merakhem zayn zikh (H-G), to have pity

der mes (H), corpse, dead man, ghost, (pl. meysim)

der mesadir kedushin (H), officiator at marriage ceremonies

mesasek zayn zikh (H-G), "to occupy oneself'

di mesekhte (H), tractate (of the Talmud)

der meser (G), a knife

"meshadekh zayn zikh" (H-Y), become connected by marriage

meshayer zayn (H-G), to assume, to presume, to suppose; "men iz meshayer", "it is understood"

der meshiekh (H), Messiah

der meshores (H), assistant, clerk, servant, (pl. meshorsim)

dos meshugas, craze, insanity, madness

meshuge (H), crazy; "meshuge makhn", to drive crazy

di meshugene, crazy woman

der meshugener, crazy-man, lunatic

dos meshugoim-hoyz, insane asylum, madhouse

der meshulekh (H), messenger

der meshumed (H), apostate, baptized Jew

meshune (H), queer, strange; "di mise-meshune", "a violent death"

der mes-les (H), twenty-four hour period

der mester (n), measure (tool), scale

dos mestl, measure

mestn (G), to gauge, to measure, to survey

mesukn (H), dangerous

di metsiye (H), a bargain, a rarity; "a groyse metsie", a big bargain (sarcastic); "khapn a metsiye", "to find a bargain"

der metupl (H), burdened person (especially one with many children)

me'uberes (H), pregnant

"mevaker-khoyle zayn" (H), "to visit the sick"

mevayesh zayn (H-G), to degrade, to disgrace, to humiliate, to shame, (stronger than "farshemen")

mevaze zayn (H-G), to abuse, to degrade

meyashev zayn zikh (H-G), "to deliberate", to take counsel; "meyashev zayn zikh mit", "to confer with", to consult

di meydele (G), little girl, (term of endearment)
di/dos meydl (G), young girl
meyle (H), "forget it", "never mind", Well!
der meylekh (H), king, (pl. melokhim)
meynen (G), to mean; "vos ikh meyn", "what I mean"
der meyukhes (H), man of aristocratic descent (with "yikhes" status); "der groyser meyukhes", "big shot"
di meyukheses (H), woman of aristocratic descent
der meyvn (H), an authority, an expert, one who understands
di mezuze (H), door post scroll (Jewish)
di mide (H), habit, manner, measure
mideye (H), "who knows?" (G-D knows how)
mien zikh (G), to exert oneself, to strive; "bamit zikh nit", "don't take the trouble"; "mien zikh far", "to intercede on behalf of"
mies (H), ugly; "mies-umoes" (H), disgusting, hideous (ugly and disgrace)
di mieskeyt (H-Y), ugliness, ugly person
mikoyekh (H), about, concerning
di mikve (H), ritual bathing pool (Jewish)
di mile (H), circumcision (Jewish)
di milkh (G), milk, milt
milkhik (adj) (G), dairy (re: Jewish dietary laws)
der milkhiker (G), dairyman, milkman
di milkhome (n) (H), war; "milkhome korbones", "war victims"
der milyon(en) (G), million(s)
der milyoner (G), millionaire
mimeyle (H), as a matter of course, perforce
mimeyledik (H), automatic, self-evident
der min (H), genus, kind, sex, species
minastam (H), probably

der mineg (H), custom, rite
di minkhe (H), afternoon prayer (Jewish)
di minut (G), minute, (time)
der minyen (H), quorum, (a congregation of a minimum of ten males) (Jewish)
mir (G), me, we
mirtsishem (H), G-D willing (mirtshem) (contraction of "im yirtse hashem")
di mise (H), death, (not used alone); "aynnemen a mise meshune", "die a violent death"; "di mise meshune", "violent death"; "onton a mise meshune", "commit suicide"
der mishebeyrekh (H), prayer for health (Jewish)
mishn, to mix, to stir
di mishne (H), (a passage of the) Mishnah, (pl. mishnayes)
mishn zikh (Y-G), to interfere, to meddle
der mishpet (H), judgment
mishpetn (H), to judge
di mishpokhe (H), clan, family
der miskher (H), business, commerce, trade
der misnaged (H), opponent of the Chasidim (Jewish)
mispalel zayn (H-G), to pray (for someone)
mistome (H), perhaps, probably
misvakeyekh zayn zikh(H-G), to argue, to debate, to dispute
mit (G), with
di mite (H), bier (Jewish)
der mitglid (G), companion, member
der mitn (G), middle; "in mitn", in the middle; "in mitn derinen" (G-Y), all of a sudden, in the midst of everything; (more commonly used than: in mitske derinen (G-Y) (sardonic form))
dos mitsrayim (H), Egypt
di mitsve (H), blessing, good deed, (commandment) (Jewish)
der mitvokh (G), Wednesday

der mizinik, pinky, youngest son
di mizinke (R), youngest daughter
der mizmer (H), psalm
der mizrekh (H), east, (front row in the Synagogue, facing the Eastern Wall)
modne (R), odd, queer (modern), singular, strange
der mogn, stomach; "a loyzer mogn", diarrhea; "hobn dem mogn", "move one's bowels"
der mol, pier
dos mol (G), time; "eyn mol", "once"
der mol, moth
mole (H), full
moln (G), to imagine, to paint
"es ken gemolt zayn", "it is possible"; "es ken nit gemolt zayn", "it is impossible"
moln zikh, to imagine
der moltsayt (G), meal, mealtime (mol is never used alone)
mon, poppy seeds, something tiny
der monat (G), month
monen (G), to dun, to demand (money)
moneshekh! (H), make up your mind, one of the two
der montik (G), Monday
der mord (n) (G), assassination, homicide, murder
di morde (R), chin, snout
di more-shkhoyre (H), melancholy (black bile)
morgn (G), tomorrow
der morgn (G), tomorrow
der moser (H), informer, spy
der moshenik (R), cheat, swindler
der moshl (H), comparison, example
motek (H), my dear, my sweet (lit. sweet)
di moyd (G), girl, lass, maiden; "di alte moyd", "old maid"
moyde zayn (H), to acknowledge, to admit, to concede
moyde zayn zikh (H-Y), to confess

der moyekh (n) (H), brains, head, mind
der moyel (H), circumciser
der moykher (H), seller
moykhl (H), "never mind", "no thanks"
moykhl zayn (H-Y), to forgive, to pardon
dos moyl (G), mouth; "onnemen a moyl mit vaser", to keep silent; "onshteln moyl un oyern", to pay close attention to
di moyre (H), fear; "moyre hobn" (H-Y), to fear
moyredik (H), dreadful, frightful
moyrevdik, fearful, timid
moysef zayn (H-G), to add (to), to append
der moyser (H), denouncer, (denounced is "gemasert")
moyshe rabeyne (H), Moses (Our Teacher)
der moyshev-skeynim (H), nursing home, old age home
der moytse (H), "makhn a moytse", "to make a benediction over bread" (Jewish)
di multer, trough
di multer-brie (Y-H), shellfish
der mum (H), a defect
di mume (G), aunt
der mumkhe (H), expert; (pl. mumkhim)
der musef (H), additional morning prayers (Sabbath and holidays) (Jewish)
der muser (H), morality, reproof
musern (H), chastize, lecture, reproach
mushve vern (H-G), to agree, to be reconciled, to come to terms
der mut (G), daring (showing courage)
di muter (G), mother
mutik, courageous
di mutikeyt, courage

mutshen (R), to torment; "mutshen zikh", "to live a wretched life", to slave, to suffer, to toil

der muz (n), essential thing, obligation; "zayn a muz", "be imperative"

muz (G) (prefix), compulsary, compulsive; "der muz-limed" (Y-H), compulsory subject

muzn (v), may, must

der muzhik (R), (Russian) peasant

der muzikant (G), musician (player)

N

der nadn (H), dowry; "silekn dem nadn", "to pay over the dowry"

der nadven (H), philanthropist

di nafke (R), prostitute, whore

di nafkemine (H), difference

naket (G), bald (figurative), naked

der nakhes (H), joy, rewards, satisfaction

di nakht (G), night

der nakhtmol (G), supper (evening meal)

der nar (n) (G), fool, (pl. naronim)

narish (H), foolish

di narishkeyt (Y-H-G), foolishness

nas (adj) (G), wet

der nash (H), a snack (coll.)

der nasher (H), greedy person, (gourmand)

dos nasheray (H-Y), snacks, sweets, tid bits

nashn (v), to snack

di natshalstve (R), authorities (humorous), officialdom

dos natskhones (H), contentiousness, disputatiousness

natskhonesh (H), contentious, disputatious

nay (G), new

nayes (G), news

dos nayes, news report, piece of news

nayn (G), nine

nayntsik (G), ninety

nayntsn (G), nineteen

nebekh (G), poor thing!, too bad, unfortunate

dos nebekhl, dupe, helpless person, sissy

di nedove (H), a charitable gift, (a trifling handout)

dos nefesh (H), creature, soul, (pl. nefashes)

dos negides (H), riches

di negidiste (H), wealthy man's wife

negl-vaser (G), nail water; "opgisn negl-vaser", ritual morning hand washing ceremony (Jewish)

nekhtn (G), yesterday; "a nekhtiker tog" (G-Y), (expression of derision), "stuff and nonsense", (lit. yesterday's day)

di nekome (H), revenge

di nekude (H), Hebrew vowel sign

nelm vern (H-G), to disappear

di nelm-verung, disappearance

nemen (G), to get to marry, to take

di nemung, military draft

der nepl (G), fog, haze, mist

nepldik (G-Y), foggy, misty, vague

der nerv, nerve

nervez (nerveyish), nervous

der nes (H), miracle, (pl. nisim)

di neshome (H), soul

di nesie (H), journey, voyage

der neyder (H), oath, vow

neyen (G), to sew

neygerik, curious, inquisitive; "neygerik tsu", anxious/eager to

neyn (G), no

di neyterke (G), seamstress

neytik, necessary

niderik (G), low

der nifter (n) (H), deceased person

nifter vern (H-G), to die (said of pious Jews, others: shtarbn)

der nign (nigndl) (H), melody (re: Jewish music)

nik (R), a suffix personifying a noun, often attatched to English words eg. "beatnik, no-goodnik"

nikhlel (H), included

der nikhne (H), humble person, submissive person

nikhshl vern (H-G), to be tempted into

nikhter (H), empty stomach, sober

di nile (H), closing prayer of Yom Kippur (Jewish)

nishkoshe (nishkoshedik) (H), "considerably", "not badly", "so-so"

nisht (G), not (same as nit)

dos nishtl, a playing card under nine, worthless trifle

nishto (G-Y), see nito

nishtoymem vern (H), amazed, astounded

nisim venifloes (H), "miracle upon miracle"

der nisn (H), Nissan (seventh month in Jewish calendar, usually coincides with March/April)

nisn (G), to sneeze

nispoel vern (H), become enthusiastic, be impressed, speechless, surprised

nistalek vern (H-G), to die, (re: a very important pious Jew)

nit (G-Y), not

nito, absent, gone, gone away (contraction of nit do - not here); "es iz nito", "there is not"; "nito far vos", don't mention it, you're welcome

der nitsokhn (H), conquest, triumph, victory; (pl. nitskhoynes); "der bal-nitsokhn" (H), conqueror, victor

di nodl (G), needle

der nodlboym, evergreen

der noged (H), wealthy man, (pl. negidim)

der nogl (negele, neygl) (n) (G), fingernail, nail, toenail; (pl. negl)

nokh (G), after, after all, another

nokhgebn (G), be permissive, give in

nokhgibik, docile, submissive

di nokhgibikeyt (G), permissiveness

nokhmalpeven, to ape, to parrot

der nomen (n) (G), name

der nopl (G), navel

nor (G), just, only

der nos, sneeze

novene, "in a novene" (R), "for a change"; "a mol a novene", "as an exception"

der novi (H), prophet; (pl. nevi'im); "zayn a novi az", to predict

der novobranyets (R), a recruit

der noyeg (H), conduct

noyeg zayn zikh, be in the habit of, be wont to

noykem zayn zikh (H-Y), to take revenge on

di noyt (n), hardship, need, want

di noz (G), nose; (pl. nez)

nu (R), "well?"; "nu-nu", "don't ask"; "nu-u-u!", "for Pete's sake get going"

der nudnik (coll. nudzh) (R), nuisance (person)

nudyen (nudzhen) (v) (R), to be a nuisance, to bore

der nus (dos nisl) (G), nut; (pl. nis); "der veltshener nus", walnut

O

ober (G), but

di obezyane, ape

odem horishen (H), Adam ("the first man")

di oder (n), blood vessel, strand, streak, vein; "trenen di odern", to annoy, to vex

oder (G), either, or

dos of (H), bird, fowl, poultry; (pl. oyfes)

ofn (adj) (G), open

okersht, a moment ago, just now, recently

der oks (G), ox

der ol (H), burden, onus, yoke
"olehasholem" (H), "of blessed
memory" (said of a dead woman),
(peace be unto her)
"olevasholem" (H), "of blessed
memory" (said of a dead man), (peace
be unto him)
di olkhe, alder (tree)
der omed (H), column (of print),
pulpit (Jewish)
omek (H), profound, wise
omeyn (H), amen
der omeynn-zoger (H-G), yes-man
(amen-sayer)
on (G), without
dos onbaysn (Y-G), lunch
onbeygn (G), to bend, to slant, to tilt
onbeygn zikh, bend, stoop
der onev (H), meek person, modest
person
der onfal (Y-G), aggression, attack, fit,
spell, stroke
onfaln (Y-G), to assail, to attack
der onfang (G), the beginning (onheyb
more commonly used)
onfangen (G), to begin (onheybn
more commonly used)
der onfreg, inquiry
onfregn zikh (G), to enquire
dos ongebl, hint
ongeblozn (G), conceited, inflated,
pompous, sulky (blown up)
ongebn (Y-G), to apply for, to pass, to
submit
ongemakht (G), did, made,
perpetrated
ongeshtoysn (Y-G), angry, hurt,
offended
ongevorn (Y-G), lost, spent,
squandered
ongeze'en, distinguished, eminent
der ongeze'ener (Y-G), distinguished
person
onhengen (G), to foist
onhengen zikh oyf, to hang on (to)
der onhenger, admirer, fan, partisan,
supporter

der onheyb (G), beginning, origin
onheybn (Y-G), to begin, to originate,
to start; "onheybn zikh mit", "to look
for trouble", to start an argument with;
"heybt zikh on a mayse", "let's not go
into that!"
der oni (H), poor man
onklepn (G), to attach to, to fasten on,
to glue, to mount (pictures), to stick
onkumen (G), to arrive, to enter
(school, organization)
onkumen tsu (Y-G), receive assistance
from
onkveln (Y), beam with joy, be
delighted by
onmakhn (Y-G), to soil (with urine or
feces), to stir up; "onmakhn a
khasene", "to stir up a holy mess" (to
cook up a wedding)
onpoyen (R), to water (animals)
onshikern (Y-H), to make drunk
onshikern zikh (Y-G), to get drunk
der onshtel, make-believe, pretense
onshtelerish, stuffy
onshteln (Y-G), to engage, to point a
gun, to set a watch; "er hot ongeshtelt
oyf ir a por oygn", "he fixed his big
eyes on her"
onshtendik (adj) (G), decent,
honourable, respectable
onteyen (Y), to delight in, to manifest
quiet glee, to smirk
dos onton, apparel, clothes
onton (G), to put on, to wear
dos ontsuherenish (Y-G), a hint, an
insinuation
der onvayz, indication
onvayzik, indicative
onvayzn, indicate, instruct
di onvayzung, instruction
der onzen (Y-G), esteem, importance,
prestige; "hobn groys onzen", "be in
high esteem"
onzen zikh (Y-G), to be conspicuous,
to look one's fill, to take a good look
der onzets (n), bankruptcy

onzetsn (Y-G), to go broke, to impose; "onzetsn zikh oyf", to gang up on, to insist

der onzog (Y-G), announcement, message, portent

onzogn (Y-G), announce, give a message to, inform, warn

opdavnen (Y-H), to complete prayers

der oper (G), sacrifice (n), ("korbn" is better Yiddish) (H)

op'esn (v), to eat up; "opgegesn", eaten up, finished eating

dos opfirekhts, laxative

opfirn (Y-G), take back (in a vehicle), take home; "vos geystu opfirn?", "what are you going to accomplish?" (pull off?)

opfregn (Y-G), to contradict, to disprove, to refute; "nit optsufregn", undisputed(ly)

der opfreser, caterpillar

opfresn (Y-G), to gobble up, to wolf

opgebn (Y-G), to cast (a ballot), to deliver, to devote, to return, to surrender, to yield; "opgebn zikh mit", attend to, devote oneself to

opgehit (Y-G), careful; "nit opgehit", not careful

opgepotert (Y-H), done, done in

opgesheyt (Y-G), separated, set apart

opgetsolt (Y-G), paid up

opgeyn (Y-G), to depart (by vehicle), to lack, to step aside; "es geyt im gornit op", "he lacks nothing"; "lozn opgeyn", to defrost, to thaw

ophaltn (Y-G), to detain, to deter, to hold (a meeting), to score (a victory)

ophaltn zikh, abstain from, refrain

ophitn (Y-G), to cherish, to take care; "got zol ophitn", "G-D forbid"

opkhayen (Y-H), to revive

opkokhn (Y-G), to boil, to cook

opkoyfn (Y-G), to buy up, to purchase

der opkum, decrease

opkumen (Y-G), to languish, to suffer

opkumen mit, get away with; "opkumen far", atone for, make amends for

dos opkumenish (Y-G), affliction, deprivation, ordeal

der opleyg, deferment, postponement

opleygn (Y-G), postpone, put aside

opleykenen, to deny

di opleykenung (Y-G), denial, (see "hakkhoshe")

opnemen (Y-G), to become numb, to call for, to deliver a baby

oprekhenen (Y-G), to deduct

oprekhenen zikh (Y-G), to get even, to take vengeance

di oprekhenung, deduction, vengence

oprikhtn (Y-G), to celebrate, perform (a ceremony); "oprikhtn khtsos", to rise at midnight for study and prayer (Jewish)

der opshats, estimation, evaluation

opshatsn (v), to evaluate, to rate, to value; "nit optsushatshn" (Y-G), inestimable, invaluable

der opshay (n) (Y-G), awe, respect, reverence

opshprekhn (Y-G), to exorcise

der opshrayb, bequest

opshraybn, to confiscate, to transfer ownership

opshrayen (Y-G), to annul, to have revoked

der opshrek, deterrent

opton (v), finish doing, play a trick

optrogn (v), return/take to owner

optrogn zikh, "to make off" (beat it); "trog zikh op fun danen", "get out of here"

optshepen (v), to detach

optshepen zikh fun (Y-G), to get rid of, to go away, to leave, to let go, to shake off

der optu, prank

oranzh (n) (adj), orange

orem (adj), poor, unhappy

der orem (n), arm (limb); (pl. orems)

der oreman (G), poor man

dos oremland (G), poor country
orn, to pray, (obsolete)
der orn (H), ark, coffin (Jewish); "der orn-koydesh", "The Holy Ark" (Jewish)
orntlekh, fair, honest, respectable
der ort (G), location, place, spot
dos ort (G), room, space; "dos gute ort", cemetery (the good place); "dos reyne ort", cemetery (the pure place)
der os (H), letter; (pl. oysyes); "zogn di oysyes (fun)", "to spell (a word)"
di osine, aspen (tree)
der osyen (R), autumn
"Ot!" (R), "like hell I will", "right away", "there!", "voila!"
otader (R-G), this (man) here
otayener (R-G), that (man) there
der otem (n), breath
otemen (v), to breathe
di oves (H), The Patriarchs: Abraham, Isaac and Jacob
ovinu (H), G-d; (Our Father)
der ovl (H), mourner
der ovnt (Y-G), evening
oy (G), oh!; "oy vey!", "woe is me!"
der oybershter (eybershter), the Lord (G-D)
oybn (G), above, on top, upstairs, up there
der oybn, top
der oyer (n), ear
oyf (G), on, up
oyfboyen (G), to construct
oyfesn (G), to eat up; "oyfesn zikh", to regret bitterly (eat oneself)
der oyffir, behaviour, conduct
der oyffirer, producer (of a film, play etc)
oyffirn (v), to stage a play
oyffirn zikh (G), to behave well
oyfhengen (G), to hang, to suspend
oyfhengen zikh (v), to hang oneself
oyfhern (G), to stop
oyfhodeven (R), to bring up children
oyfkhapn zikh (v), to awaken oneself, to wake

der oyfkum, origin
oyfkumen (v), to awaken, to come into existence, to ripen
der oyfn (H), manner, way
der oyfnem, reception
oyfnemen (G), to entertain, to receive (guests)
der oyfnemer, receiver (radio), receptionist
oyfnemik, receptive
oyfrikhtik, sincere
di oyfrikhtikeyt, sincerity
oyfrikhtn (G), to restore
der oyfruf (n), appeal, call, call to the Torah (Jewish)
oyfrufn (G), to call up to the Torah (Jewish), to call up troops
der oyfshnit, cold cuts
der oyfshtendler(s) (n) (Y-G), rebel(s)
der oyfshtertsler, bottle opener
oyfshteyn (G), to awake, to get up, to revolt, to stand up
dos oyg, eye; (pl. oygn)
der oygnblik (G), glimpse, instant
oykh (oykhet) (G), also
der oylem (H), audience, crowd, public
der oylem-habe (H), the Hereafter, (the world to come)
der oylem-haze (H), this world, (in contrast to the hereafter)
oylem-hazenik (H), sensual, voluptuous
der oynesh (H), penalty (moral), punishment
der oyrekh (pl. orkhim) (H), guest, one who is welcomed as a visitor
oys (G), no more, over, through; "oys-khasene", the project is over, the wedding is off; "oys-shabes", the Sabbath is over
oysbrekhn (Y-G), to break out, to vomit
oysdreyen (Y-G), sprain, turn, twist, wring; "oysdreyen zikh", turn around
oyser (G), except

der oysfir, conclusion, deduction, inference

oysfirlekh, feasible, workable

oysfirn (Y-G), to accomplish, to succeed, to work; "nit lozn oysfirn", to frustrate; "oysfirn dayns", to have your way

di oysfirung, performance

oysgebn (Y-G), marry off, pretend, spend money; "oyf doktoyrim zol er es oysgebn", "may he spend it all on doctors" (curse); "oysgebn zikh far", impersonate

di oysgebung, pretense; "unter falshe oysgebungen", under false pretenses

oysgematert (Y-G), exhausted

oysgemutshet (Y-R), whacked out

oysgetriknt (Y-G), dried out, old and wrinkled

oysgetseykhnt (Y-G), excellent, extraordinary, outstanding

oysgetseylt (Y-G), accounted for

oysgeyn (Y-G), to die, (genteel way of saying "pass away"), to starve

der oysher (H), wealthy person; (pl. ashirim)

oys'hitn (Y-G), to guard against, to protect from

oysklaybn (Y-G), to choose; "oysklaybn far", "to elect"; "oysklaybn zikh tsu", "get around to (at last)"

oyskoylen (Y-G), to slaughter all (of a group)

oyskrenken (Y-G), to agonize, to suffer for, to sweat out

oysleygn (Y-G), to interpret (dreams), to lay out (money), to set out (things), to spell; "oysleygn kortn", "to tell fortunes by cards"

dos oysleyzgelt, ransom

oysleyzn (Y-G), to deliver (ransom), to redeem, to save; "leyz undz oys", "deliver us"

oyslozn (v), to end, to leave out, to omit

oyslozn zikh (Y-G), to result, to turn out

oysmatern (Y-G), to exhaust, to tire out

oysmekn (Y-G), to erase

oysmutshen (Y-H), to exhaust, to run down; "zi hot mikh oysgemutshet, oysgematert", "she tormented the life out of me, left me a wreck"

der oysnem, exception

oysnemen (v), be a success, make a hit, take out on a date

oysnemen bay . . . az (Y-G), to stipulate

dos oysnemenish, stipulation

dos oysnemens (Y-G), special period during services (removal of Torah from ark) (Jewish)

oysnemik, exceptional

oysraysn (Y-G), to rip out

der oysred (Y-G), pretext, reprimand, reproach

oysredn, to rebuke, to reprimand; "oysredn zikh tsu", to confide in

oysshekhtn (Y-G), slaughter completely (mass murder)

oyssheygetsn (Y-G), to dress down, to rebuke sternly

oysshpayen (Y-G), to spit out

oysshrayen (Y-G), to cry out, to exclaim, to shout out

oysshteln (Y-G), to display, to exhibit, to expose; "oysshteln oyf", subject to; "oysshteln zikh mit", to flaunt

oysshtrekn (Y-G), to stretch out

oystaynen (Y-G), to argue it out, to present one's arguments to

di oystralye (G), Australia

oystsien (Y-G), to drag out, to stretch; "oystsien di fis" (Y-G), to die (to stretch out the feet); "oystsien zikh", "to stretch out"

oystsvogn (Y-G), to shampoo, to wash one's hair

oysyes (H), fine print; "der kener in di kleyne oysyes", "Jewish scholar"

oyszayn (Y-G), to have been in many places (not used in present tense); "ikh vel gants frankraykh oyszayn", "I shall visit all of France"

dos oyszen (Y-G), appearance

oyszen (Y-G), to appear to be, to resemble, to seem; "vi es zet oys", to all appearances

oyszukhn (Y-G), to pick, to seek out

der oytomobil (oyto) (I.O.), automobile

der oytser (H), treasure, treasury; "natirlekhe oytsres", natural resources

di ozhene (R), blackberry

P

di padloge (R), floor

der pak (G), bundle, package

der pakhed (H), fear, terror

der pakntroger (G), pack-carrier

di palme (G), palm (tree)

der palmes, autopsy

pamelekh (R), slowly, "watch your step"

di pamunitse (pamoynitse) (R), household slops, slop pail

pani (panye) (R) (title), lord, sir

dos papir (G), paper

dos papiros (R), cigarette

der pare (H), Pharaoh

pareve (H), neither meat nor milk, person without character, ("neither fish nor fowl")

der parkh (R), blemish, scab, stingy person

di parnose (H), living, subsistence; "dayges parnose", "worry for one's livelihood"

di parshe (H), chapter

der parshoyn (G), character (in book), passenger, person

di partey, party (political); "di arbeter partey", "worker's party"

pashen, tend (grazing animals)

pashen zikh (R), to graze

dos pasirl, pass (permit)

pasirn, to happen, to occur

di pasirung, adventure, event, occurence

paskenen (H), to give a decision

paskudne (adj) (R), filthy, loathesome, nasty, rotten, terrible; "a paskudne yid", "an unpleasant fellow"

der paskudnyak (paskudnik) (R), a nasty, evil man (worse than "son-of-a-bitch")

di paskutstve (R), abomination, a nasty, evil woman (also paskudnyatshke), filth

dos pasles (H), delinquency (crime), dishonesty

pasn (v), be becoming, be proper, fit, to suit; "es past nit", "it is unbecoming"

der pastekh (R), shepherd

di pastke (R), a trap

der patsh (R), a box on the ear, a slap

patshn (R), to slap

pavolye (R), by and by, slowly, "take it easy"

der payn (n) (G), suffering

der pedler (Y), peddler

dos pekl (n) (G), bundle, package

dos pekl-fleysh, corned beef

der pelts (G), fur, pelt; "iberkern dem pelts", "be converted to another religion" (turncoat) (hum.); "raysn dem pelts", "strain oneself" (tear the pelt)

di pen, a pen

dos pepl (R), penis

di perednye (R), anteroom, lobby

di perene (R), feather bed

di petrishke (pyetrushke) (R), parsley

di peye (H), earlock, sideburn; "es ligt im in der linke peye", "he doesn't care" (hum.) (it lies in his left earlock)

der peyger, carcass

peygern (G), to croak (die, re: lowest classes and animals)

di peyre (H), fruit

der peyrek (H), chapter, chapter in the Mishnah (Jewish), section

der peyresh (H), commentary

der peysekh (H), Passover

der pidyen (H), payment to Rabbi for advice, ransom

"der pikuekh-nefesh" (H), "saving of a life" (when ritualistic laws are suspended) (Jewish)

di pil (G), pill

der ping-pong, ping-pong

der pint, pint

pintelekh (Y) (reference to Hebrew), vowels (little points)

dos pintl, dot, point; (pl. pintelekh); "trefn in pintl", hit the nail on the head

pintlen, blink; "pintlen mit di oygn", to wink

dos pishekhts (Y), urine (coll.)

pishn (G), to urinate

der pisk (R), jaw, mouth (of animal), yap; "efenen dem pisk", to open one's big mouth (trap, yap)

pitsik (pitsink) (R), tiny, (coll.)

pitsimoninke (Y-R), tiny

dos pitsl, shred, tiny bit

der plant, railroad track

der plats, crack, place, site

der plats'halter, governor general

platsirn, to locate, to position

platsn, to be agitated, to burst, to faint, to lose patience

di pleytse (n) (R), back, shoulder; "kvetshn mit di pleytses", to shrug one's shoulders; "oysdreyen zikh mit der pleytse tsu", to give the cold shoulder to; "untershteln a pleytse", to lend a hand

der plimenik, nephew

di plimenitse, niece

der ployt (R), a fence; "der lebediker ployt", hedge

plutsling (plutsem), abruptly, suddenly

der plyukh (plyushk) (R), splash

plyukhen (R), to rain cats and dogs

der plyukhregn (R-G), downpour, torrential rain

plyushken, to splash

pofn, to sleep, (coll.)

di pokrishke (R), pot lid

di pole (n), lap of a garment

der polk (R), regiment

di polke, drumstick (of a fowl)

di polke, Polish woman, polka

der polkovnik (R), colonel

der pomerants (marants) (G), orange

der pomidor (I), tomato

der pomyeshtshik (R), land lord, landowner

dos ponem (H), appearance, face; "a ponem", apparently, seemingly

di por (n), few, pair; "a por", a couple (of), a few

der porekh, dust; "ash-un-porekh", dust and ashes

der porets (H), landowner, rich gentile (coll.), (pl. pritsim)

dos por-folk (Y), married couple

dos porl, unmarried couple

der poroykhes (H), curtain before Holy Ark (Jewish)

porn, to mate, to pair

porn zikh, be a match, copulate

di portsye (R), a portion, a scolding

der posek(h) (H), Biblical verse; "vi in posek shteyt" (hum.), "by the book", properly

der poshe (H), sinner; "der poshe Yisroel", "heretic"

poshet (H), clearly, definitely, simply

di post (G), mail, mails, post office

der post-ba'amter, postal-clerk

dos postkestl, mailbox, post-office box

poter (H), finished, rid of, washed up; that's that

poter vern fun (H-G), dispose of, get rid of

der poyer (R), peasant; (f., poyerte)

der poyezd (R), railroad, train

poylish, Polish

dos poyln (G), Poland

di poymene (R), kidnapped children in Czarist Russia forced into the army

poyser-kholem zayn (poyser zayn) (H-G), to interpret a dream, ("poyser" not used alone)

di pozemke (R), strawberry (wild)

di pratse (n) (R), toil

praven (R), to celebrate, to perform

pravozhitelstvo (H), the right to establish residence in Russia (R)

di priline(s) (G), praline(s)

prima(t), first-rate, tops

der priml, (G), primrose

der pristav (R), commissioner of police in Czarist Russia

der priziv (R), conscription, recruiting officer in Russia

di problem (G), problem

problematish, problematic, questionable

prost (G), coarse, ordinary, simple

der protest, protest

der protestir, protester

protestirn (v), to protest

der psak (H), scolding, verdict

der psak-din (H), judgement, verdict

der pshat (H), literal interpretation

di psure (H), announcement, message, news, tidings

dos pudele (P), cardboard box, carton, little box

dos pultsl, young girl

punkt (G), exactly, just

der pupik (R), gizzard, navel; "er ligt mitn pupik aroyf", "he's dead" (he's lying with his navel up)

der purim (H), "lots", (M.S.)

di pushke (R), coin box (used to collect charitable offerings), tin can

pust (R), empty

der pustepasnik (m.) (R) (di pustepa snitse (f.) (R)), idler, loafer

di puter (G), butter; "es geyt im mit der puter arop", he is having a streak of bad luck (with him the buttered side lands down)

dos puterbroyt, bread and butter sandwich

di putermilkh, buttermilk

di puternitse, butter dish

di pyate (n) (R), heel/sole of foot; "hobn in der linker pyate", to hold in contempt, to not care about (to have in the left sole)

R

raboysay (H), GENTLEMEN!

rak (H), only

der rakhmen (H), merciful man

dos rakhmim (H), charity, mercy

dos rakhmones (H), mercy (quality of . . .), pity

der ramay (n) (H), cheat, imposter

ramen, to clean house, to clean up, to clear away; "oysramen", "to clean out", to clear away

der rash (H), noise

rashn (v) (H), make noise; "rashn zikh", "make a big to-do", "make a fuss"

rateven (R), to rescue, to save

der rats, nick, rat, scratch

raybn (G), to grate, to rub

di raye (H), (piece of) evidence, proof

der rayen (H), idea, thought; (pl. rayoynes)

raykh (G), rich

dos raysn, Belorussia

raysn (G), to tear

di rayze (n) (G), journey

reb (H), Mr. (Jewish)

der rebe (H), rabbi, teacher

di rebetsn (H), rabbi's wife

der reboyne-sheloylem (H), the Almighty

dos redl (G), dial, fortune, group, small crowd

dos redls, a dance (Jewish)

redn (v), to talk

156

di refue (n) (H), healing, medicine
di refue-shleyme (H), a cure
di rege (H), instant, moment; "oyf der
rege", for the moment
regenen (G), to rain
der regn (n) (G), rain, rainfall
regndik, rainy
dos regndl, drizzle, shower
der rekhener, computer
di rekhenung (G), account, bill,
calculation
dos rekhiles (H), gossip, slander;
"traybn rekhiles", to gossip
der rekhilesnik (m.) (di rekhi
lesnitse (f.)) (H), slander-monger
rekhnen (v) (G), calculate, count, to
figure; "rekhnen far", consider (as);
"rekhnen oyf", count on
di rekhn-mashin, calculator
rekht (adj) (G), allright, proper
dos rekht (n), right; "mit rekht", justly
rekht'hantik, right-handed
rekhtlekh, legal
rekhts (G), (to the) right
der remez (H), allusion to, hint
dos rendl, coin, (gold) ducat
der resh-khoydesh, beginning of a
Jewish month
der reshus (H), authority, jurisdiction,
power; "hobn in reshus", have at one's
disposal, possess
der restoran, (G), restaurant (I.O.)
dos retenish, mystery, puzzle, riddle
retenishdik, mysterious, puzzling
der retsept (G), prescription, recipe
reyd (n) (G), discourse, language,
speech, talk; "harbe reyd", strong
language
reyn (adj) (G), clean, net, pure
di reynikeyt (G-Y), Torah scroll
reynikn, to clean, to purify; "khemish
reynikn", to dry clean
di reynkeyt (G), cleanliness, pureness
rikhtik (G), correct (right)
rikhtn zikh oyf (G-Y), to expect (a
child), to prepare for
rind (G), cattle

dos rind(er) (G), head of cattle
rindern (adj), beef
dos rinderns, beef
rinen (G), leak, ooze, run over
der rir, touch
rirevdik, agile, lively, mobile
ririk, mobile
rirn (G), to budge, to move; "rir zikh",
"get a move on"
di rod (G), circle, wheel
di roe (H), bad, disservice, harm,
wrong
der rog, intersection, street corner
der roman (F), love affair, novel,
romance
der roshe (H), villian, wicked man;
"der roshe merushe" (H),
"irreclaimably wicked man"
der rosheshone (H), New Year
(Jewish)
der rosl, brine, broth
der rotsn (n) (H), desire, will
der rov (H), rabbi
der royfe (H), not formally trained,
old-time physician (Jewish)
der roykh, fume, smoke; "avekgeyn
mitn roykh", to go up in smoke
roykhern (reykhern) (v), to smoke
der royshem (H), impression
royt, red; "royt vern", to blush
di royz (G), a rose
di rozhinke(s) (R), raisin(s)
der ruekh (H), devil; (pl. rukhes)
der ruf (G), appeal, call
rufn (G), call, page; "rufn zikh", answer
to the name of, be called
ruik (G), calm, quiet; "zay ruik", "be
still!"
der rukn, (a person's) back
"ruk un hemd", "mere skin and bone"
(back and shirt)
der rus (der rusish) (n), Russian
(language and person)
rusish (adj) (G), Russian
dos rusland, Russia
ruslendish, Russian (pertaining to
Russia)

S

sakh ("a sakh"), a lot, many, plenty

sakh ... (prefix), multi; "sakh-talantirt", multi-talented

di sakone (H), danger; "shteln in sakone", to endanger, to threaten; "shteyn in a sakone fun/tsu", to run the risk of

sakonedik (H), dangerous

dos sakones-nefoshes (H), "mortal danger"

sakones-nefoshesdik (H), deadly

der sam (H), poison, venom

di sam-oborene (R), self-defense

saydn, unless

"say vi say", anyhow, anyway, "at any rate", "be that as it may"

"say ... say", "both ... and", "whether ... or"

dos sdom (H), Sodom, (any form of evil); "di mayse-sdom" (H), "homosexuality"

se (Y), it's (same as "es")

di semitshke(s) (zhemeke(s), zhe mitshke(s)), sunflower seeds

der seyder (H), ritual meal of Passover (Jewish)

der seyfer (H), any important book, book (Talmudic etc.) (Jewish); (pl. sforim)

der seykhl (H), brains, intellect, reason, sense, wisdom, wit

di sgule (H), a remedy, a solution

sha!, be still!, hush

der shabes (H), Sabbath, Saturday; "makhn shabes far zikh", one does as one sees fit

shabesdik (adj) (H), festive (as Sabbath preparations)

der shabes-goy, gentile hired to do chores for Jews on the Sabbath

der shabes-zuntik (H-Y), weekend

der shadkhn (H), marriage broker

shadkhnen (H), attempt to match; "shadkhnen zikh tsu", to court, to woo

di shadkhnte (H), female marriage broker

dos shadkhones (H), matchmaker's fee, matchmaking

di shafe (R), closet, cupboard

der shakh (shokh) (R), chess, chess set

der shakhres (H), morning prayer (Jewish)

di shakhte (Y), elevator shaft, mine shaft

der/dos shaleshudes (H), third Sabbath meal, (Saturday lunch) (Jewish)

der shames (H), caretaker of a synagogue, sexton

di shand (shande) (G), disprepute, shame

dos shand'hoyz, brothel

der shap, industrial workshop

sharf (G), acute, keen, sharp, spicy

di sharf (n), blade, edge, scarf

sharn (G), push, rake, scrape

shatn, to harm, to hurt

shayekh (H), pertinent, relevant; "nit shayekh", "irrelevant"; "shayekh tsu", "re:"; "vos shayekh", "as for"

dos shaykhes (H), connection, relation

di shayle (H), question, question re: ritual purity

der shed (H), devil, spectre

shekhtn (H), to slaughter (Jewish) (ritual)

der shel-rosh (H), phylactery which is placed on the forehead (Jewish)

der shem (H), fame, G-d (The Name), reputation; "zikh koyne-shem zayn" (Y-H-Y), "to gain a reputation"

der shem-dover (H), fame, renown

shemen zikh (G), to be ashamed, to be shy; "megst zikh shemen", "you ought to be ashamed of yourself"; "shem zikh nit", "don't be shy"; "zolst zikh shemen in dayn vaytn haldz", shame on you!

der/di shenk, bar, pub, saloon, tavern

shenken (v) (G), bestow, grant, present

der shenker, saloonkeeper

der shenkl, cabinet, locker

shenst (G), finest, most beautiful

shepn, to derive, to draw

der sheps(l) (G), lamb, sheep

der sheptsh, whisper

sheptshen (v), to whisper

der sher, a lively Jewish dance, sher

di sher, shears

der sher-blat, title page

der sherer (G), barber

shern, clip, cut, shear; "lernen zikh shern oyf bord", to use someone as a guinea pig

der sheygets (H), any wild boy, gentile boy; (pl. shkotsim)

sheyln (G), to peel, to shell

sheyn (G), beautiful, pretty

di sheynkeyt (G), beauty

dos shfikhes-domim (H), aggravation

der shidekh (H), a match (in betrothal); "redn a shidekh tsu", to propose a match to

shier (G), almost, (accompanied by "nit" or "nisht"), nearly, would-be

der shier (n) (H), lesson in Talmud (Jewish), limit

shif (adj), slanted

di shif (G), a ship; "arop fun shif", ashore, overboard; "oyf der shif", aboard ship

dos shifl, boat

shiker (adj) (H), drunk

der shiker (H), drunkard

shikern (H), to drink habitually

shikn (G), to send

dos shikres (H), drunkenness

di shikse (H), gentile girl

der/dos shikyingl (G), errand boy, messenger

shiltn, to curse

shisn (G), to shoot

shitn (v) (G), to pour

dos shitsblekh, fender

di shive (H), seven day mourning period after death of a close relative (Jewish); "zitsn shive", observing the seven day mourning period (Jewish)

di shkape (R), mare

dos shkheynes (H), vicinity; "in shkheynes (mit)", next door (to)

shkheynesdik (H-Y), adjacent, adjoining

di shkhine (H), the Divine Presence (G-D)

der shkhiv-mera (H), dangerously ill person

der shklaf (G), a slave

dos shklaferay, slavery

di shkole (R), school

di shlakht (G), battle, combat

der shlaks(regn) (G), downpour

shlekht (G), bad

der shlemiel, clumsy person, consistently unlucky person (somewhat pitiable), fool; (see shlimazl) "the shlemiel" spills hot soup in the lap of the shlimazl

der shlep, jerk, pull

der shleper (G), bum, hanger-on, hobo, vagabond

shlepn (G), to draw, to pull

shleykes (R), reins, suspenders

der shlimazl (G-H), a born loser, dolt, unlucky person

der shlisl (G), clue, key, wrench; "der frantseyzisher shlisl", "monkey wrench"

shlisn (v), to close, to conclude

der shlof, sleep; "der harter shlof", sound sleep

di shloflozikeyt, insomnia

dos shlofmitl, sleeping pill

shlofn (G), to sleep; "leygn zikh shlofn", to go to bed/sleep

der shloftsimer (G), bedroom
shlogn (G), to beat, to hit, to punish
der shlos (n), castle, joint, lock
der shlump (G), sloppy person
di shlumperke (G), slattern (female)
shmadn (H), to convert from Judaism
    to another religion; "er is geshmadt",
    "he is converted"
dos shmalts (n) (G), fat
shmaltsik (G), fat, greasy, gutsy tear-
    jerker (coll.)
di shmate (R), a rag
shmates, tatters
"shma-yisroel" (H), "Hear, O Israel"
    (Jewish credo said in prayers)
der shmays (G), a whack
shmaysn (G), to thrash, to whip
der shmek (n) (G), pinch, smell, sniff,
    whiff
dos shmekl (G), penis (coll.)
shmekn (G), to smell; "dos shmekt mir
    nit", "I don't care for this"
shmekn mit, to reek, to smell of
der shmeykhl (G), a smile
shmeykhlen (G), to smile
shmontses, folly, nonsense, trifles
der shmoysh, lambskin, sheepskin
di shmue (n) (H), rumor
der shmues (H), chat
shmuesn (H), chat, consider,
    deliberate, discuss
dos shmuts (G), dirt
shmutsik (G), dirty
der shnaps (G), brandy, (hard liquor)
der shnar (n), scar
di shnaydbret, carving board, cutting
    board
der shnayder (n) (G), tailor
shnaydn (G), to cut
der shnaydveg (n), crossroads
der shney (G), snow; "dos shneyele",
    snowflake; "di shneykoyl", snowball;
    "der shneyshturem", snow-storm
der shnips, a tie
der shnorer (G), mendicant, parasite,
    scrounger
shnorn (Y-G), to beg

di shnur (G), daughter-in-law
di sho (H), hour; (pl. shoen); "ale sho
    tsu der sho", every hour on the hour
di shoa (H), The Holocaust
der/di shof (G), sheep
der shok, a shock
der/di shok, sixty, threescore
der shokhn (H), neighbour (male);
    (pl. di shkheynim)
di shokhnte (shkheyne) (H),
    neighbour (female)
der shokl (G), nod, shake; "gib zikh a
    shokl", "get a move on"
shoklen (G), to rock, to shake;
    "shoklen mitn kop", to nod
di/dos sholekhts (n), peel, rind, shells
der sholem (H), peace
der sholem-bayes (H), domestic
    peace, harmony
sholem gebn (H-G), to greet, to
    welcome by shaking hands
der shop (n), raccoon
der shorabor (H), mythological bull
    whose flesh is a delicacy (Jewish)
der shoyfer (H), trumpet (ram's horn,
    ritual use: Rosh Hashana) (Jewish)
der shoyfet (n) (H), judge, referee,
    umpire
der shoykhed (H), a bribe, bribery,
    graft
der shoykhet (H), Jewish ritual
    slaughterer
di shoykhetke (H), wife of slaughterer
shoymer-umatsl zayn (H-Y), to
    protect and save; "got zol undz
    shoymer-umatsl zayn", Heaven protect
    us!
shoyn, already
der shoyte (H), blockhead, fool
shpakuln (R), spectacles
der shpalir, lane
shparn (v), to press, to push
shparn zikh, to dispute; "shparn zikh
    az", "to insist"
der shpatsir, excursion, stroll, walk
shpatsirn (G), to go for a walk, to stroll
dos shpayekhts (G), saliva, spittle

shpayen (G), to spit

dos shpendl(ekh), splinter(s), wood chip(s)

shpet (G), late (in time)

shpeter (G), later

der shpigl (G), mirror

di shpilke (R), pin; "zitsn oyf shpilkes", to sit on tenterhooks

shpiln (G), to play

der/dos shpitol, hospital, (M.S.)

shpogl nay (G), brand new, spic-and-span

di shprakh (G), language

shpreyen (G), drizzle

shpringen (G), to jump, to leap

di shprintse (G), lively good-natured daughter

der shprits (G), shower, squirt; "makhn zikh a shprits", "to take a shower"

di shpritsbret (n), dashboard

dos shpritsekhts, spray

shpritsn (v), splash, sprinkle, squirt

der shprokh (n), incantation, magic formula

di shraybmashin, typewriter

shraybn (G), to write

shrayen (G), to shout, to yell

der/di shrek (G), fright; "onvarfn a shrek oyf", "to terrify" (to throw a fright on)

shreklekh (G), terrifying

shrekn (v), to frighten, to terrify; "shrekn zikh", "to be frightened/terrified", "to fear"

der shtam, clan, race, stem, tribe, trunk

shtamen (G), to be descended, to come from, to stem

der shtar (H), bill, deed; (pl.) shtorim

shtarbn (G), to die

shtark (G), greatly, strong

dos shtaygl (G), bird cage

der shtekhl-khazer (G-H), porcupine

shtekhn (G), to prod, to stab, to sting

der shtekn (shtekl) (n) (G), cane, club, stick

shtekn (v), to stick; "shtekn in", "be involved in"; "shtekn zikh", "to meddle"; "shtek(t) zikh nit", "mind your own business"

der shtel, attitude

di shtel, stall, (newspaper) stand

di shtele, job, position; "di halbe shtele", part-time job

shteln (G), to put, to set up

shtendik (G), always, continually

der shter, drawback, handicap, inconvenience, obstacle

der shtern (G), brow, forehead

der shtern (G), star; "der falndiker shtern", "falling/shooting star"

shtern (v), to be in the way of, to disturb, to interfere; "shtern tsu", "to prevent someone from"

dos shtetl (G), small town

der shteyger, kind of, manner, way; "a shteyger", for example; "der shteyger lebn", way of life; "vi der shteyger iz", as usual

shteyn (v) (G), (clock) to have stopped, to stand; "shteyt im nit on", "not becoming to him"

der shteyn (n) (G), rock, stone

di shtibl, home, house, room

dos shtibl, (G), small Chasidic house of prayer

di shtifmuter (shtifmame) (G), step-mother

dos shtifmuterl (G), pansy (flower), (little step-mother)

shtifn (G), to be naughty, to carry on, to play pranks

shtik, pranks, whims; "makhn shtik", to carry on

di/dos shtik (G), piece; "a shtik tsayt", "for some time"

dos shtikl (G), bit, cake (of soap), head (of cattle), little piece; (pl.) shtiklekh; "mir zaynen shtiklekh makhatonim", "we are slightly related by marriage"

shtiklekhvayz (G), "little by little", piece meal

shtikn (v), to choke, to suffocate

shtil (G), quiet, silent; "in der shtil", quietly

shtilerheyt (G), secretly, unobtrusively

di shtim (n) (G), ballot, voice, vote; "opgebn di shtim", cast one's ballot

shtimen (G), to vote; "shtimen mit", accord with, be compatible with, "fit in", tally

di shtinke (n), smelt

shtinken (G), to stink

der shtinker (n) (G), a stinker

der shtokh (G), (sarcastic) dig, insinuation, shock, stab, stitch; "a shtokh in hartsn", "a stab in the heart"

shtokh (G), last trick in a card game, (Clubbyish, Pinochle)

shtolts (adj), proud

der shtolts (n), pride, stilt

shtoltsirn (G), to be proud of, to exult in

shtopn (G), to feed poultry, to stuff

di shtot (G), city; "in shtot", downtown

der shtoyb, dust

shtoydriyohu (R), tall, (coll.)

der shtraf (R), a fine

shtrafirn, to fine

dos shtrayml, fur hat worn by East European Jews and Chasidic Jews

shtrekn zikh (G), extend, strain

shtreng, severe, stern, strict

di shtrof (n), penalty, punishment, sentence

shtrofn (n), to punish

shtrofreyd (n), reproof

der shtroy (G), straw

der shtroys (G), ostrich

der shtshav (R) (schav), sorrel, spinach borsht

di shtub (shtibl) (G), home, house, room; "in shtub", at home, indoors

shtudirn (G), to study (secular only)

di shtudye, investigation, study

di shtunde (G), hour

der shtunk (G), stink, stinker

der shtup, impetus, push, shove

shtupn (G), to bribe (coll.), to push

der shturem (G), assault, (thunder) storm

der/dos shtus (H), folly, nonsense

der shukh (shikhl) (G), a shoe, (pl. shikh)

di shul (G), school, synagogue

di shuld, blame, fault, guilt; "aroyfvarfn di shuld oyf", to blame

shuldik (G), guilty

di shule (G), school

der shulkhn-orekh (H), code of religious laws (Jewish)

di shup, dandruff, fish scale

di shure (H), line (reading or writing), row; "di naye shure", a new paragraph

der shuster (G), cobbler, shoemaker

shustergas (G), "arayngeyn in shustergas", "lose its exclusiveness" (to go into the street of the shoemakers)

di shusterke (G), shoemaker's wife

der shutef (H), partner

shutfesdik (H-G), in partnership

shvakh (G), weak

der shvants (n), penus (coll.), tail

shvarts (G), black

der shvartsmeyenik (G-H-R), member of "the Black Hundreds" (Russian Reactionaries)

der shvarts-yor (n) (H-Y), devil (black year); "der shvarts-yor zol im nemen", "the devil (should) take him"; "geyn tsum shvarts-yor", "go to the devil"

shvaygn (G), to be silent, to stop talking

di shvebele, match (sulphur match)

der shvebl (n), sulphur

di shvegerin, sister-in-law

der/di shvel (G), doorstep, threshold

der shver (G), father-in-law

shver (H), difficult, heavy

di shverd (G), sword

shvern (G), to swear

di shvester (G), sister

dos shvesterkind (G), cousin

der shveys (n) (G), sweat

di shveyts, Switzerland

di shviger (G), mother-in-law

der shvoger, brother-in-law

di shvue (H), an oath

der shvues (H), Feast of Weeks, Shabuot (Jewish)

di sibe (H), accident, cause, reason

der sider (H), book (for daily prayers) (Jewish)

der sikhsekh (H), conflicts, controversy, feud

der silek (H), settlement

silekn (H), to pay off debts, to settle

der simen (H), a sign, (pl. simonim)

di simkhe (H), joyous occasion

der skhar (H), reward, salary

dos skhires (H), pay, reward, salary

di skhoyre (H), cloth, merchandise; "toyre iz di beste skhoyre", "Torah is the best merchandise"

"skotsl kumt", "look who's here", "welcome"

skutshne (R), boring, dull; "zayn skutshne", be bored (by)

di slikhes (H), penitential prayers (Jewish), said on the High Holidays

di smetene (shmetene) (R), sour cream

di smikhe (H), rabbi's license

smoktshen, to suck

der sobvey (Y), subway. (M.S.)

der sod (H), mystery, secret; (pl. soydes)

der sof (H), conclusion, end, turn (of century); "sof kol sof", "eventually"

der sofek (H), doubt, suspicion

sokhrish, business like

der soldat (G), soldier

der sosn (H), joy

di sosne (R), fir, pine tree

der sotn (H), Satan

der soykher (H), businessman, merchant, seller

der soyne (H), enemy; (pl. sonim)

der spodik (R), high fur hat (worn by Jews), saucer; "dreyen a spodik", annoy, to bother (to turn a hat)

di sreyfe (n) (H), fire

stam (adv) (H), just, simply

stayen (R), last, suffice, to be sufficient

staytsh, "how is this possible?", "what is the meaning of it?", (contraction of "vi heyst es oyf taytsh?")

di stelye (R), ceiling

der stolyer (R), cabinet maker, carpenter

dos stolyeray, cabinet making, carpentry

der strash (n) (R), scarecrow

strashen (R), threaten

di strashidle (R), scarecrow

der strazhnik (R), police officer

der strozh (R), building superintendent, janitor; (f.) di strozhke

der sud (R), court of justice

di sude (H), banquet, feast, festive meal; "praven a sude", "give a festive meal (kosher)"

di suke (H), sukkah, (festival booth), tabernacle (Jewish)

der sukes (H), Festival of Booths (Jewish)

di svore (H), guess, hypothesis

T

di ta'are (H), ritual cleansing of body before burial (Jewish)

der tabak, tobacco

di tabik (tabike) (R), snuff, tobacco

take (R), honestly, really; "take?", (implying incredulity) "do you mean it?"

der takef (H), influential, powerful person

der takhles (H), practical goal, purpose

takhrikhim (H), grave clothes, shroud

der tales (H), praying shawl (Jewish)

der tales-kotn (H), Jewish religious undergarment (see arbe-kanfes)

der talmed (H), student (m.)
der talmed-khokhem (H), Jewish
  scholar, learned man
di talme-toyre (H), Jewish school
  (Torah study)
di talmide (H), student (f.)
der tam (n) (H), good taste, taste; (pl.
  taymim)
der tam (H), half-wit, moron, naive
  person
tamevate (H-R), feeble-minded, foolish,
  naive; "makhn zikh tamevate", to play
  the fool
der tanakh (H), Jewish Bible
der tants (dos tentsl) (G), dance
tantsn (G), to dance
der tantszal, ballroom, dance hall
der tap, touch; "a tap ton", get a feel of,
  touch
tapn (G), to touch
der tareram, fuss; "makhn a tareram
  (iber)", make an issue (of)
dos tarfes (H), non-kosher food
  (Jewish), non-kosherness of food
  (Jewish)
der tate (R), father; "tatenyu!", "dear
  little father" (exclamation)
der tate-foter (R-G), G-D
tate-mame (R-G), parents
tayer, dear, expensive, precious; "haltn
  tayer", to treasure, to value; "kostn
  tayer", to cost a lot
tayere (G), darling! (f.), "dear ones"
tayerer (G), "dear one" (m.)
di tayne (H), argument, claim,
  complaint
taynen (H), argue, complain, contend,
  maintain
der taytsh (G), interpretation, meaning
taytshn (v), to interpret
di tayve (n) (H), lust, passion
tayvedik (H-Y), passionate, voluptuous
der tayvl, devil, fiend
der tel (H), ruin, shambles, to wreak
  havoc; "makhn a tel fun", "to create
  destruction", to ruin, "wreak havoc";
  "vern a tel (fun)", "to be ruined"

der teler (G), plate, (dinner)
der tenenboym (G), fir tree, spruce
dos tentsl (G), dance, jig
dos tepl, cup, small pot
der terets (H), answer, excuse,
  justification, pretext
di teve (H), habit, nature
di tey (G), tea
teykef (H), immediately
di tfile (H), prayer
tfiln (H), phylacteries (Jewish)
di tfise (n) (H), grasp, understanding
di tfise (H), prison
tif (G), deep
di tifle (H), church
der tikn (H), improvement, redress
der tilim (H), Book of Psalms (Jewish)
der tipesh (H), a dolt, a fool
tipish, typical
di tir (G), door, doorway
der tish (G), panel, table
der tishebov (H), fast of the ninth of
  Av, in commemoration of the
  destruction of the Holy Temple, (coll.
  "mourning") (M.S.)
der/dos tishtekh, tablecloth
der tkhies-hameysim (H),
  resurrection of the dead
der tnay (H), condition (pl. tnoyim)
to (R), so, well
der toes (H), error; "a toes hobn", "to
  be mistaken", to err
der tog (G), day; (pl. teg); "esn-teg",
  "the daily feedings of Yeshiva bokhers
  by various households" (eating days);
  "tog-teglekh" (adj), day-to-day
der tokhes (H), ass (bottom) (coll.),
  seat (coll.); "shteln tokhes oyfn tish"
  (G), "lay your cards on the table" (put
  your rear end on the table) (coll.)
di tokhter (G), daughter
der tolk (R), agreement, result, sense,
  understanding
tomed (H), always, invariably
tomer (H), if, in case, perhaps
der ton (n), note, tenor, tone; "der
  falsher ton", a sour note (a false note)

ton (v), to do; "ton zikh", to be going on, to be happening

der tones (H), fast day; (pl. taneysim)

der top (G), cooking pot

di topolye (R), poplar tree

di torbe (R), a sack, (a beggar's sack)

torn, to be allowed; "me tor nit", "one musn't"; "mir torn?", "may we?"

der toter, Tartar (Tatar)

dos toterish, Tartar (Tatar) language; gibberish (hum.)

toye, "zikh toye zayn" (H-Y), "to make a mistake"

toygik (adj), fit

di toygikeyt, fitness

toygn (v), to be adequate, to be worth, to qualify; "es toyg oyf kapores", "it's good for nothing"; "vos toyg", what good is, what use is?

di toykhekhe (H), list of afflictions (rel.); "oyslozn di toykhekhe oyf", "heap curses on"

di toyre (H), law, (five books of Moses) (Jewish)

di toyre-shebalpe (H), oral law (the Talmud)

di toyres-moyshe (H), Law of Moses

toyt (adv), dead

der toyt (n), death

der toytn, a dead person

di toyve (H), a favour, a good deed; "maysim toyvim", "good, pious deeds"

toyvl zayn (H-Y), to immerse (Jewish ritual); "toyvl zayn zikh" (H-Y), to immerse oneself for ritual purification (Jewish)

der toyznt (G), thousand

trakhtn (G), to think

der trask (R), a bang, a blow (slap), a crash; "er lebt mit trask", "he's living it up"; "er trasket mitn gelt", "he throws his money around"; "firn zikh mit trask", "to live in high style"

dos traybholts, driftwood

dos traybl, telephone receiver, tube

traybn (G), to drive, to force, to goad; "traybn rekhiles", to gossip

der tref, clubs (in cards), guess, impact

trefn (G), to guess, to happen, to meet

trenen, to fornicate (coll.)

di trep, stairs (flight of); "di halbe trep", landing

di trer(n) (n), tear(s)

trern (v), to fill eyes with tears

treyf (adj) (H), non-kosher food (Jewish), shady

der treyfnyak (H-R), one who eats "treyf"

treyslen (R), to shake, to shudder

treystn, to comfort, to console; "treystn zikh in", to take comfort in

trinken (G), to drink

dos trinkgelt (n), tip

trogedik (Y), pregnant; "makhn trogedik", to impregnate

der trog-farhiter (Y-G), contraceptive (pregnancy preventor)

trogn (v) (G), be pregnant, carry

trukn (adj) (G), dry; "opshnaydn trukn", to come out unharmed

der trumbanik (trombenik) (R), troublemaker

der trunk (G), a drink, a swig

der tsad (H), party, side, side of a family (pl. tsdodim)

der tsadik (H), saint (Jewish); (coll.), smart alec

der tsank, flicker

tsanken, to fade, to flicker, to grow dim

der tsap, he-goat

der tsar (H), grief, sorrow; "tsum tsar", "unfortunately"

der tsar (R), Czar

di tsatske (R), ornament, toy, trinket; "tsatsken zikh" (v), to fuss over (with pride or delight)

di tsavoe (H), a bequest, a testament, a will

tsaygn (G), to point out, to show (old usage)

di tsayt (G), era, time

di tsaytung (G), journal, times

di tsdoke (H)   **dos tsitkes (H)**

---

di tsdoke (H), charity; "es toyg oyf tsdokes (tsitkes)", "it's only good to give away" (snide remark)

tsebrekhn (G), to break, to crush, to fracture

tsebrokhn (adj), broken

der tsederboym (G), cedar tree

tsedreyen (v), to confuse, to distort, to twist

tsedreyt (G), crazy, mixed up, turned around, twisted

tsegeyn, melt, thaw; "tsegeyn zikh", to disperse

tsekhapt (G), snapped up

tsekneytsht (G), crumpled, wrinkled

tsekrokhn (G), slovenly

der tseleyger (f. di tseleygerke), hotshot

tseleygn (G), to arrange, to lay out; "er tseleygt es oyf zibn telerlekh", "he makes a great show of little (learning)"

der tselokhes (H), defiance, spite, (from Hebrew "lehakh'is", "to anger"); "oyf tselokhes", "for spite"

tsen (G), ten

dos tsener (tsendl, tsenerl) (coll.), a tenner, a ten-spot (ten dollar bill); "tsener-yorn", teens

di tsenerene, devotional book for women (Jewish)

tseraysn (G), to rip apart, to tear

di tseraysung, denunciation (of an agreement)

tserinen zikh (v), to dissolve

tseshpaltn, to split (with an axe)

tsetreyslen (v), to rattle, to shake up (emotionally)

tsetreyslt, shaken up (emotionally)

tsetrogn, absent-minded, beside onself, upset

tsetumlt, confused

der tseylem (H), cross, crucifix

tseylemen zikh (v), to make the sign of the cross

tseyln (G), to count, to number; "tseyln sfire", "telling (counting) the count" between Passover and Shabuoth

der tseynveytik, toothache

der tshad (Y), carbon monoxide, charcoal fumes

der tshadnepl (Y-G), smog

der tshaynik (R), kettle, teapot; "hakn a tshaynik", to argue endlessly, to bother, to chatter (to bang a teapot)

tshepen (R), to bother, to plague, to touch; "tshepen zikh tsu", badger, bother, bully, pick on

di tshernitse (R), huckleberry

tshikave (R), curious

tsholent (F), Tsholent (a dish kept warm for the Sabbath) (Jewish); (lit. warm)

di tshuve (H), answer, penitence; "tshuve ton", to atone, to do penance

der tshvekl, small nail

der tshvok, large nail; (pl. tshvekes)

tsi (R), if; "tsi . . . tsi", "whether . . . or"

der tsi (n) (G), jerk, pull, stretch, stroke; "a tsi ton", to jerk, to pull

di tsibele (R), flower bulb, onion; "di bitere tsibele" (bitter onion), wet-blanket (fig.); "di tsibele-trern" (onion tears), crocodile tears

tsien (G), to draw out, to pull, to stretch; "tsien zikh", to continue, to last

dos tsien (H), Zion

der tsienist (H), Zionist

der tsienizm (H), Zionism

der tsig (G), goat

der tsigayner (G), gypsy

tsiklen zikh, cantor's ecstatic repetition of a musical phrase

di tsilbret (G), target

der tsimer (G), a room

der tsimes, pudding, vegetable stew; "makhn a tsimes", "to make a federal case" (coll.) (to make a stew of it)

tsitern (G), to shiver, to shudder

dos tsitkes (H), charity, piety, saintliness, virtue

der tsol (n), customs duty, inch, tariff, toll

di tsol (n), number; "on a tsol", countless, innumerable

tsoln (G), to pay (money)

der tson (G), tooth; (pl.) di tseyn, di tseyner

der tsop (n), a braid; (pl.), tsep

der tsop, he-goat, (pl.), tsopes

di tsore(s) (H), hardship, misery, sorrow, trouble

tsu (G), apiece, to, too, towards; "tsu tsvey bikher", two books apiece

tsu, closer, (as prefix) shut, some more

der tsudek (G), cloak, covering, mantle

tsudekn (v), to cover

tsufridn (G), happy, satisfied

der tsugang, approach

tsuganvenen (H-G), to rob, to steal

dos tsugebekhts, additive

tsugebn (G), to add, to admit, to concede

tsugeyn (G), to approach, to step over

der tsugob (G), accessory, an addition

tsugreytn (Y-G), to prepare

der tsuker (G), diabetes, sugar

tsuleygn (G), to add to, to apply; "tsuleygn zikh", "lie down for a while"

tsulib (G), for the sake of; "vos tut nit a yid tsulib parnose", "what won't a Jew do for a livelihood"

tsumakhn (G), to close, to shut; "tsumakhn an oyg", to die (to shut an eye) (G)

der tsung (G), tongue

di tsure (n) (H), face

tsurik, back; "gey tsurik", "go back"

tsurirn (G), to approach, to touch

tsushikn (G), to send

tsuzamen (G), together

tsuzamenfirn (G), bring together (tsunoyffirn), collate; "er ken tsuzamenfirn a vant mit a vant", "he's a great wrangler" (he can bring together a wall with a wall)

der tsuzamenshtoys, collision, conflict, crash

tsuzetsn zikh (Y-G), to take a seat for a moment; "tsuzetsn zikh tsu", "to sit in on"

tsuzogn (G), to promise

der tsuzung, chorus, refrain

tsvantsik (G), twenty

tsvelf (G), twelve

tsvey (G), two

der tsveyfl (n), doubt

tsveyflen (v), to doubt

tsveyt (G), second

tsveytns, secondly

tsvishn (G), between

der tsvuyak (H-R), hypocrite (tsvuak); (f.), di tsvuatshke

di tube (n), tuba, tube (sqeezable)

der tuman (R), fog, mist

tume (H), impurity (morally)

der tuml (G), clamour, noise, racket; "makhn a tuml", "create a stir"

tunkl (G), dark, dim, dull, sinister; "tunklte gesheftn", "monkey business" (dark businesses)

di turme (R), jail

der tuts, dozen

di tvue (n) (H), cereal, grain

U

di ugerke, cucumber; "zoyere ugerke", dill pickle, wet blanket (fig.) (sour pickle)

di ume (H), nation, people; "umes-ho'oylem", nations of the world

der umet, gloom, sadness

umetik, disconsolate, gloomy, lonesome, restless, sad

umetum (Y), everywhere

umetumik (Y), ubiquitous

umfaln (G), to collapse, to fall, to tumble

dos umglik (G), accident, misfortune

der umkum, holocaust, mass death

umkumen, to die a violent death, to perish

umnisht, for no reason, in vain, to no avail

umshuldik, innocent

der umyoysher (Y-H), injustice

umyoysherdik (Y-H), unfair, unjust

umzist, in vain, to no purpose

undzer (G), our

unter (G), under

der unterban (G-Y), subway

unterdrikn (G), to oppress, to suppress

der unterfirer (G), one who accompanies or leads

der unterfirer (Y-G), best man at wedding

di unterfirerin, bridesmaid

unterganvenen zikh, to sneak up on

untergebn (G), to add (small amounts of); "zikh untergebn", "to surrender"

untergeyn (G), to go down, to go under, to sink

unterhaltn (Y-G), to bear out, to support, to sustain

unterhern (Y-G), eavesdrop, overhear

unterhinken (Y-G), be faulty, limp; "zayn entfer hinkt unter a bisl", "his reply doesn't hold water"

unterhungern (Y-G), to go on a starvation diet

unterhustn (Y-G), to cough slightly, to sputter (engine)

unterkoyfn (Y-G), to bribe

unterlekn zikh (Y-G), to toady

unterlenen (Y-G), "unterlenen zikh dos harts", have a bite to eat (give the heart a boost)

unterleygn (Y-G), to lay beneath; "unterleygn an aksl", "put a shoulder to the wheel"

di unternemung (G), enterprise, undertaking

der unteropteyl, subdivision

untershmirn (Y-G), to bribe (hum.), to grease; "az me shmirt, fort men", "if you grease you ride"

untershraybn (G), to sign your name

di untershrift, signature

untershteln (Y-G), to place underneath

untershteln zikh (Y-G), to dare; "vos shtelt ir zikh unter?", "how dare you?"

untershtupn (Y-G), to bribe (hum.), to push along

untertantsn (Y-G), to be obsequious (sycophant), to toady

untertentslen (Y), to dance obedience

dos untertetsl (n), coaster (under glasses)

untertraybn (Y-G), to drive hard, to goad, to urge on

untertrogn (Y-G), exasperate, shock, wait on

untervarfn (Y-G), abandon (a child), plant (stolen goods); "untervarfn a kind", "to abandon a child on a doorstep"

untervarfn zikh, to submit

untervisik (adj) (Y-G), subconscious

di untervisikeyt (n), subconscious

unterzindikn (Y-G), to sin continuously (petty sins)

unterzogn (Y-G), to prompt (furtively)

untn (G), below, downstairs, underneath

der untn (n), bottom, downstairs

der utshastok (R), branch, district, field, police station

der utshenik (R), high school student

V

vaksn (G), to grow

der vald (G), forest, woods

dos vald, timber

valn, election(s)

di vane, bath tub; "makhn a vane", "take a bath"

di vant (n) (G), wall; (pl. vent); "redn tsu der vant", "to waste your breath" (to talk to the wall); "rirn a vant", "move a stone to tears"

di vants, bedbug

varem (adj) (G), warm

di varemflash, hot-water bottle

der varenik (n) (R), cheese or jam filled dumpling (also varenishke)

di varenye, jam

varg, ware (suffix)

dos varg, equipment, gear

varum (G), why

dos vaser (n) (G), water

vashn (G), to wash

di vate, absorbent cotton

der vatn-makher (Y-G), devil (coll.); "khapt im der vatnmakher", "may the devil take him"

di/dos vayb (G), wife

vayb, women

vayberish (G), feminine, women's

der vayhi (H), calamity; "in eyn vayhi", in a jiffy

vayivrekh (H), (lit. "and he fled") (Jacob); "makhn vayivrekh" (hum.), to flee, to run away, to take to one's heels

vayl (G), because

di vayl (vayle) (n) (G), while; "ale vayle", frequently, intermittently

di vaylinke (G-Y), a little while

der vayn (G), wine

der vaynshl (G), a cherry (sour); "makhn a vaynshl", "pucker one's lip"

vays (G), white

vayt (G), far

di vebshtul (G), a loom

der veg (G), path, road, way

vegn (G), about, regarding; "er hot gefregt vegn dir", "he asked about you"

vegn (G), to weigh

vekn (G), awaken, to wake

velkhe (G), which

veln (v) (G), shall, to boil, will; "veln zikh", "have a yen for"

di velt (G), world; "di velt", "This life"; "yene velt", far away, life to come, the sticks

veltlekh (G), secularized, worldly

vemen, whom

vemens, whose

ven (G), for, when

der verb, verb

di verbe (R), willow tree; "di veynendike verbe", weeping willow

vern (G), to be; "zol vern", "may it be"

vert (G), worth, worthy; "hobn/zayn (di) vert", be entitled to, be worth, deserve

der/di vert (n), merit, value, worth

der/dos verterbukh (G), dictionary

dos vertl (G), saying

dos vesh (G), laundry, linen, underwear, wash

di vesne (R), spring (season)

der veter (G), weather

di vetshere (R), supper

der vey (G), hurt, woe; "es tut mir vey", "it hurts"; "vey iz mir" (vey z'mir), "my goodness!"

veynen (G), to cry

der veytik (G), ache, hurt, pain

vi azoy (G), as, how, like

di vide (H), deathbed confession; (pl.), di viduim

vider (G), again

vifl (G), how many, how much

der vifler (Y), quotient

vign (G), to rock, to swing

viklen, roll up, twist, wrap

viklen zikh, to spin, to wind

di vikltrep (der escalator) (Y-G), escalator

der vikuekh (H), debate, disputation; (pl.), di vikukhim

vild (adj) (G), wild

viln (G), to want, to wish

vinkl (n) (G), corner

der vint (n) (G), wind

der vinter (G), winter; "vinter", in the winter

vintshn, to wish

vintsheven, to congratulate

visik (Y), conscious

visn (G), to know; "ikh veys?", "do I know?"; "veys ikh vos?", "fiddlesticks", "how do I know?"

der vogn (G), buggy, carriage, cart, wagon

di vokh (G), week

der vokzal (R), depot, railway station, (see I.O.), station building, terminal

der volkn (G), cloud

der volknbrokh, cloud burst

der volkn-kratser, skyscraper

volvl, cheap

di vontse (vontses, vontsn), moustache

vorem (Y-G), because (or "vorn")

der vorem (G), worm; "yeder vorem hot zayn dorem", "there's a reason for everything" (every worm has it's intestines)

der voron (R), a raven

di vorone (R), crow

dos vort (G), word (pl. verter)

vos (G), that, what; "far vos", "why?"; "vos nor", whatever

vosara (vos far a) (Y-G), "what a . . . " (what kind?)

voyl (G), good, happy, nice, pleasant; "zol es dir voyl bakumen", you are welcome

dor voyl, welfare

voynen, to reside

vozhe (Y-G), what for, what then, why

vu (G), where; "ergets vu", "someplace"; "vu geystu?", "where are you going?"

di vund (n) (G), injury, sore, wound

der vunder (n) (G), wonder

Y

der yadn (H), expert, knowledgeable person, widely informed person (in Talmud)

di yagde (R), berry; "di shvartse yagde", "blueberry" (black berry)

der yakhsn (H), a man with "yikhes" (status), privileged person; "zayn a glaykher yakhsn mit", "be as good as"

di yakhsnte (H), feminine of "yakhsn"

der yalovets (R), juniper (tree)

der yam (H), ocean, sea; "a yam", a lot of; "der yam-suf" (H), "Red Sea"

dos yapan, Japan

der yapaner, Japanese person

yapanish (adj), Japanese

dos yapanish (n), Japanese (language)

der yarid (H), bazaar, fair; "me ken nit zayn mit eyn tokhes oyf tsvey yaridn", "you can't be in two places at one time" (you can't be with one behind at two fairs)

di yarmulke (H), skull cap

yarshenen (H), to inherit

di yashtsherke(s) (R), lizard(s); "lakhn mit yashtsherkes", "to laugh through tears" (crocodile tears)

di yasine, ash tree

di yasle, chewing gum

der yasmin (G), jasmine

di yatke (R), butcher shop

yeder (G), each, every; "yeder tsveyter", alternate, every other

der yedeye-hakl (H), G-d, (the Omniscient One)

yedue (H), (generally) known

di yelole (H), lament, wail; "makhn yeloles", to wail

"yemakh-shmoy" (H), "let his name be wiped out" (curse); "yemakh-shmoy-vezikhroy", "and his memory" (even stronger curse)

der yemakh-shmoynik (m.) (n) (H), scoundrel; (f.), di yemakh-shmoynitse

yener (G), that, the other; "yener velt", out in the sticks, "the beyond"

der yerey-eloyhim (H), G-D-fearing person

der yerey-shomayim (H), G-D-fearing person (fearful of the heavens)

dos yerusholaim (H), Jerusalem

di yerushe (H), heritage, inheritance, legacy

di yeshive (H), Talmudic Academy; "der yeshive-bokher" (H), "yeshiva student"

di yesoyme (H), orphan (female); (pl.), di yesoymes

yesurim (H), anguish, suffering; "hob nit keyn yesurim", don't worry; "onton yesurim", to cause suffering to

der yetsies-mitsrayim (H), the Exodus of Jews from Egypt

der yeytser (H), (psychological) drive, inclination, urge

der yeytser-hore (H), evil inclination, sexual impulse

der yeytser-toyv (H), good inclination, moral sense

der yid (G), a Jew (male)

di yidene (G), a petty, sentimental, talkative Jewess

yidish (adj), Jewish, Yiddish

dos yidish (G-Y), the Yiddish language

di yidishke (dos yidish-kind), Jewess

yidishn (v), to circumcise (Jewish)

der yikhes (H), aristocracy (Jewish), distinguished ancestry, importance (hum.), lineage, pedigree, status

yingele, dear little boy

der/dos yingl (G), boy

der yishev (H), colony, settlement (community), village

der yishev-hada'as (H), consultation, deliberation, reflection

yishevn zikh (H-Y), to consider, to deliberate, to hesitate

di yodle (R), fir, spruce tree

der yom-hadin (H), day of reckoning, doomsday

"yomim-nero'im" (H), "days of awe", (Rosh Hashanah and Yom Kippur)

der yonkiper (H), Day of Atonement (Yom Kippur) (Jewish)

der yontef (H-Y), (H. "yomtov"), festival, holiday, (pl. "yontoyvim")

yontevdik (H-Y), festive, gala

dos yor (G), year

der yorhundert (G), century

der/di yortsayt (G), anniversary of death (Jewish)

dos yortsayt-likht (G), anniversary candles (for the dead) (Jewish)

der yosem (H), orphan (m.); (pl. di yesoymim)

der yovn (R), a Russian, a soldier; (pl. yevonim); "ale yevonim hobn eyn ponim", "all soldiers (Russians) look alike"

di yoykh (yaykhl) (R), broth, gravy; "di gildene yoykh" (G-R), "fat chicken soup"

der yoysher (H), fairness, justice; "alpi yoysher" (H), "by right", "in all fairness"

yoysherdik (H-Y), fair, just

di yugnt (G), young woman, youth (collective)

yukl fayvish, nincompoop

yung (adj) (G), young

der yung (n) (G), a boy, a fellow, a youth

der yungatsh (G-Y), brat, rascal, scamp

der yunger-man (G), a young man

Z

di zakh (G), thing; "dos iz di zakh", that's the point; "keyn zakh nit", nothing; "nit dayn zakh", none of your business; "nit tsu der zakh", irrelevant; "tsu der zakh", relevant, to the point

dos zaklayvnt (n) (G), sackcloth

di/dos zalts (G), salt

der/dos zamd (G), sand
zamen zikh (G), to return late, to saunter, to stay behind
zamlen (G), to collect, to gather
di zaverukhe (P), a blizzard
zaydn (G), gentle, kind, silken; "zaydene hentshkes", "kid gloves" (figurative) (silken gloves)
dos zaydns, silk
zayn (G), his; "zayns", his, "his own way"
zayn (G), to be; "zayt azoy gut", "please" (be so good); "zayt gezunt", be healthy/well (a fairwell greeting)
zaynike (G-Y), his own way
di zayt (G), page (of a book), side
der zay-visn, message
zekhtsik (G), sixty
zekhtsn (G), sixteen
zeks (G), six
der/di zelbshuts, (organization for) self-defence
der zelbstmord (aleynmord) (G), suicide
der zelner, soldier
der/di zeml, roll (for eating)
dos zemlmel, best flour, "cream of the crop"
zen (v), to behold, to see
der zeneft, mustard
zey (G), them, they
der zeyde (R), grandfather
di/dos zeyf (G), soap
der zeyger (G), clock; "siz fir azeyger", "it's four o'clock"
dos zeygerl, wrist-watch
zeygern (v), to time
di zeygerung, timing
zeygervaylekhts, clockwise
der zeykher (n) (H), remembrance, remnant, trace
der zeykher-lekhurbn (H), memorial of the destruction of the Temple
der zgal (n), kind, sort, species; "siz nit far zayn zgal", "it's not for the likes of him"

zhaleven (R), to begrudge, to economize on, to give reluctantly; "nit zhaleven", "be extravagant with"
zhe (R), (a floating particple, cannot be used alone), now, then, well; "ven zhe vet ir kumen?", "so when will you come already?"
der zhid (R), a Jew (very derogatory)
der zhulik (R), crook, good-for-nothing, rogue
di zhurekhline (R), cranberry
der zhurnal (G), newspaper (journal)
zi (G), she
zibetn (G), seventh
zibitsik (G), seventy
zibitsn (G), seventeen
zibn (G), seven
zidlen, to call names, to curse, to scold
der zifts, a sigh
ziftsn (v), to sigh
zikh (G), each other, self
zikher (G), certain, for sure
zikhroyne-livrokhe (H), of blessed memory (said after the mention of a name of a respected deceased Jewish man/woman)
der zikorn (H), memory
dos zilber (G), silver
der zilzl (H), abuse, defamation, humiliation, vilification
zilzldik, abusive, derogatory
di zind (G), sin
zindikn (G), to sin
zingen (G), to sing; "hobn tsu zingen un tsu zogn", "to have no end of troubles"
zis (G), cute, fresh (water), sweet
der zits, seat
zitsn, to sit
di zitsung, conference, meeting, session
der ziveg (H), a pairing, marriage, mate; "mayn ziveg", "my preordained mate"; "dos ziveg-lebn" (H-Y), "married life"; "di zivegshaft" (H-Y), marriage, matrimony, wedlock

der zkhus (H), justification, merit, privilege; "melamed-zkhus zayn" (H-Y), justify, speak favourably about, "to give the benefit of the doubt"

der zman (H), period, semester, term, (alloted) time

zogn (G), to say; "zogzhe", "please speak"

der/di zok(n) (n) (G), sock(s), stocking

zok, hose (stocking)

der zokn (H), old man

zol (v) (G), shall

di zorg, care, worry; "on zorgn (zorg'loz)", carefree

zorgn (G), to care fore; "zorgn far", to cater to

zorgn zikh, to worry

zoyer (G), pickled, sour

di zoyere ugerke, dill pickle (sour cucumber), (fig. wet blanket)

di zoyermilkh (G), buttermilk, (sour milk)

zoykhe zayn (v) (H-G), be worthy of, have the honour of, live to see

der zukhenish, searching

zukhn (G), to search, to seek

der zukhtsetl, index

di zukhung, search

dos zukhvort, entry word

zumer (zumertsayt) (G), in the summer

der zumer (G), summer

zumerdik (G), summery; "sof zumerdik", "late summer"; "sof zumerdik teg", "last days of summer" ("eleldike teg", same as "sof zumerdik teg")

dos zumer-feygele, butterfly

der zun (G), son

di zun (G), sun, sunshine

der zunele (G), dear little boy

der zuntik, Sunday; "zuntik", on Sunday

der zup, sip

di zup (G), soup

dos zupfleysh, boiled beef

zupn (G), to sip, to slurp

The Plant World
Di Velt Fun Flantsn

alder (tree), di o̧lkhe (R)
almond(s), der mandl(en)
apple, der epl
apricot, der apriko̧s (R)
artichoke, der artisho̧k
ash, dos ash
asparagus, di sparzshe (R)
aspen (tree), di osine (R), der topo̧l̩
(R)
avocado, der avokado
bamboo, der yamsh
banana, der banan̩
bay leaf, der lo̧rberblat
bean, dos bebl (pl. di beblekh), der bob
(R) (pl. di bobes), di fasolye (pl. di
fasolyes)
beech, der buk (R)
beet, der bu̧rik (R); (pl.) bu̧rikes
berry, di yagde (R)
birch tree, di bereze (R)
blackberry, di o̧zhene (R)
blade (of grass), dos grezl
blossom, der kveyt, der tsvit
blossoms, dos bliekhts (pl. only)
blueberry, di shvartse yagde (G-R)
bough, di tsvayg
branch, der optsvayg, di tsvayg
Brussels sprouts, dos brisler kroyt (Y-
G)
bud, der buto̧n, der knosp
bulb, di (blu̧men-) tsi̧bele
bunch (of grapes), dos hengl
bush, der kust
cabbage, dos kroyt (G)
cactus, der kaktus
cantaloupe, di dinke (R)
caraway, der kiml
carnation, dos nȩgele
carrot(s), di mer(n)
cauliflower, dos blu̧menkroyt, der
kalifyo̧r
cedar tree, der tsȩderboym
celery, di sȩlerye
cherry, di karsh, der vaynshl (sour
cherry)
chestnut, di kest
chicory, di tsikorye

citron (Succoth), der esreg (H)
(Jewish)
climbers, kleterbleter
cinnamon, der tsimring
clove(s), dos nȩgele(kh), dos tseyndl
(of garlic)
clover, di konishine
cocoanut, der ko̧kosnus
coffee, di kave
cone (of a tree), di shishke (R)
conifer, der no̧dlboym
corn, der papsho̧y (R), di kukuruze (R)
cotton, der bavl
cotton batting, di vate
crabapple, dos erts-isro̧el-epele
cranberry, di bru̧snitse (mountain)
(R), di zhurekhli̧ne (R)
cucumber, di u̧gerke (R)
currant, dos va̧ymperl
cypress, der tsiprȩs
daffodil, der geler nartsi̧s
daisy, di margeri̧tke
dandelion, dos luftl
date, der teytl
date-palm tree, der tȩytlboym
dill, der krop
dill pickle, di zoyere ugerke
eggplant, der patlezhan̩ (R)
eggwhite, dos vaysl
elm, der knupboym
eucalyptus, der eykali̧pt
evergreen, der nodlboym
farina, di mane
fern, dos federgroz
fig, di fayg
filbert, dos valdnisl
fir, di sosne (R), di yodle (R)
flower, di blum, der kveyt
forest, der vald
forget-me-not, dos fargȩsnitl
fruit, di peyre (H), di frukht (G)
fungus, der shvom
garlic, der knobl
ginger, der ingber
gooseberry, der agres (sing. and pl.)
(R)
grape, di vayntroyb

grapefruit, der greypfru(kh)t
grapevine, di pantofl-post
grass, dos groz
greenhouse, di oranzherie (R)
hazelnut, dos hozn nisl
herb(s), dos kraytekhts(er)
honeydew, di tsesarke
horseradish, der khreyn (R)
huckleberry, di tshernitse (R)
hybrid, der mishling
ivy, kleterbleter, der plyushtsh, der vilder vayn
jasmine, der yasmin
juniper, der yalovets (R)
leaf, der blat; (pl.) bleter
leek, di pore-tsibele
lemon, der tsitrin, di limene
lettuce, der salat, shalatn
lilac, der bez, der may
lily, di lilye
lime, di grine limene, der laym
mahogany, der mahon
maple, der nezboym
melon, di dinye (R), der melon
mint, di mints
mushroom, der shvoym (pl. shvoymen), dos shveml (pl. shvemlekh)
mustard, di gortshitse (R), der zeneft
myrtle, der hodes (H), di mirt
nettle (stinging), di kropeve (R), di shtekhavke
nut, der nus (pl. nis)
nutmeg, der mushkat
oak tree, der demb (P), der domb (P)
oats, der hober
olive(s), di masline(s), der eylbert (n)
onion, di tsibele
orange, der marants
orchard, der sod (R)
orchid, di orkhideye
oyster, der oyster
palm branch (Succoth), der lulev (H) (Jewish)
palm tree, di palme
pansy, dos shtifmuterl (G), dos khaneles eygele (H-Y)

parsley, di petrishke (R)
parsnips, der pasternak (R)
pea, der arbes (same in pl.)
peach, di fershke
peanut, dos rebe-nisl (H-Y), di stashke
pear, di barne (di bar)
pecan, der pekan
peel, di sholekhts
pepper, der fefer
peppermint, dos fefermints
pickle (dill), di zoyere ugerke (G-R)
pineapple, der ananas (R)
pine tree, di sosne (R)
plant, di flants, der geviks
plum, di floym
poison ivy, sam-bletlekh (H-G)
pollen, der (blumen)shtoyb
pomegranate, der milgroym (R)
poplar, di topolye
poppy, der mon
poppy seed(s), der mon
potato, di bulbe (R), der kartofl (R)
praline(s), di priline(s)
prickly, shtekhik
primrose, der priml
prune, di (getriknte-)floym
pumpkin, di dinye (R), der kirbes
radish, der retekh
radish,(red), dos (resh-)khoydesh-retekhl (H-R)
raisin, di rozhinke (R)
raspberry, di malene (R)
reed, der ayir, der ror (H)
rhubarb, der rabarber
rice, der rayz
root, der vortsl
rose, di royz
rush, der kamish (R)
safflower, di zeyfblum
saffron, der zafren
salt, di zalts
sap, der sok, der zaft
sapling, dos shprotsl
seaweed, dos yam-groz (H-Y)
seed, di zere (H), der zoymen
sheaf, der garb
shrub, der kshak (R)

snapdragon, dos leybnmoyl
soy beans, di soye
spice, dos gevirts
spinach, der shpinat (R)
spruce, der tenenboym (G), di yodle
  (R)
squash, der kabak (R)
stalk, dos shtengl, di zang
stamen, der shtoybfodem
stem, der shtam, dos shtengl
straw, di shtroy
strawberry, di pozemke (wild) (R), di
  truskafke (R)
string bean(s), di grine fasolye(s), dos
  lopetkele(kh)
sugar, der tsuker
sugar cane, der tsukerror
sunflower, di zunroyz
sunflower seed(s), di semitshke(s) (di
  zhemishke, di zhemitshke)
sweet potato, di batate
tea, di tey, di tshay (R)
tea leaf, dos teyele
thistle, di shtekhlke
thyme, der timyan
toad-stool, dos (sam-)shveml
tobacco, der tabik, di tabike, der titun
tomato, der pomidor (I)
tree, der boym
trunk, der shtam
tulip, der tulpan (R)
turnip, di brukve (R)
twig, dos ritl, dos tsvaygl
vegetable, dos grins
vegetable plant, dos geviks
vine, kleterbleter, der vaynshtok
vineyard, kleterbleter, der vayngortn
violet, di fyalke (R)
walnut, der veltshener nus
watermelon, der arbuz (R), di kavene
  (R)
weed, dos vildgroz
wheat, der veyts
whortleberry, di (shvartse) yagde (R)
wilderness, di vildenish
willow, di verbe (R)
wood, dos holts (G)

wood-chip(s), dos shpendl(ekh)
woods, der vald
yam, der yam (pl. yamen)

The Animal World
Di Velt Fun Khayes

animal, der bal-khay (H), di khaye (H)
ant, di murashke (R)
anthill, der murashnik
ape, di malpe, di obezyane
badger, der taks
to bark, biln, havken
bat, di fledermoyz
bear, der ber
beast, di beheyme (H), di khaye (H)
beaver, der biber
bedbug, di vants
bee, di bin
beehive, der binshtok
beetle, der zhuk, der khrushtsh (R)
bird, der foygl; (pl.) feygl
birdy (birdies), di feygele(kh) (Y-H)
bison, dos vizltir
bitch, di klafte (H), di tsoyg
blackbird, der amstl
bloodhound, der shpirhunt
bray, shrayen
brood, der plid, dos zetsl
buffalo, der bufloks
bug, der knayper, der zhuk
bull, der bik (R), der buhay
bulldog, der buldog
bumblebee, di zhumzhe (R)
butterfly, dos flaterl, dos zumer-feygele
calf, dos kalb
camel, der keml
canary, der kanarik
carp, der karp
carrier pidgeon, di posttoyb
cat, di kats (pl. di kets), der koter (pl. di koters) (male)
caterpillar, der opfreser, dos shleyerl
chicken, dos hindl, di hun
chipmunk, der (geshtrayfter) vevrik
chirp, tshiriken, tsirlen
clam, der klam
claw, di krel
cockroach, der tarakan (R)
cod, der dorsh
coo, torklen, vorken
coop (chicken), der katukh (R)
coop (pidgeon), der toybnshlakh
cow, di beheyme (H), di ku; (pl.) di ki

cowhide, der yukht
crab, der krab
crane, der kran(ikh), der zhuravl
crawl, krikhn
crayfish, der rak (R)
cricket, di gril, der tshirkun (R)
crow, di kro, di vorone
cub (bear), dos berl; (lion), dos leybl
cuckoo, di kukavke
cud (to chew c.), malegeyren (H)
deer, der hirsh, di sarne (R)
doe, di hind
dog, der hunt
doghouse, di bude
dolphin, der delfin
donkey, der eyzl
dove, di toyb
down, der pukh (feathers) (R)
dragonfly, di libele
drake, der kotsher
drumstick, di polke (chicken) (R)
duck, di katshke (R)
dung, dos mist
eagle, der odler
egg, dos ey; (pl.), di eyer
eel, der venger
elephant, der helfand
elk, der los
fawn, di hirshele
feather, di feder
ferret, di fret-vizele
fin, di flusfeder
firefly, der glivorem
fish, der fish (same in pl.)
flea, der floy; (pl. di fley)
fleece, di fel
flock, di stade, di tsherede; (of birds) (R), di tshate
fly, di flig
fly (v), flien
flying (adj), fliendik
fowl, dos of (H) (pl. di oyfes)
fox, der fuks
foxhole, di fuksnlokh
frog, di frosh, di zhabe (R)
fur, der futer, der pelts, dos roykhvarg
gander, der goner

gill, di zhabre
giraffe, der zhiraf
gizzard, der pupik
gnat, di muk (R)
gnaw, grizhen, khromtshen
goat, der bok (male) (pl. di bek), der
    tsap (male) (pl. di tsapes), di tsig
    (female) (pl. di tsign)
goose, di ganz; (pl.) di genz
gopher, der grizun
gorilla, di gorile
grasshopper, der shpringer
graze, fitern zikh, pashen zikh
greyhound, der khart (R)
growl (n), der vortsh
growl (v), vortshen
guinea-pig, dos yam-khazerl (H)
gull, di meve (R)
halibut, der halibut
hamster, der hamster
hare, der hoz (R)
hatch (to be h.), brien zikh, (oys) pikn
    zikh
hawk, der falk (R)
hedgehog, der shtekhler
heifer, di telitse (R)
hen, di hun; (pl.) di hiner
herd, di stade (R), di tsherede
herring, der hering
hibernate, vintern
hippopotamus, der hipopotam (R)
honey, der honik
hoof, di kopete, di tlo
hornet, di ferdbin
horse, dos ferd (sing. and pl.)
horseshoe, di potkeve (R)
hound, der shpirhunt
howl (n), der rev, der voy
howl (v), reven, voyen
insect, der insekt
ivory, der helfandbeyn
jackal, der shakal (R)
kangaroo, der kenguru
kennel, di hintarnye
kitten, dos ketsl
lady-bug, dos meshiyekhl (H), dos
    moyshe-rabeynes kiyele (H)

lair, di nore
lamb, di lam (pl. di lemer), dos leml (pl.
    di lemlekh)
lambskin, der shmoysh (R)
lark, dos trilerl
larva, di larve, dos shleyerl
leather, di leder
leech, di piavke (R)
leopard, der lempert
lion, der leyb
lioness, di leybikhe
litter, der plid
livestock, dos fikh, der lebediker
    inventar
lizard(s), di yashtsherke(s) (R)
lobster, der homar (F)
locust, der heysherik
louse, di loyz (pl. layz)
lynx, der luks
maggot, di mod (R)
mammal, der zoyger
mane, di grive (R)
manger, der zholeb (R)
manure, dos mist
mare, di kliatshe, di shkape (R)
mew, kanoyken, myauken (R)
migrate, ibervandern
migration, di vanderung
mink, der mink
mite, di milb
mole, der krot (R), der multvorem
molehill, dos krotbergl (R-G)
monkey, di malpe
moo, muken
mosquito, der komar, der moskit
moth, der mol (R)
mouse, di moyz
mule, der moyleyzl
neigh, hirzhen
nest, di nest
nightingale, der solovey (R)
nocturnal, nakhtik
oink (n), der khruk
oink (v), khruken
ostrich, der shtroys (R)
otter, di vidre (R)
owl, di sove (R)

ox, der oks
oyster, der oyster
pack (of wolves), di staye, di tshate (R)
panther, der panter
parakeet, der langekiker popugay (di
    papuge)(P), der parakit
parrot, der popugay (di papuge)(P)
partridge, di kuropate (R)
paw (large), di lape (R)
peacock, di pave (R)
perch, der okun (R)(pl. di okunyes)
pet, der gletling
pheasant, der fazan (R)
pig, der khazer (H)
pigeon, di toyb
pigsty, der khazer-shtal (H-G)
pike, der hekht
polar bear, der vayser ber
pony, der poni
poodle, der pudl
porcupine, der shtekhl-khazer (Y-H)
    (pl. di shtekhl-khazeyrim)
poultry, oyfes (H)
praying mantis, der heysherik
prowl, lugn, shlaykhn zikh
prowler, der nakhtshlaykher
pup, dos hintl, der tsutsik (R)
pupa, dos goyleml (H)
purr, mruken
pussycat, di kotinke
quack, kvaken
quail, der vakhtl
quill, di feder
rabbit, dos kinigl
rabies, dos (hintishe) meshugas (Y-H),
    di vasershrek
raccoon, der shop
ram, der baran (R), der vider
rat, der rats, der shtshur
rattlesnake, di klapershlang
raven, der rob, der voron (R)
reindeer, der renifer
reptile, di reptilye, der sherets
rhinoceros, der noz'horn
roar, der bril, der brum
roar (v), briln, brumen, reven
robin, dos royt'heldzl

rodent, der noger
roe (deer), di sarne (R)
roe (fish), der royg
rooster, der hon (pl. di hener)
salmon (smoked), der laks
sardine, der sardin
scale (fish), di shup
scallop, der skalop
scorpion, der ekdish, der skorpyon
seafood, dos filyervarg, di yam-shpayz
    (H-G)
sea gull, di meve
seal, der yam-hunt (H-G)
seashell, dos meyerkepl, dos yam-
    multerl (H-Y)
serpent, di shlang
shark, hayfish
sheep, der sheps, di shof
sheepskin, der shmoysh
shellfish, di multer-brie (Y-H)
shrimp, der rakl, (fig. der shnek), der
    shrimp
skunk, der tkhoyer
smelt, di shtinke
snail, di poyle-royle, der shnek
snake, di shlang
snout, der pisk
sole, di yam-tsung (H-Y)
sow, di khazerte (H), di lyokhe
sparrow, der shperl
sparrow hawk, der shparber
spider, di shpin
spider web, dos shpinveb
sponge, der shvom
squid, der tintfish
squirrel, di veverke (R); "grey
    squirrel", der fey
stag, der hirsh
stallion, der oger
steer, dos eksl
stork, der botshan, der bushl
stud (horse), der zavod (R)
sturgeon, der balik
swarm, der roy, der shvorem, di staye
swine, der khazer (H)
tadpole, dos kopekl
tail, der ek, der veydl

termite, der termit
tick, der klieshtsh
tiger, der tiger
toad, di broske, di luhashke (R), di
   ropukhe
tongue, di tsung (pl. di tsinger)
tortoise, di tsherepakhe (R)
trout, di stronge (R)
trunk, der shnuk
tuna fish, der tunfish
turkey, der indik (R)
turtle, di (vaser-)tsherepakhe
udder, der ayter
vixen, di fuksikhe
vulture, der grif
walrus, der morzh, dos yam-ferd (H-G)
wasp, di vesp
weasel, dos vizele
web-footed, pletvedik
whale, der valfish
whiskers, vontselekh
wildcat, di valdkats
wing, der fligl
wolf, der volf (pl. di velf)
woodpecker, der pik'holts
wool, di vol
worm, der vorem (pl. di verem)
wren, der rob
zebra, di zebre

The Weather
Der Veter
(Der Droysn)

blizzard, di zaverukhe (P)
blow, blozn
clear, klor
cloud, der volkn, (pl.) volkns
cloudy, volkndik
cold (adj), kalt
cold, di kelt
damp, faykht
dew, di rose, der toy
drizzle (n), dos regndl, der shpreyregn
drizzle (v), shpreyen
dry, trikn
fog, der nepl
foggy, nepldik
freezing (to be), zayn a frost
freezing weather, der frost
frost, dos gefrir
frosty, frostik
hail (n), der hogl
hail (v), hoglen
heat, di hits
hot, heys
how's the weather?, vi iz es in droysn?
humid, dempik
hurricane, der huragan
it's blowing rain, snow, wind etc, es
   blozt a regn, a shney, a vint
lighten (v), blitsn
lightning, der blits
mist, der tuman (R)
moon, di levone (H)
mud, di blote
muddy, blotik
new moon, der moyled (H)
pour (rain), khlyapen
rain (n), der regn
rain (v), regnen
rainbow, der regn-boygn
rainfall, der skhum regn (H)
rainy, regndik
sleet, der graypl-regn
snow (n), der shney
snow (v), shneyen
snowstorm, der shneyshturem
snowy, shneyik
star, der shtern
starry, oysgeshternt

sun, di zun
sunny, zunik
sunshine, di zun
thunder (n), der duner
thunder (v), dunern
tornado, der tornado
warm, varem
wet, nas
weather, der droysn, der veter
what's it like out?, vi iz es in droysn?
wind, der vint
windy, vintik

der blits, lightning
blitsn, to lighten
di blote, mud
blotik, muddy
blozn, to blow
dempik, humid
der droysn, weather
der duner, thunder
dunern, to thunder
es blozt a regn, a shney, a vint, it's
   blowing rain, snow, wind, etc.
faykht, damp
der frost, freezing weather
frostik, frosty
dos gefrir, frost
der graypl-regn, sleet
heys, hot
di hits, heat
der hogl, hail
hoglen, to hail
der huragan, hurricane
kalt (adj), cold
di kelt, cold
khlyapen, to pour rain
klor, clear
di levone (H), moon
der moyled (H), new moon
nas, wet
der nepl, fog
nepldik, foggy
oysgeshternt, starry
der regn, rain
der regn-boygn, rainbow
regndik, rainy
dos regndl, drizzle
regnen, to rain
di rose, dew
der shney, snow
shneyen (v), to snow
shneyik, snowy
der shneyshturem, snowstorm
shpreyen, to drizzle
der shpreyregn, drizzle
der shtern, star
der skhum regn (H), rainfall
der tornado, tornado
der toy, dew

trikn, dry
der tuman (R), mist
varem, warm
der veter, weather
vi iz es in droysn?, what's it like out?,
   how's the weather?
der vint, wind
vintik, windy
der volkn, (pl.) volkns, cloud
volkndik, cloudy
di zaverukhe (P), blizzard
zayn a frost, to be freezing
di zun, sun, sunshine
zunik, sunny

Family Relations
Di Kroyveshaft

adopt, adoptirn
adoption, di adoptirung
aunt, di mume (di tante)
baby, dos eyfele (H)
boy, der/dos yingl
brother, der bruder, (pl.) di brider
brother-in-law, der shvoger
child, dos kind, (pl.) di kinder
children (small), kinderlekh
cousin (f), di kuzine, (pl.) di kuzines, dos shvesterkind
cousin (m), der kuzin, (pl.) di kuzinen, dos shvesterkind
daughter, di tokhter, (pl.) di tekhter
daughter-in-law, di shnur, (pl.) di shnir
descendant, der opshtamling
father (parent), der tate (der foter)
father-in-law, der shver
father of daughter-in-law or son-in-law, der mekhutn (H)
girl, di/dos meydl, (pl.) di meydlekh
grandchild, dos eynikl
granddaughter, dos eynikl
grandfather (grandparent), der zeyde
grandmother (grandparent), di bobe
grandparents, zeyde-bobe
grandson, der/dos eynikl
great (ancestor) (prefix), elter
great (progeny) (prefix), ur
great-grandchild, der ureynikl
great-granddaughter, dos ureynikl
great-grandfather, der elter zeyde
great-grandmother, di elter bobe
great-grandson, der/dos ureynikl
lass, di moyd
little boy, der boytshik (anglicism), dos yingele
little girl, di meydele
maiden, di moyd
mother (parent), di mame (di muter)
mother-in-law, di shviger
mother of daughter-in-law or son-in-law, di makheteneste (H)
nephew, der plimenik
niece, di plimenitse
only daughter, di bas-yekhide (H)

only son, der ben-yokhed (H)
orphan, der yosem, (pl.) di yesoymim (H)
parent (father), der tate (der foter)
parent (mother), di mame (di muter)
parents, eltern, tate-mame
predecessor, der foroysgeyer (der firgeyer)
progeny, der nokhkum, der opshprots
quadruplets, der firling
quintuplets, der finfling
relative, der korev (H), der eygener
relative by marriage, di makheteneste (f) (H), der mekhutn (m) (H)
siblings, der geshvister
sister, di shvester (sing. and pl.)
sister-in-law, di shvegerin
son, der zun, (pl.) di zin
son-in-law, der eydem, (pl.) di eydems
step-brother, der shtif-bruder
step-father, der shtif-foter
step-mother, di shtif-muter
step-sister, di shtif-shvester
teenager, der tsenerling
triplets, der drayling
twin brother, der tsviling-bruder
twin sister, di tsviling-shvester
twins, der tsviling
uncle, der feter (der onkl)

adoptirn, to adopt
di adoptirung, adoption
di bas-yekhide (H), only daughter
der ben-yokhed (H), only son
di bobe, grandmother, grandparent
der boytshik (anglicism), little boy
der bruder; (pl.) di brider, brother
der drayling, triplets
elter . . . (prefix), great . . . (ancestors)
di elter bobe, great grandmother
eltern, parents
der elter zeyde, great grandfather
der eydem (pl. eydems), son-in-law
dos eyfele (H), baby
der/dos eynikl, grandson
dos eynikl, grandchild
dos eynkil, granddaughter
der feter (der onkl), uncle
der finfling, quintuplets
der firling, quadruplets
der foroysgeyer (firgeyer),
  predecessor
der foter, father, parent
der geshvister, siblings
dos kind (pl.) kinder, child
kinderlekh, children (little)
der korev (H) (der eygener), relative
der kuzin (m.), (pl.) kuzinen, cousin
di kuzine (f.), (pl.) kuzines, cousin
di makheteneste, mother of daughter-
  in-law or son-in-law, relative by
  marriage (f.)
di mame (di muter), mother
der mekhutn, father of daughter-in-law
  or son-in-law, relative by marriage
  (m.)
di meydele, little girl
di/dos meydl; (pl.) di meydlekh, girl
di moyd, lass, maiden
di mume (di tante), aunt
di muter, mother, parent
der nokhkum (der opshprots),
  progeny
der opshtamling, descendant
der plimenik, nephew
di plimenitse, niece
di shnur (pl. shnir), daughter-in-law

der shtif-bruder, step-brother
der shtif-foter, step-father
di shtif-muter, step-mother
di shtif-shvester, step-sister
di shvegerin, sister-in-law
der shver, father-in-law
di shvester (sing and pl), sister
dos shvesterkind, cousin
di shviger, mother-in-law
der shvoger, brother-in-law
der tate (der foter), father
tate-mame, parents
di tokhter; (pl.) di tekhter, daughter
der tsenerling, teenager
der tsviling, twins (pair of)
der tsviling-bruder, twin brother
di tsviling-shvester, twin sister
ur . . . (prefix), great . . . (progeny)
der ureynikl, great grandchild
der/dos ureynikl, great grandson
dos ureynikl, great granddaughter
dos yingele, boy (little)
der/dos yingl, boy
der yosem, (pl.) yesoymim (H),
  orphan
der zeyde, grandfather, grandparent
zeyde-bobe, grandparents
der zun; (pl.) zin, son

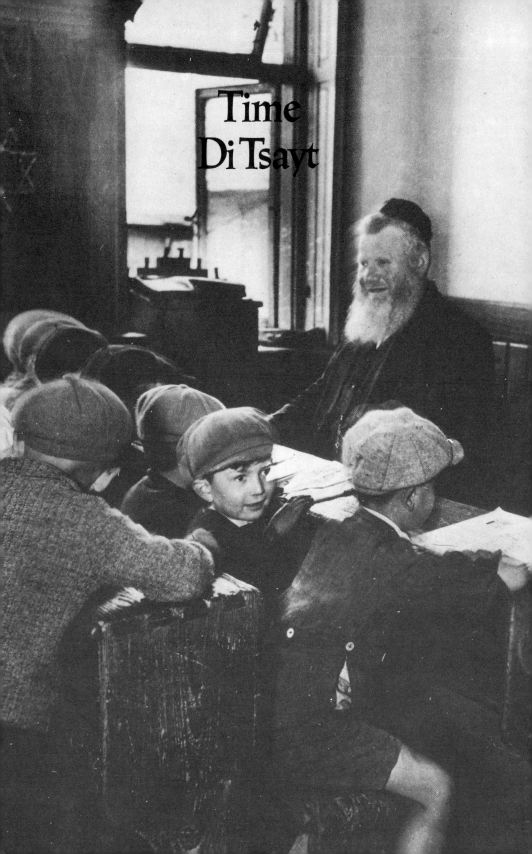

Time
Di Tsayt

dos gev̲erk	clockwork
dos h̲ant-zeygerl	wristwatch
der minutnik	minute hand
der sekundnik	second hand
der sh̲oen-plan (H-G)	timetable
der sh̲oen-vayzer (H-G)	hour-hand
der stoper	stopwatch
vayzn di tsayt	to clock
der v̲ekzeyger, (pl.) di v̲ekzeygers	alarm clock
vifl iz der zeyger?	what time is it?
der zeyger; (pl.) di zeygers	clock
zeygerdik	clockwise
dos zeygerl; (pl.) di zeygerlekh	watch
z̲eygervaylekhts	clockwise
eyns azeyger (eynse)	one o'clock
eyn minut nokh eyns	one minute after one
fuftsn minut nokh eyns,	
a fertl nokh eyns	one fifteen or a quarter after one
eyn (un) draysik,	
a halb nokh eyns	one thirty or half-past one
nayn un tvantsik tsu tsvey	twenty-nine minutes to two
a fertl tsu tsvey,	one forty-five, a quarter to two,
fuftsn minut tsu tsvey,	fifteen minutes to two
tsvey azeyger (tsveye)	two o'clock
dray azeyger (draye)	three o'clock
fir azeyger (fire)	four o'clock
finf (finef) azeyger (f̲ineve)	five o'clock
zeks azeyger (zekse)	six o'clock
zibn azeyger (z̲ibene)	seven o'clock
akht azeyger (akhte)	eight o'clock
nayn azeyger (nayne)	nine o'clock
tsen azeyger (tsene)	ten o'clock
elf azeyger (e̲leve)	eleven o'clock
tsvelf azeyger (tsv̲eleve)	twelve o'clock
tsvelf azeyger bay tog, mitog	twelve o'clock p.m., noon
tsvelf azeyger bay nakht, halbenakht	twelve o'clock a.m., midnight
baginen	at dawn
bay nakht	at night
baynakhtik (adj)	nighttime
bay tog	in the daytime
baytogik (adj)	daytime
dos beynashmoshes (H)	twilight
far nakht	at dusk
farn̲akht, in ovnt	in the evening
der farn̲akht	dusk
far tog	at the crack of dawn
der fart̲og, der kay̲or	dawn

di halbe nakht	midnight
der halber tog	noon
in der fri	by day, daytime
mitn tog glaykh	at daybreak
di mitog-sho	noon hour
mitogtsayt	at noon
di mitogtsayt	noon
di nakht	night, nighttime
der ovnt	evening
dos toglikht	daylight
di sekunde; (pl.) di sekundes	second
di minut; (pl.) di minutn	minute
di sho; (pl.) di shoen (H)	hour
di shtunde; (pl.) di shtundes	hour
der tog; (pl.) di teg	day
di vokh; (pl.) di vokhn	week
der khoydesh; (pl.) khadoshim (H)	month
der monat; (pl.) di monatn	month
dos yor; (pl.) di yorn	year
der dor; (pl.) di doyres	generation
der yorhundert; (pl.) di yorhunderter	century
di ere, di tkufe (H)	era

Di Fir Sezonen (Tsaytn)   The Four Seasons

der sezon(en)	season(s)
di tsayt	season
der farpeysekh (Y-H)	spring
der friling	spring
der vesne (R)	spring
friling(tsayt)	in the spring, springtime
der zumer	summer
zumerdik	summery
zumer (tsayt)	in the summer, summertime
der khezhvn-zumer (H-Y)	Indian summer
der harbst, der osyen	fall, autumn
der vinter	winter
vinterdik	wintery
vinter(tsayt)	in the winter, wintertime

Di Yidishe Khadoshim (Monatn)   The Jewish Months of the Year

der tishre	Tishre
der khezhvn	Heshvan
der kislev	Kislev
der teyves	Tebeth
der shvat	Shebat
der oder	Adar
der oder tsvey (in a leap year)	Adar Two

der nisn	Nissan
der ier, der iyer	Iyar
der sivn	Sivan
der tamez	Tammuz
der ov	Ab
der elel, der elul	Elul

Di Englishe Khadoshim (Monatn) — The English Months of the Year

der yanuar	January
der februar	February
der marts (merts)	March
der april	April
der may	May
der yuni	June
der yuli	July
der oygust	August
der september	September
der oktober	October
der november	November
der detsember	December

Di Zibn Teg Fun Der Vokh — The Days of the Week

di vokh	week
der zuntik	Sunday
zuntik	on Sunday
der montik	Monday
montik	on Monday
der dinstik	Tuesday
dinstik	on Tuesday
di mitvokh	Wednesday
mitvokh	on Wednesday
der donershtik	Thursday
donershtik	on Thursday
der fraytik	Friday
fraytik	on Friday
der shabes (H)	Saturday
shabes	on Saturday

Numbers
Di Numern

Di Grunttsoln	Cardinal Numbers
eyns	one
tsvey	two
dray	three
fir	four
finf (finef)	five
zeks	six
zibn	seven
akht	eight
nayn	nine
tsen	ten
elf	eleven
tsvelf	twelve
draytsn	thirteen
fertsn	fourteen
fuftsn	fifteen
zekhtsn	sixteen
zibetsn	seventeen
akhtsn	eighteen
nayntsn	nineteen
tvantsik (tsvontsik)	twenty
eyn un tvantsik (tsvontsik)	twenty one
tsvey un tvantsik (tsvontsik), u.a.v.	twenty two, etc.
draysik	thirty
eyn un draysik, u.a.v.	thirty one, etc.
fertsik	forty
fuftsik	fifty
zekhtsik	sixty
zibetsik	seventy
akhtsik	eighty
nayntsik	ninety
hundert	hundred
hundert un eyns	hundred and one
hundert un tsvantsik	hundred and twenty
tsvey hundert, u.a.v.	two hundred, etc.
toyznt	thousand
tsvey toyznt	two thousand
milyon	million
bilyon	billion

Di Seyder-Tsoln (Di Ordenung-Tsoln)	Ordinal Numbers
ershter	first
tsveyter	second
driter	third
ferter	fourth
finfter	fifth
zekster	sixth
zibeter	seventh
akhter	eighth
naynter	ninth
tsenter	tenth
elfter	eleventh
tsvelfter	twelfth
draytseter	thirtheenth
fertseter	fourteenth
fuftseter	fifteenth
zekhtseter	sixteenth
zibetster	seventeenth
akhtseter	eighteenth
nayntseter	nineteenth
tsvantsikster (tvontsikster)	twentieth
eyn un tsvantsikster (tvontsikster) u.a.v.	twenty first, etc.
draysikster	thirtieth
fertsikster	fourtieth
fuftsikster	fiftieth
zekhtsikster	sixtieth
zibetsikster	seventieth
akhtsikster	eightieth
nayntsikster	ninetieth
hundertster	hundredth
hunder ershter	hundred and first
hunder eyn un tsvantsikster (tvonsikster)	hundred and twenty-first
toyzntster	thousandth
milyontster	millionth

Proper Names
Di Prat-Nemen
(Di Familyes)

Adlman (Adelman, Eydlman), nobleman
Atles (Atlas), satin
Aynbinder (Einbinder), bookbinder
Ayzn (Eisen), iron
Barg (Berg), hill
Berger, miner
Bikl (Bikel), marble (toy)
Birger (Berger, Burger), citizen
Blok (Block), pulley
Bodner, barrel-maker
Boyer, drill (n)
Boytshik (Boytchuk), youth (n)
Breg, shore
Bremen, eyebrows
Brenen (Brennan), burn
Brener (Brenner), burner
Bril (Brill), roar
Buk (Buck), beech
Dayen (Dayan), rabbi's associate
Drayfus (Dreyfus), tripod
Falk, hawk
Farb, dye
Fefer, pepper
Feler, defect
Fingerhut, thimble
Finkel, sparkle (n)
Fleysher (Fleisher), butcher
Fokh (Foch), flutter (n)
Fokher (Fokker), fan (n)
Freylekh (Frelick), happy
Fraynd (Friend), friend
Frits (Fritz), chump, novice
Freyd (Freud), joy
Frost (Frosst), freezing weather
Gelernter, learned man
Glezer (Gleyzer), spectacles
Greb, thickness
Grenetshteyn (Granatstein), landmark
Grinshpon (Greenspan), verdigris
Gris (Griss), regards
Harts (Hartz), heart
Heler (Heller), fair
Helfand, elephant
Heyber (Haber), lever
Hilka (Hilkka), bat (wood)

Himel, sky, heaven
Hoyt, skin
Kant, region
Katerinke, barrel organ, jalopy
Kats (Katz), cat
Keler (Keller), basement, cellar
Keml (Kemel(man)), comb
Kern, turn (v)
Kestn (Keston), boxes
Keyle, instrument
Keymen (Kayman), smokestack
Kheyfets (Keyfets), object (aim)
Khronik (Kronik), chronicle, annals
Kinig (Koynig), king
Kintsler (Kunsler), artist
Kirzhner, furrier, hatter
Kling, blade
Korb, basket
Kormen (Korman), feed (v)
Korn, rye
Kotsher (Kotser), drake
Kotz (Kats), blanket
Krankeyt (Kronkite), disease
Krug, jug
Kurts (Kurts(man)), short
Landsman, countryman
Langer, longer
Lempert (Lampert), leopard
Lerer, teacher
Lind, gentle
Lombard, pawnshop
Mark, market place
Melamed (Melamud), teacher
Muter, permissible
Naft, kerosene
Neyder (Nader), vow (n)
Neygl (Nagel), fingernail
Nodlboym (Nodelbaum), evergreen
Odler (Adler), eagle
Okun, perch (fish)
Pasternak, parsnips
Poter (Potter), dispose
Pulver, gun-powder
Raye (Riah), proof
Redner (Radner), orator, talker
Sam, poison
Shants, ditch

Shats (Shatz), value
Shef (Sheff), boss
Shenk (Shankman, Shenkman), pub (owner)
Sheyfer (Shafer), trumpet
Shir (Shier), poem
Shier (Sher, Shier), limit
Shif (Shiff), ship
Shmukler (Smukler), lacemaker
Shnayder (Snider, Snyder), cutter, tailor
Shpayzer (Spizer), provider
Shpigl (Spiegel), mirror
Shtern (Stern), forehead, stars
Shtrom (Strom), scar, stream, tide
Shuster, shoemaker
Solovay (Solway), nightingale
Sosn (Sossin), joy
Teler, dish
Teper(man), potter(man)
Top, cooking pot
Toyb (Taub), dove
Tselnik (Selnik), notions (goods)
Tshaynik (Chainek), kettle, teapot
Vayngarten (Winegarden), vineyard
Vaynshtok (Winestock), vine
Vayntrob (Winetrob), grape
Yeger (Jaeger), hunter
Yung (Jung), youth

Anecdotes
Di Anekdotn

araynfaln, "araynfaln vi a yovn in suke", to barge into a conversation, (lit. to fall like a Russian soldier into a Sukkah)

araynleygn, "shtarbn iz nokh vi es iz, ober dos araynleygn in drerd, dos bagrobt a mentshn", "dying isn'too bad in itself, it's laying the man in the earth that buries him"

aynredn, "es ret zikh ayn!", "that's what you say!"

azoy, "is that so?"

bagrobn, "do ligt der hunt bagrobn", this is the unknown factor, (lit. there lies the dog buried); "zayn oder nit zayn, do ligt der hunt bagrobn", "to be or not to be, that is the question"

der bal-tshuve (H) (a penitent), "There, where the bal-tshuve stands, even the saints cannot stand." the godless reply: "Because of the smell"

bela'z (H), (sarcastic) English equivalent: " . . . if you'll pardon my French", "otherwise known as", (lit. in the language of the strange people)

betsedek (H) (with righteousness), (Ironically) . . . B, TS, D, K,-"biz tsu der keshene", (lit. as far as the pocket)

boykh svores (Y-H), "Hogwash!", (lit. belly surmises)

der dank, "a dank dir in noz arayn", you needn't have bothered, (lit. thank you in your nose)

di dayge (H), "mayn bobes dayge", "I should worry" (lit. my grandmother's worry)

daygen (H), "nit gedayget!", "Buck up!", (lit. not worried)

di deye (H) (opinion), "a breyte deye hot er", "He does all the talking" (lit. he has a wide idea)

dreyen (to turn), "er dreyt mitn grobe finger", "He argues the point speciously" (lit. he turns with a fat finger (thumb))

foyl (lazy), "siz a foyler terets", "Your answer doesn't hold water", (lit. that's a lazy excuse)

feygelekh (little birds), "leyg nit feygelekh in buzem", "Don't count your chickens before they're hatched", (lit. don't put little birds in your bosom)

di gdule (H) (glory, grandeur), "a gdule oyf zayn bobe", "much glory to his grandmother" (mocking sarcasm)

geshtoygn, "nit geshtoygn, nit gefloygn", entirely untrue, (lit. neither arose nor flew) (in reference to Jesus Christ)

hakn (to bang, chop), "hakn a tshaynik", to chatter, argue endlessly, (lit. to bang a teapot)

der haldz (throat, neck), "du zoltst zikh shemen in dayn vaytn haldz", "Shame on you" (lit. blush deep down in your throat)

hefker tsibeles (H-Y) (lit. worthless onions); hefker petrishke (H-R) (lit. worthless parsley), "Everything goes!"

der honik (honey), "bay im hob ikh keyn honik nit gelekt", I did not succeed with him, "I didn't have an easy time with him", I had no success with him, (lit. I didn't lick any honey by him); "ir hot in belsen keyn honik nit gelekt?", "You had a hard time in Belsen?"; "MENTSH! men hot undz gor keyn sakharin gegebn", "Man, they hardly gave us any saccharin"

di kapore (H), "a sheyne reyne kapore", "Good riddance", (lit. a beautiful, pure scapegoat fowl)

kapores (H) (rel. ceremony), "es toyg oyf kapores", "It's good for nothing"; "oyf kapores!", (idiomatically) "like a hole in the head"

di kashe (R) (porridge), "farkokhn a kashe", "to brew up trouble" (lit. to cook up a stew)

di keyle (H) (vessel), "di puste keyle", "an empty-headed person", "windbag", (lit. empty vessel)

der khazer (H) (pig), "az men est khazer, zol rinen iber dem moyl", Go the whole hog, In for a penny, in for a pound, (lit. When one eats pig, it should run over his mouth); "lebn a khazershn tog", "Living it up", (lit. living a pigish day); "vil men zayn a gvir, darf men zikh farshraybn oyf tvantsik yor a khazer", "If one wants to become a rich man, one must sign up for twenty years as a swine"

khlebn, honestly, I should live so, (contraction of "ikh zol azoy lebn")

di khutspe (H) (arrogance, gall), This word is difficult to define accurately, but perhaps this story will help: A young man, convicted of mudering his mother and father, is asked by the judge if he had anything to say before sentence is passed. He throws himself on the mercy of the court on the plea that he is an orphan. That's khutspe.

kimat (H) (almost), "kimat hot amol dem taytsh fun gornit", "A miss is as good as a mile", (lit. 'almost' can sometimes be translated as 'nothing')

dos knipl (knot), "er hot a knipl", "he has a hoard of savings (some money)", (lit. tied in a corner of a handkerchief or in a sock)"

der kop (head), "geyn mitn kop durkh der vant", "To knock yourself out to do the impossible" (lit. to go with one's head through the wall); "zikh shlogn kop in vant", "To beat your brains out", To carry on without hope, (lit. to bang one's head against the wall)

kosher (H) (ritually clean, honest), "der khazer shtelt aroys dos koshere fisl", putting over a fraud, (lit. The pig thrusts out its kosher little leg)

koyln (to slaughter), "er hot mikh gekoylet on a messer", "He ruined me" (lit. he slaughtered me without a knife)

di kushvokh, honeymoon, (lit. kiss week)

der laybserdak (religious Jewish undergarment), Those who resented its introduction in the Shtetl gave it the contemptuous expression "laybserdrek"

lebedikerheyt (living), "bagrobn lebedikerheyt", lost his shirt, ruined, (lit. buried alive)

matse-vaser (matzo water), "bilik vi matse-vaser", "Cheap as dirt"; "me hot es tsekhapt vi matse-vaser", "It was snapped up like hot cakes"

di mayse (H), story; "a mayse on a sof", "A dragged out affair" (lit. story without an end); "arbetn maysim", "Make a great to-do" (lit. work stories); "di emese mayse", "cancer" (lit. the real story); "gekhapt in der mayse", "caught in the act"; "gor a mayse!", "What kind of a story is that?"; "herst a mayse!", "What a story!" (lit. do you hear a story?); "heybt zikh on a mayse!", "Once you begin there'll be no end" (lit. a story starts); "opton a mayse", "Play a dirty trick"; "vos iz di mayse?", "What's wrong?" (lit. what's the story?); "zikh onton a mayse", "Commit suicide" (lit. do a story on oneself)

maysim toyvim (H) (good deeds), Parent's prayer, "toyre, khupe un maysim toyvim", "Torah, wedding canopy and good pious deeds"

mendl un vaybl, hook and eye (lit. Mendl and wife)

onmakhn (to stir up), "onmakhn a khasene", "To stir up a holy mess", (lit. stir up a marriage ceremony)

di peye (earlock, sideburn), "es ligt im in der linke peye", "He doesn't give it a thought" (lit. it lies in his left earlock)

der pupik (navel), "er ligt mitn pupik aroyf", "He's dead" (lit. he's lying with his navel up)

der shokl (a shake), "gib zikh a shokl!", "Get a move on!", (lit. give yourself a shake)

shtiklekh (little bits), "mir zaynen shtiklekh makhatonim", "We are slightly related by marriage" (lit. we are bits of relatives)

skotsl kumt, "look who's here", "welcome"

staytsh (Contraction of "vi heyst es oyf taytsh?"), "What is the meaning of it?" (How is this possible) (lit. what is it called in translation?)

der tog, day; "a nekhtiker tog", "stuff and nonsense", (lit. yesterday's day)

der trog-farhiter, contraceptive (lit. pregnancy preventor)

tseleygn (to lay out), "er tseleygt es oyf zibn telerlekh", he explains in detail, he spells out (lit. he lays it on seven plates)

tsiklen zikh, a cantor's ecstatic repetition of a musical phrase

der tsimes (stew), "makhn a tsimes", "to make a hash of it" (a federal case), (lit. to make a stew)

tsuzamenfirn (bring together), "er ken tsuzamenfirn a vant mit a vant", "He's a great wrangler" (lit. he can bring together a wall and a wall)

untershmirn (to bribe), "az me shmirt fort men", "If you grease you ride"

di vant (wall), "redn tsu der vant", "To waste your breath" (lit. to talk to the wall); "rirn a vant", "Move a stone to tears", (lit. move a wall)

visn (to know), "veys ikh vos", "Fiddlesticks" (lit. do I know what)

der vorem (worm), "yeder vorem hot zayn dorem", "There's a reason for everything" (lit. every worm has its intestines)

di yevonim (soldiers, Russians), "ale yevonim hobn eyn ponim", "All soldiers (Russians) look alike" (lit. all Russians have one face)

Curses
Di Kloles

aynleygn (to lie still), "lig ayngeleygt!", "Shut up!", (lit. lie still, stay still)

aynnemen a mise meshune (H), To suffer a violent death

bentshn (to bless, to say grace), "got zol im bentshn mit dray mentshn, eyner zol im haltn, der tsveyter zol im shpaltn, der driter zol im bahaltn", "may G-D bless him with three men: one to hold him, the second to split him, the third to bury (conceal) him"

der blits (a stroke of lighting), " a blits im in kop", "A lighting stroke in his head"

drikn (to have heaviness), "zol im drikn in hartsn", "may he have heaviness of the heart"

der duner (thunderbolt), "a duner zol im trefn", "may a thunderbolt strike him"

di gdule (H) (glory, grandeur), "a gdule oyf zayn bobe", "much glory to his grandmother" (An expression of mockery or sarcasm)

hargenen (H) (to kill, to murder), "ver geharget!", "Drop dead!" (lit. get killed)

di khoḻere (kholerye) (cholera), "a khoḻere oyf im!", "To hell with him" (lit. a plague on him)

oysgebn (to spend), "oyf doktoyrim zol er es oysgebn", "May he spend it all on doctors"

der parkh, canker, ulcer, rat (person), stingy person

der paskudnyak (R) (paskudnik), a most evil person (Worse than son-of-a-bitch), scoundrel

paskudne (paskudnye), filthy, nasty, rotten, loathsome; "a paskudne man", "A rotten fellow"

di paskutstve (R), feminine of "paskudnyak", (also filth and abomination)

di tsibele (onion), "zolstu vaksn vi a di tsibele, mitn kop in drerd un di fis aroyf", "May you grow like an onion with your head in the ground and your feet in the air"

yemakh shemoy (H), let his name be wiped out; yemakh shemoy vezikhroy, let his name be wiped out and his memory too

"zolstu voynen in a hoyz mit a toyznt tsimern, un in yeder tsimer zolstu hobn a bọykhveytik", may you live in a house with a thousand rooms, and in each room may you have a stomach-ache

Death, Cemeteries, God
Der Toyt, Di Bes-oylens,
Der Got

Der Toyt, Death

The Jews of Eastern Europe displayed an unusual preoccupation with death not
unnatural considering the times and the locale. These are some of the many words
and phrases they used to approach the subjects of death, cemeteries, G-D and the
Beyond, sometimes directly, sometimes tangentially and tragi-comically.

ariberpeklen zikh, to die (lit. to bring over bag and baggage)
aveksharn zikh, to die (lit. move oneself aside)
der bar-menen (H), a corpse
di emese velt (H-Y), the Hereafter (lit. the true world)
farbay, passed away
der gan-eydn (H), paradise
dos gehenem (H), hell
krepirn, to croak
di kvure (H), burial
maabid atsmoy lodaas (H), one who commits suicide
der/dos mes (H), corpse, dead man, ghost; meysim (pl.), corpses
der nifter (H), deceased person
nifter vern (H-Y), to die (said of a pious Jew) (others "geshtorbn")
nistalek vern (H-Y), to die (said of a very important pious Jew)
opgepotert (Y-H), done in
der oylem-habe (H), the Hereafter (lit. the world to come)
oysgeyn, to die (genteel)
oystsien di fis, to die (lit. to stretch out the feet)
oysvern, to cease to be
peygern, to die (lowest classes)
pupik, "er ligt mitn pupik aroyf", "he's dead" (lit. he's lying stomach up)
shive (H), Jewish seven day mourning period after death of a close relative (lit.
  seven); zitsn shive, to sit shiva
der shoykhn-ofer (H), sleeper in the dust
shtarbn, to die
toyt, dead
der toyt (v), death
tsumakhn an oyg, to die, (lit. to shut an eye)
yener velt, the Beyond

Di Bes-Oylems (Yidishe), Cemeteries (Jewish)

der bes-almen, cemetery (lit. house eternal)
der bes-oylem (H), cemetery (lit. house eternal)
der beysakvores (H), cemetery (lit. house of burials)
der beys-khayim (H), cemetery (lit. house of life)
dos feld, cemetery (field)
feld-mestn, the measuring of graves with a string which is later used as a
  candlewick in the synagogue service
der keyver (H), grave
di levaye (H), funeral
ort, "dos gute-ort", cemetery (lit. the good place)
dos heylike-ort, cemetery (lit. the Holy place)

"dos reyne ọrt", cemetery (lit. the pure place)

Der Got, G-d
adenoy (H), the Lord (lit. my Lord)
der almekhtiker, Almighty
der bashẹfer, Creator
der ẹybershter (ọybershter), the All Highest, the Lord
eyli, eyli (H), MY G-D! MY G-D!
eyl rakhum vekhanun (H), merciful and gracious G-d
der got, G-d
gotenyu, dear G-d
hakodesh-bọrkhu (H), the Holy one, blessed be He
hashẹm-yisborekh (H), Blessed Name
di hashgokhe (H), Providence
ovinu (H), Our Father
der rebọyne-shel-oylem (H), the Almighty (Lord of the world)
der shem (H), the Name
di shkhine (H), the Divine Manifestation, the Divine Presence
der yedeye-hạkl (H), the Omniscient One

Signs of the Zodiac
Di Mazoles

Aquarius, der vaser treger, der mazl dli (H), (the water carrier)
Aries, der baran, der mazl tale (H), (the ram)
Cancer, der rak, der mazl sartn (H), (cancer)
Capricorn, der shteyn bok, der mazl gdi (H), (the mountain goat)
Gemini, der tsviling, di mazl tomen (H), (the twins)
Leo, der leyb, der mazl arye (H), (the lion)
Libra, di vogn, di mazl mazonim (H), (the scales)
Pisces, der fish, di mazl dogim (H), (the fish)
Sagittarius, der fayln-boyger, der fayl un boygn shiser, der mazl kshos (H), (the
    archer)
Scorpio, der ekdish, der mazl ekrev (H), (the scorpion)
Taurus, der bik, der buhay, der mazl shor (H), (the bull)
Virgo, di psule (H), der mazl psule (H), (the virgin)
Astrology, di astrologye
sign, dos mazl (H)
zodiac, mazoles (H), der zodiak

Editors: Richard Bassett and Eleanor Koldofsky
Design: Eleanor Koldofsky

Published by
Proclaim Publication Inc.
Box 130, Station Z
Toronto, Ontario
M5N 2Z3
Telephone: 416/226-9608

Acknowledgements

Edited by Richard Bassett and Eleanor Koldofsky
The publisher acknowledges with thanks:

Richard Bassett B.A., M.S.W., Editor
Mr Bassett was largely responsible for the introduction of a Yiddish class into the curriculum of the Associated Hebrew Day School in 1974. He continued his education with an advanced course in Yiddish Literature at the University of Toronto. He is actively involved in furthering the Yiddish language, especially among Jewish youth. He is vice-president of the 'Fraynt Fun Yiddish Club', writes for the cultural publication 'Dos Bletl', and is on the Yiddish Committee of the Toronto Jewish Congress.

Brad Sabin Hill
Curator of The Lowy Collection, Rare Books and Manuscripts Division, National Library of Canada.

Zachary M. Baker
Head of Technical Services and Yiddish Department, Jewish Public Library, Montreal.

Joseph Klugman M.A.
Principal of Borochov School, Toronto, and Yiddishist, member of Polar Zion, late editor of *Unser Weg.*

Ben Kayfetz
Retired Director of the Canadian Jewish Congress, National Joint Community Relations Committee, and a lover of Yiddish.

Isaac Shoichet
Professor of Germanic Studies, University of Toronto.

Morley Torgov
Twice winner of the Stephen Leacock Award for humour. Author of *A Good Place to Come Home From, Abramsky Variations,* and *The Outside Chance of Maximilian Glick.*

Elizabeth Abraham
For kindness, friendship, and total support.

Roman Vishniac, New York
For permission to use the photograph of the rabbi and children.

Other Proclaim Publications:

This Is My Beloved-Sometimes, Drawings by Helen Lucas,
Deluxe Limited Edition of 250.
ISBN 0-919415-00-8

A Fragile Tree-Has Roots, Poetry. John C. Walker
ISBN 0-919415-01-6

Of the Bird, Flying, Poetry. Sol Mandlsohn
ISBN 0-919415-02-4